Perspectives in Metropolitan Research V

Published with the kind support of the ZEIT-Stiftung Ebelin und Gerd Bucerius

The series "Perspectives in Metropolitan Research" is edited by the Vice President for Research at HafenCity University, Gesa Ziemer

HafenCity Universität Hamburg
Referat für Forschung
Überseeallee 16
20457 Hamburg
forschung@hcu-hamburg.de

Imprint

© 2018 by jovis Verlag GmbH
Texts by kind permission of the authors.
Pictures by kind permission of the photographers/holders of the picture rights.

Cover: abseiten (Mehmet Alatur | Katrin Bahrs)

Editors of this volume: Michael Koch, Amelie Rost, Yvonne Siegmund, Renée Tribble, Yvonne Werner
Editorial team: Michael Koch, Amelie Rost, Yvonne Siegmund, Renée Tribble, Yvonne Werner
Editorial team support: Luis Pototzky
Editorial coordination: Nora Kempkens
Translation: Mahrt Fachübersetzungen GmbH
Copy-editing and proofreading: Christen Jamar, Urban Edits
Design and layout: abseiten (Mehmet Alatur | Katrin Bahrs)
Lithography: Bild1Druck, Berlin
Printed in the European Union

Bibliographic information published by the Deutsche Nationalbibliothek
The Deutsche Nationalbibliothek lists this publication in the Deutsche Nationalbibliografie; detailed bibliographic data are available on the Internet at http://dnb.d-nb.de

jovis Verlag GmbH
Kurfürstenstraße 15/16
10785 Berlin

www.jovis.de

jovis books are available worldwide in selected bookstores. Please contact your nearest bookseller or visit www.jovis.de for information concerning your local distribution.

ISBN 978-3-86859-515-4

Changing Perspectives in Metropolitan Research

New Urban Professions—
A Journey through Practice and Theory

Michael Koch, Amelie Rost, Yvonne Siegmund,
Renée Tribble, Yvonne Werner (eds.)

Contents

PHENOMENA: Practitioners & Practices, Reflections & Reflexes

TRANSFER: Education—Further Learning

Preface of the ZEIT-Stiftung Ebelin und Gerd Bucerius

Perspectives in Metropolitan Research
Vol. V: New Urban Professions—A Journey through Practice and Theory

"Co-creation," understood in the urban context as a mixture of co-design, co-production, and co-implementation, is the leading approach of the Mistra Urban Futures project. This initiative was established in 2010 in Gothenburg and created an international research and knowledge center. The goal of the project, funded by the Swedish Foundation for Strategic Environmental Research, is to address current challenges of sustainable urbanization. It uses the joint knowledge production from both practice and research experiences to enable innovative ways of solving complex social problems. Multilevel governance, urban empowerment, or urban games bring new actors into the urban planning and decision-making processes. The overall aim is to design and test a complement to the approach based on traditional academic disciplines and well-predefined professional roles.

The fifth volume of *Perspectives in Metropolitan Research*, entitled *New Urban Professions—A Journey through Practice and Theory*, concentrates also on major transformations in urban development occurring today and looks for new academic and professional approaches for the future. It invites reflection on professional requirements, standards, and self-definitions in urbanism, experimentation within the novel fields of urban theory and practice, and a discussion of challenges that arise when creativity intermingles with joint ownership and authorship.

On behalf of the ZEIT-Stiftung, I would like to congratulate the editors of the volume—Michael Koch, Amelie Rost, Yvonne Siegmund, Renée Tribble, and Yvonne Werner—on this rich collection of reflections on theory and practice in today's urbanism. We hope that the current edition of the journal, echoing the academic and professional discussions conducted at the HafenCity Universität in Hamburg, will be a valuable source for readers interested in the future of urban studies and professions.

Hamburg, February 2018
Anna Hofmann
Program Director Research and Scholarship
ZEIT-Stiftung Ebelin und Gerd Bucerius

Introduction

Professional Challenges

Michael Koch/Amelie Rost/Yvonne Siegmund/ Renée Tribble/Yvonne Werner

"The architect as a species is going extinct."[1]

"Regional planning must redefine itself today. The tasks it now faces are indeed fundamentally different after fifty years."[2]

"Art no longer tries to represent utopias; it is trying to construct concrete spaces.*"*[3]

1.1.4 ▶

The arts sections of newspapers are full of statements like these on the relevance of specific professional groups to a future-proof design of our cities. They are equally full of assertions of the relevance of certain professional groups to the solution of urban problems. This and our own experience prompted us to hold a symposium in 2016 and now to make this book.

Talking over Approaches

Amelie Rost (AR): Every time I walk through new, unfamiliar cities, I wonder why does this space so touch me? Why does this one not? Why do I feel good? As planners, we are aware that what gives a place its identity is always a combination of spatial, social, cultural, visible, and invisible elements and structures—an identity that is not firmly established, but instead is constantly developing and changing.

2.1 ▶

Yvonne Werner (YW): But that means that when we consider contributing to the making of cities, we have to do justice to the specifically local, dynamic circumstances, which calls for a procedural, flexible, cooperative, and transdisciplinary approach. This also holds when we want to explore the idea of the city.

2.6.1 ▶ / 1.4 ▶

2.2 ▶

1 Carlo Ratti in *Der Standard*, June 5, 2017

2 Sieverts, T. (2013). "A Golden Age of Regional Planning: The Long Decade 1960-1975 Revisited from a Time of Uncertainty." Wilhelm, K. and K. Gust, eds. *New Cities for a New State: The Invention of Town Planning in Modern Israel and Reconstruction in the Federal Republic of Germany, A Rapprochement*. Bielefeld, p. 207.
3 Nicolas Bourriaud, poster at the Institution Urbane Künste Ruhr (March–December 2017)

Michael Koch (MK): To do so, however, we must question the routines of thought and structures of action of the disciplines. We must decisively leave behind us the "God the Father model" of planning (Walter Seibel) and thus allow for a new understanding of the co-production of the city. This is a discussion that has also been going on for some time in Brazil.

▶ 2.5

4 Vinicius Andrade is an architect, professor at Escola da Cidade in Sao Paolo and partner in www.andrade-morettin.com.br. He is involved in a German-Brazilian exchange program.

▶ 1.5

Vinicius Andrade (VA)[4]**:** Challenged by huge urban problems in São Paulo, we discuss that urbanism must be seen not as a specialization but as a field of activity, where not only architects and town planners are involved, but economists, anthropologists, engineers, etc. also act. And especially in today's reality, real estate market agents, legislators, administrators, and public managers.

Yvonne Siegmund (YS): Actually, the planning disciplines are struggling with this, like all disciplines separated since the Enlightenment: they have solidified their logics and theoretical references more and more, yet have given short shrift to the necessity of seeing the whole, as well as productive reference and supplement …

YW: In Germany, we were able to observe concretely that the separations of disciplines in the reality of work have long been overcome: far more than merely the conventional professions are now involved in planning and building processes.

▶ 2.7.3

VA: To be successful, these different professionals must work together in a co-productive way: interpretations and urbanistic proposals can only be fostered in a manner consistent with the joint participation of representatives of the public administration, the private sector, and civil society.

▶ 1.2

Renée Tribble (RT): Processes must be reshaped, especially to achieve the goal of integrating civil society, such as government and the economy, into urban development processes. For this purpose, we need knowledge from all disciplines at the intersection of the city and perhaps even beyond.

AR: My impression is also that the disciplinary boundaries drawn up at universities are becoming rather blurred in everyday life and that new professional fields have long ago arisen at these intersections between established professions, which are being managed by their actors with new methods and tools.

▶ 1.6

MK: I share this impression, but if you want to be prepared for these new professional fields, you need to go beyond traditional disciplinary boundaries and have to discuss the curricula. What is required therefore is a rethinking of professional needs within urbanist practice.

2.2 ▶

VA: In short, the challenge is to construct a transdisciplinary narrative to try to develop a capacity for cross-cutting articulation from this common field of action that is the city. A curiosity: in the face of this task, the question of language is, little by little, imposed as a central challenge.

Professional Needs

While an approach that crosses disciplinary boundaries has long become the practice in everyday life, it does not seem to have arrived at the core of disciplinary self-conception. This is what first led us to hold the above-mentioned Crossing Disciplinary Boundaries symposium—sponsored by the VW Foundation—at which we discussed this topic with around 120 participants in the summer of 2016.

The exchange between "boundary-crossers" in the established disciplines confirmed that once sharply drawn boundaries had long become boundary regions in which the boundary-crossers have developed their own remits. To describe this in more detail and bring its relevance into focus, it appears to us time, considering increasing differentiation, for an in-depth exchange on this topic. Here we are less concerned with negating, delimiting, and redefining traditional/existing disciplines than with expanding into new professions. This volume would like to make a contribution to procuring for these new professions of procedural understanding and city-making their due social recognition. Transdisciplinarity in teaching, research, and practice is proving to be an important criterion for this, despite being anchored in disciplinary core competences.

These new professions entail new questions, which in this volume are to be illuminated from a wide variety of perspectives:
- What should be the nature of the professional and personal social competences?
- What kind of understanding of authorship is needed?

1.6 ▶

- Which relationship between creativity and multiple authorship is to be taught and lived?

▶ 2.1 / ▶ 2.4

- What form might a sustainable exchange of experience take, what curricular consequences would appear necessary, and in what roles, spaces, and spatiotemporal contexts must one prepare for the co-production of the city?

A look at the world in figures. Can the changes already be shown and thus proved in today's practice?

Approach with Statistics: Participants
Who participates in planning and building?
The 2016–17 building culture report shows how much the professional fields have differentiated in building practice.

Figure 1: Employees in select planning and building professions in Germany 2015–16, © Yvonne Werner in accordance with *Baukultur Bericht 2016/17*, BSBK (2017).

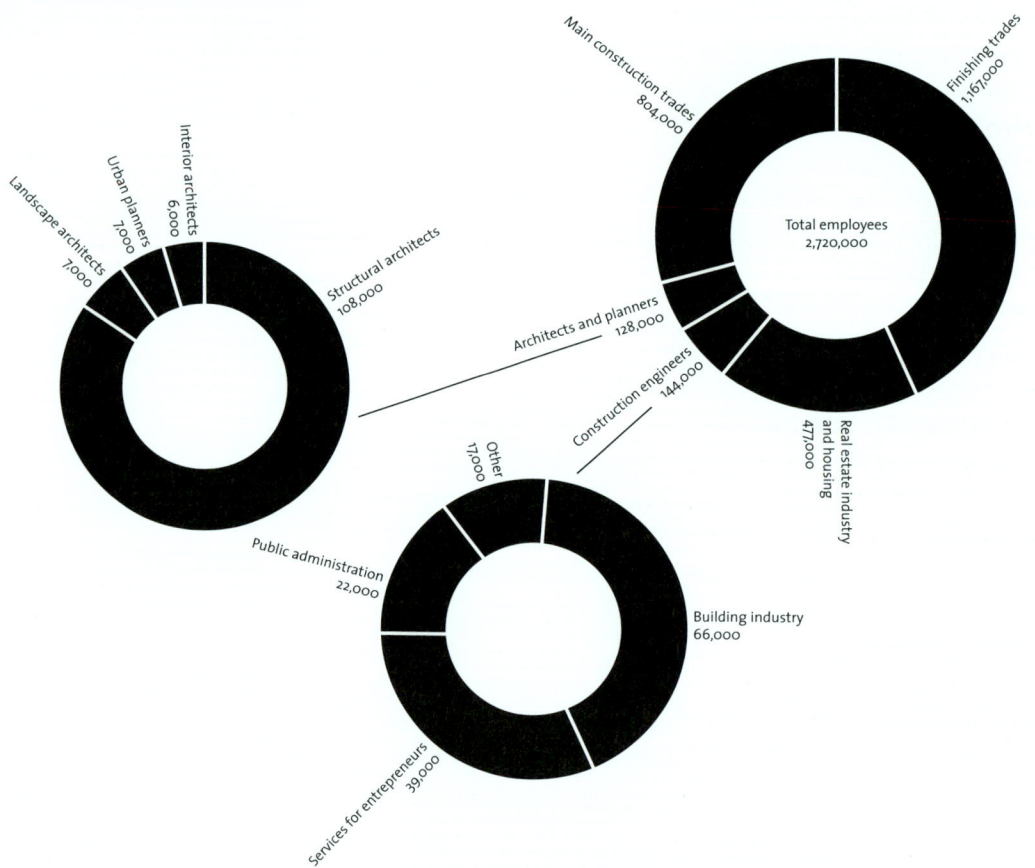

In the building culture report 2016–17, the breakdown of the building industry gives an impression of the differentiation of the trades, crafts, service providers, and participants in politics and government. Civil society gets shortchanged, as well as the actors in the gaps and holes, the forgotten places and areas of city planning. Does this still do justice to our society as it ever more strongly demands rights of co-determination? 1.1.4 ▶

Professional Fields
Quote from Klaus Selle[5]:

"The word 'discipline' comes from 'discipulus,' or 'pupil.' Thus it refers to the training phase—for example, at a 'school' called a technical university. This leads to a degree in the 'discipline' of X, for instance, city planning. And with the degree you also get the certification that 'you are now a city planner' or 'you are an architect.' And you remain so for your entire life ... At least, this is how it appears when you hear how the word 'discipline' is often used in Germany: you impute the 'career' in later life from the training. Once a teacher, always a teacher; once an architect, always an architect. In fact, however, a lot happens in later life—and very many people later work in professional fields that have little or nothing to do with what they originally learned. That is to say, professional biographies—at least today—are not straight roads, but often winding paths. This begins in the educational biographies themselves, for instance, through dividing up technical training into bachelor, master, and postgraduate courses of study. If you first study architecture, then get a master's in urban planning followed by postgraduate work in real estate—what 'discipline' is this then supposed to be? And then you may work for a decade in a bank or as a gallery owner. What are you now? In a word, various training courses and experiences add up to a specific profile in the career biography of a given person. And that is why we can all be part of a professional community even though we may have started off in quite different disciplines."

A sharp division according to disciplines is given at universities, but as a rule is not reflected in the scope of duties in practical work. The professional fields in which graduates of city planning at HafenCity University work are already enough to show how diverse the scope of duties in practical work can be.

5 Klaus Selle is an urban planner and urban researcher. He is professor at RWTH Aachen University, where he holds the chair of planning theory and urban development.

Approach with Statistics: Professional Fields of City Planning Graduates at HCU

A survey of graduates at HCU illustrates how much professional fields in city planning have differentiated.

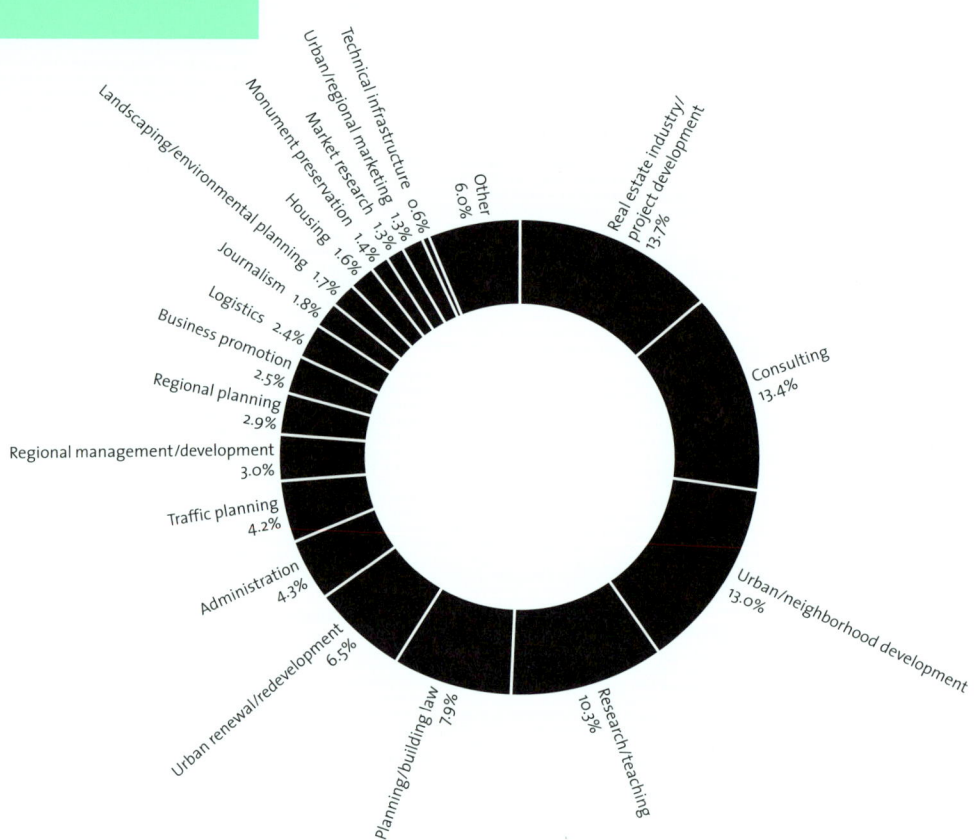

Paradigms of Understanding

Architect and planner collectives have been building disciplinary bridges for some time already.

▶ 1.6 From the super studio in the nineteen-sixties up to today's bureau spectacular, there have been and still are many different urban boundary-crossers who dissociate themselves in collaborative groupings from singular authorships of the (star) architect or from omnipotent planners' promises.

These collectives often have several (disciplinary) languages at their command and thus have made indispensable contributions to the production and reflection of urban spaces. In this sort of "multilingual" collaborative work process, it is important to recognize the various languages and to illustrate the various related conceptualizations.

At our 2016 symposium, we attempted to enable the participants to experience this necessity in a playful manner; we played the Monday Painter (German for Pictionary) where quickly drawn pictures had to be guessed at by others to uncover the different (disciplinary) backgrounds of the participants. A common awareness of the multidimensionality of concepts proved to be fundamental to successful understanding in collaboration. Then there has to be a struggle for their suitability in specific research or practical situations, until the participants are able to act together in a goal-oriented manner.

Monday Painter—"Detail"

Figure 3–5 (p. 21–23): Participants with varying disciplinary backgrounds draw concepts that had to be guessed by the auditorium.

Facade

Vertical Projection

Scale

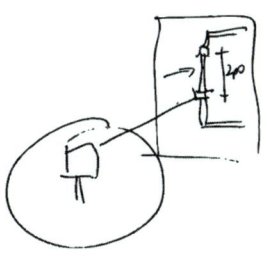

Section

Ground Plan

Proportion

Neufert

Building Code

DETAIL

Monday Painter—"Image"

Spacing

Ground Plan
    Addition of Stories

    Landscape

    Distant View
Frameword

    Cityscape

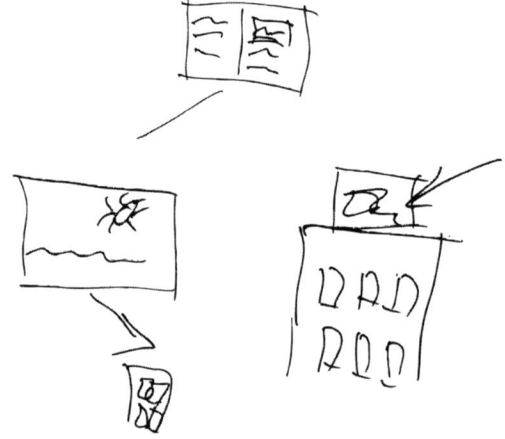

Window
    Planning Error

    Construction Window

Skylight

    Manifesto

    Vacancy

Politics
    Rally

Scandal
    Environment

Forecast
    Capital

    Environmental Impact

Environmental Pollution

    Climate Change
Ecological Footprint

IMAGE

Monday Painter—"Process"

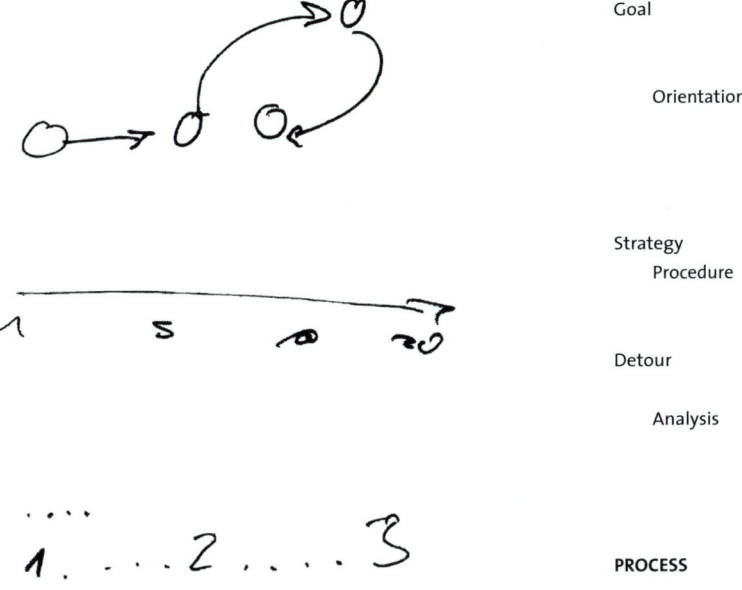

Goal

Orientation

Strategy
Procedure

Detour

Analysis

PROCESS

"New" Urban Studies

A reaction to changing demands placed on training in the urban design and research courses of study has also been observed in Germany since the mid-2000s. Some new courses of study arose that work in these research areas and intersections.

Figure 6: Selection of new courses of study in urban development and urban research since the mid-2000s

Timeline of New Courses of Study

2013 Planung und Partizipation • Universität Stuttgart
Urban Design—Revitalization of Historic City Districts •
BTU Cottbus

2011 Integrated Urbanism and Sustainable Design • Universität Stuttgart
Urbanistik • TU München

2009 Kultur der Metropole • HafenCity Universität Hamburg

2008 Urban Design • HafenCity Universität Hamburg
Resource Efficiency in Architecture and Planning •HafenCity Universität Hamburg
Urbanistik • Bauhaus-Universität Weimar

2007 Raumstrategien • Kunsthochschule Berlin-Weißensee

2006 Urban Design • TU Berlin

2004 Advanced Urbanism • Bauhaus-Universität Weimer

These new training courses promise to qualify students for a new understanding of their tasks and work methods, thus professionalizing, so to speak, disciplinary boundary-crossers. Indications of a "Twilight of the Disciplines"?

▶ 1.5.2

"Professionalizing Niches"

Quote from Sabrina Gieron[6]:

"We must actively take on responsibility for our own discipline. We need to undertake the tasks before us with courage, joy, and generosity. It requires professional strength to develop an assignment towards a solution and finalize an idea towards a concept. Meanwhile we need to be open to critical discourse and sharpen our solutions until we finally bring them to the world."

In view of the complex challenges of our living environments, we will need in the future more bridge builders who can exchange ideas in transdisciplinary collaboration! This also includes the expanded competence to transform processes, to appropriate and design urban spaces within self-created free zones step-by-step, or even to indicate room for social creativity by means of ingenious experiments.

▶ 2.8 / ▶ 2.3.1

▶ 1.5.1

▶ 1.4.2

Quote from Martin Kohler[7]:

▶ 1.3

"Professionalizing niches! Artistic interventionistic projects are further developed and professionalized. Is art then still necessary? Who are the new bearers of responsibility? What are the new areas of duties? Are architect swarms, that is, temporary or project-related groupings as a kind of 'professional collective intelligence,' a possibility for competitiveness?"

▶ 1.3.4

We must rethink structures and framework conditions. Even the monetary turnover in building and planning underscores how necessary the long-term success of the projects is in order to ensure responsible handling of resources. Thus the question of fees is also raised, since after all, how will we pay for the fields of activity of these new professions in the end if fees are determined according to tables for specified occupational profiles?

▶ 1.4.4

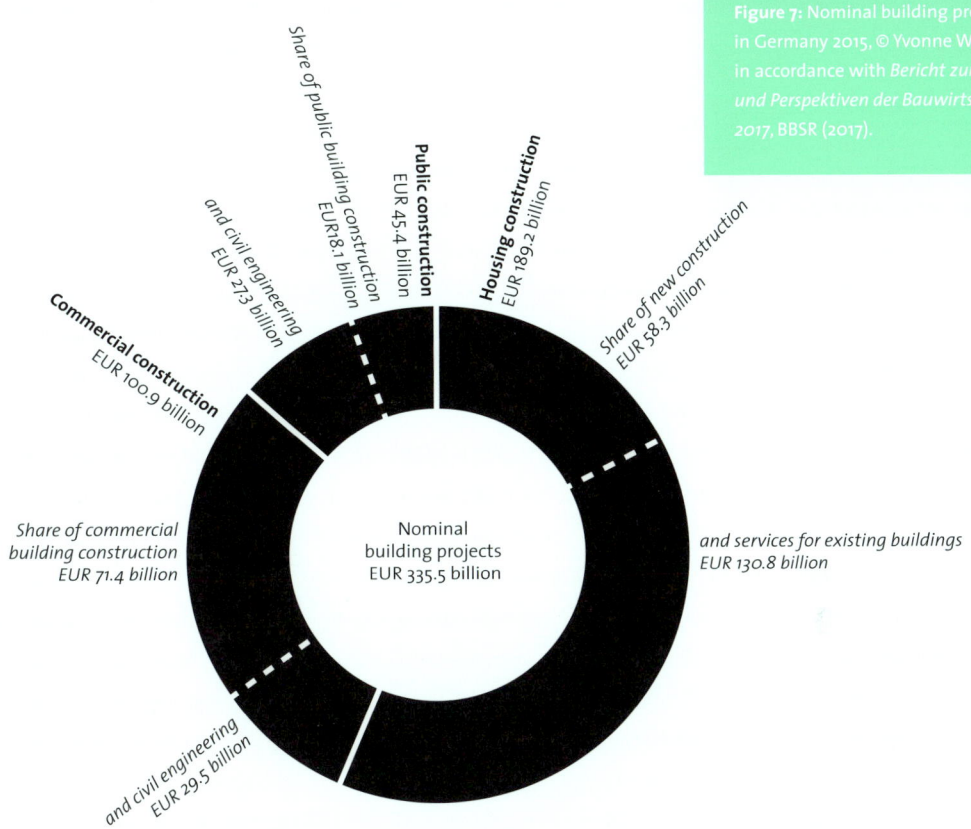

Figure 7: Nominal building projects in Germany 2015, © Yvonne Werner in accordance with *Bericht zur Lage und Perspektiven der Bauwirtschaft 2017*, BBSR (2017).

Share of public building construction and civil engineering
EUR 273 billion

Public construction
EUR 45.4 billion

EUR 8.1 billion

Housing construction
EUR 189.2 billion

Share of new construction
EUR 58.3 billion

Commercial construction
EUR 100.9 billion

Share of commercial building construction
EUR 71.4 billion

Nominal building projects
EUR 335.5 billion

and services for existing buildings
EUR 130.8 billion

and civil engineering
EUR 29.5 billion

This book tries first to describe this complex, dynamic network of new professions and secondly to sound it out in view of the transfer of experience and educational possibilities. Hence the first chapter, **PHENOMENA: Practitioners & Practices, Reflections & Reflexes**, concentrates on reflecting the phenomena of urban practices, supplemented by thematic side glances. It is a matter of places—processes—structures—strategies— competencies—authorships.

The articles in the second chapter, **TRANSFER: Education—Further Learning**, describe how and what knowledge is acquired in these practices and link the corresponding realizations with references to necessary learning processes and curricular implications. Here, too, thematically focused considerations on the transfer and exchange of knowledge in education, training, and research supplement the overview on multiscale—spatial agency—transformation—temporalities—co-production—improvisation—multidisciplinarity—exchange.

Every single article is to be understood as an independent but additional perspective on future urban tasks and fields of work.

PHENOMENA: Practitioners & Practices, Reflections & Reflexes

1.1. Places

WandererUni Rounding the World

Ton Matton

space&designSTRATEGIES of the Art University of Linz (Austria) researched the Austrian mountains, German cities, an African village, and a small Austrian town in an educational wandering tour, a nonlinear geographic journey to discover, improvise, and learn from new experiences. This is the essence of Grenzgänger. Through new confrontations with reality students subjectify circumstances; they attach new meanings and thus improvise their way through the world. This is what our space and design practice is about.

The journey is described as a search for new and practical philosophies for **space&designSTRATEGIES**. The key lies in quick changes in focus and confrontations between the local conditions and the responsive, improvised actions. These actions can be globally inspired as the difference between European and African locations shows.

1. Identity, space&designSTRATEGIES

In 2017 the faculty of **space&designSTRATEGIES** moved across the Danube. From the laboratories in Linz Urfahr in the south, the department moved to the main square in the center of Linz. The most direct way would be over the bridge that spans the Danube, a 950-meter walk. We decided to go the opposite direction; instead of the bridge, we go around the world to arrive at the new atelier via Halle, Freiburg, Cologne (Germany), Charleroi (Belgium), Tankwa (South Africa), Totope (Ghana), Milan (Italy), and Marchtrenk (Austria) to arrive finally at the central square in Linz. This is a condensed summary of this journey.

On our way we developed a view of the identity of **space&designSTRATEGIES** studies. The main goal is clear: a design based on research for a better world. This cannot be a theoretical and abstract vision: when confronted with local circumstances, we adopt

1.1.1

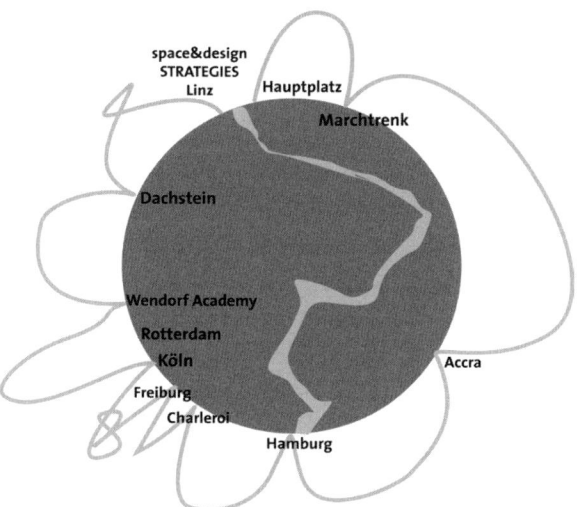

Figure 1: WandererUni rounding the world, © space&designSTRATEGIES

▶ 2.6.1 a flexible approach, apply a talent for <mark>improvisation</mark>, and develop strategies based on doubt and critical thinking.

Before we go any further, it is good to understand the following: We are not urban planners, who generally work in terms of structures and organization and less in terms of daily life and personal experiences. We are not architects, who often hold on to their conceptual designs even when they don't work for the building. Neither are we interior architects or designers, who start from feelings and emotions, often dismissing designs because they are not beautiful or don't comply with those feelings and emotions. Are we artists then? Artists work from a place that is more personal, more autobiographical and therefore more activist, based on direct experiences and local conditions, much more in tune to the changing present. So our preliminary conclusion on identity politics: probably **space&designSTRATEGIES** is found somewhere in between shaping society, ecological space planning, and artists' activism. This can only to be experienced through action on location.

2. The Fragility of Mankind

Austrian mountains
October 4–6, 2016 / snow, storms, and cold

*Thirty-seven **space&designSTRATEGISTS** feel the power of nature and the fragility of humans and human culture. We are neither in the classic modernist category of recreation nor in a mode of mobility.*

At the semester's start we walked into the Austrian mountains. Some students are familiar here and bounced like goats over the rocks and stones. Others had less experience and walked in linen summer shoes. After a restful night in an Alpine shelter (*Berghut*), we headed for the mountaintop the next morning. Quite soon, however, we were caught up by a snowstorm. After four more hours climbing, in ever heavier snow, we arrived at a cable car station. Unfortunately it was closed because of unexpected heavy weather. So we had to go on to the next station on the other side of the mountain, another three hours by foot, as the men at the station told us without any pity.

Then Waleed stood up. The year before, he had come as a refugee to Europe, by foot and over the Mediterranean by rubber boat. "If this is the biggest problem..." he said, moving his backpack to his front, putting a Chinese student's backpack on his back, and supporting the student with his arm. "Let's go!" And the group went on, frozen, exhausted, some crying, but we made it.

This event was a super discovery of the essence of wandererUni. It became clear that our society, our culture, takes on a different meaning high up in the mountains; we felt the violence of the mountains, the fragility of mankind, the thinness of our cultural layer. We were no longer in the classical modernistic category of "recreation," nor were we simply in mobility mode.

Order and disorder no longer exist. Insecurity is not calculable, unlike in Cedric Price and Archigram's understanding of the cybernetic system theory. The world is a process and it is not in our control; but still there are places to be discovered and improvised upon with design.

3. Design Deconstructs Old Meanings

Freiburg, Germany
November 5–9, 2016 / rain, cold

*Seven **space&designSTRATEGISTS** invented an instrument to view the city in a different way and at a different angle in order to dismantle conventional ways of urban planning where democratic rules and laws prohibit entrance to certain citizens and to develop new enriching views and interpretations.*

When we arrived in Freiburg we got involved in the preparations of the Dietenbacher Festspiele. Dietenbach is a new suburb that is in the planning stages, envisioned as rather classic modernistic with a focus on living, working, recreation, and transport, but also planned with an eye to the investors' money and a sales message of comfort. The Freiburg theatre wanted to research both of the adjacent neighborhoods, Rieselfeld and Weingarten, to generate a program for the new area of Dietenbach. In the context of this research, some students considered alternative instruments to research the city in another way, that is, not to assume that the plan would be driven by the capitalist urban-planning-machine. If we use functionalism

1.1.1

as a framework for urban planning, as Jane Jacobs asked over fifty years ago, what actually happens in our cities? We wanted to find new mapping forms to show, as Kevin Lynch did, that functionalism cannot cover the city. We acted, like in the Chicago School, with participative observations.

It is amazing what happens in our minds when our view is redirected with mirrors, shows the work of student Ayan. Suddenly the concepts of the frog's perspective or the bird's eye view are realized in front of your eyes and immediately adapted by your brain. To observe the city from the perspective of a mole, an ant, a cat, a giraffe, or a drone opens another dimension of perception. The incredible amount of rules and regulations that of course become valid in a new suburb are questioned in the *neulandteppich* of yet another student Romy. An Euclidean space in a tabula rasa mind, which shows how quickly the pores of the city are filled with an acne of laws: where to (not) park the cars; how high fences should be between neighbors; how far the trees should be from the facade so the branches do not hit the windows, requiring an employee to come with a ladder to cut them off, and in the meantime, the roots of the tree should not grow to clog the sewer pipes; when to dispose the empty green bottles, and when the brown. Another student's project *newland-carpet* is a Lefebvrian attempt to get in contact with inhabitants and to understand their everyday lives in relation to freedom, rules, and utopia. Fear creates an entitlement that the suburb of Dietenbach (and many others) are accessible only to a certain clientele, for those who can afford it, who shield themselves with democratic rules and regulations that automatically deny access to others.

4. Rich Empty Spaces

Halle and Leipzig
November 24–26, 2016 / sun, cold, Christmas atmosphere

*Nine **space&designSTRATEGISTS** need friends with a power generator and some beers to improvise within the luxury of empty buildings.*

The luxury of emptiness is our next research task: what is the potential of deserted buildings? Both cities, Halle and Leipzig, are full of gaps between buildings, abandoned areas, and ramshackle huts. For example, behind the main station, where the infrastructure is badly connected, a derelict slaughterhouse attracts the attention. There is no bakery, no supermarket, but there is the old former GDR ice cream parlor with the best name in town.

You only need friends with an electricity generator and a six-pack of beer, and then the party in some deserted building starts, says a Leipzig philosophy student with compassion for improvisation.

In the city center, meanwhile, a great deal has been cleaned up, and the city is selling off its low-rent apartments, beloved by artists and people with little or no income, in order to create space for young families who are willing to pay good

Perspectives in Metropolitan Research

money for their soy chai lattes. Gentrification ends the creative and open process of filling empty spaces.

5. Niches, Biotopes, and Pioneers

Cologne and Mülheim
June 24–30, 2017 / rain showers, windy, and cold

*Twenty-nine **space&designSTRATEGISTS** have doubts on the technologization of laws, neoliberal market behavior, and the disappearance of social cultures.*

How come theatre managers have to care for the future of living in the cities? Isn't that the job of urban planners? Our performative, urbanistic research project in the village of Gottsbüren in 2015, where we, with about forty students, squatted some empty houses for a month, brings us the invitation from two theatres to do research with them. First, the Theater Freiburg invited us the previous November; then Schauspiel Köln invited us to participate in the festival Die Stadt von Morgen.

Two requests from two other small villages had stopped in the first rounds of talking because of planning formalities. Do

1.1.1

Figure 3: Cooking in the neighborhood, © space&designSTRATEGIES

traditional urban planning departments have more problems with informality and improvisation? Do they still see the city as a *Werk* (piece of work) in the sense of Heidegger? Or are they more sensitive to the interests of investors and their lobbyists?

Under the Mülheimer Bridge, in the pouring rain, we have a lot of time to doubt the city of tomorrow; and, as a university, we should be doubting. That is exactly our task in contemporary society, where too much research is done on commission with the goal being prove the hypothesis, instead of requestioning it and research.

Some students attended a hygiene course—otherwise they would not be allowed to cook in public spaces—and learned that you should wash your hands before dinner. There was a time, back then when the bridge was being rebuilt after the bombing, when no laws were needed and to wash your hands before dinner was obvious. Today you have to build an extra sink. The law does not say that hands should be washed, but establishes the technical neoliberal requirements so you can wash your hands. The possibility of using one of the ninety-seven sinks in the surrounding houses is not part of this regulation. One could even say it contradicts it. Own your own instead of asking others—that is the neoliberal motto.

Despite the demand for transparency, we buy *Gammelfleisch* (rotten meat), clothes made by modern slaves, coffee in plastic-and-paper cups, manipulated Volkswagen diesel, obscure finance papers, and so on. So contemporary politics is based on an incorrect statement, which Alan Greenspan, the founder of neoliberalism, already in 2008, recognized as a lie and apologized in public: that neoliberalism is in the end a utopian thought, the consumer has proven he can buy everything, including the stuff that he doesn't want. Instead of starting a revolution, today you start a company of your own, finding a market gap and try, with Adorno, the right life in wrong (*das richtige Leben im Falschen*).

A niche delivers the requirements for a protected biotope and so delivers the freedom for the pioneers. So a city needs niches like under the Mülheimer Bridge, where you can kiss secretly or smoke your first cigarette. Or a niche behind the Turkish curtains on Keupstraße, where you can withdraw. Therefore the niche has to be discovered and recognized, like the empty office buildings at night that are longing for human attention.

In the project *Botschaft* (Embassy) thousands of rules structure the twelve-square-meter representative embassy and guide the visitors properly through an accurate collection of pictures of the city. The collection changes your perception continually, by sorting again and again. It makes it immediately clear that it is based on subjectivity, and so the point of view changes continuously.

The embassy exposes the construct of efficiency, the categorization and regulation as a questionable attempt to order/organize the city. It is a way of looking at the city, a view, nothing more, nothing less. It helps to see some things, but is blind to others. With the equipment it seems everything is in order, but that only counts within the self-build system. It is a point of view that leaves out the city and the subjective experiences of its inhabitants. But what happens when you go under the skin

1.1.1

and the city is caught in flagrante? A reinterpretation changes reality again and again. De facto it is exactly the reinterpretation that we should consider design.

What if the subjectification is so important that you have to do subjective research in a real situation, is it possible to make this provided subjectivity universal without to concluding it? asks the urban philosopher and improvisational musician Christopher Dell, who we meet in a lecture in Cologne. How to get into a fluid subjectivity is a question that grabs our attention in the coming semester.

6. City of the Future

Totope, Ghana
April 13–30, 2017 / sun, heat, heat, and even more heat

*Five **space&designSTRATEGISTS**, their skin full of dust, meet the chief and the elderly of the village Totope. Climate change threatens the village through rising sea levels. Finding solutions for the city of the future takes on quite a different meaning.*

The porosity of the asphalt roads is on our way to the village of Totope to be taken literally—maintaining asphalt streets is much more complicated than dirt roads. The holes have sharper edges; slaloming around the road is has metaphorical parallels in the society. Almost everything takes place in public space; actually you only go inside the hut to sleep. Cooking, washing, eating all happens in public space. It feels like a mixture of living, working, recreation, and mobility, without being able to differentiate between them. Also shops and workshops open towards the street or are directly situated on the roadside.

Every product from the range in our supermarkets is being presented on the street here. Piled on the side of the road, in baskets and plates on the head, or in market stands. The saleswomen and men offer their articles every second: roll-on deodorant, biscuits, handkerchiefs, meatballs, soap, towels, toothbrushes, cotton swabs, skipping ropes, cookies, curry powder, jewelry, skirts, corn, apples, sugar cane, more cookies, medicine, toothpaste, bread, combs, beer, more deodorant, even more cookies, kitchen rolls, body spray, headphones, shoes, ice cream, cloths, prepaid SIM cards, warning triangles, eggs, coconuts, rope, Chinese cups, shirts, avocados, navigation-device-holders, chewing gum, maps, lessons on the Koran, chips, torches, bananas, radios, steering-wheel covers, sunglasses , socks, belts, black Adidas sneakers, bath slippers, high-visibility clothing, ladies' hats, tree-shaped air fresheners, towels, second-hand books, English grammar notebooks, toilet paper, ...

Full of sweat and dust are the pores of the city, like the pores of our skin. It is impossible to see what is taking place—a clear vision on Ghana society seems impossible. All these world problems in a small village alone is too much to deal with, and we from **space&designSTRATEGIES** are overwhelmed at first. It feels like a continuing blur; everything is fuzzy. Here we bounce at the externalization of the modernistic world. All the waste seems to be outsourced to here.

Figure 4: The table is set,
© space&designSTRATEGIES

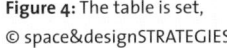

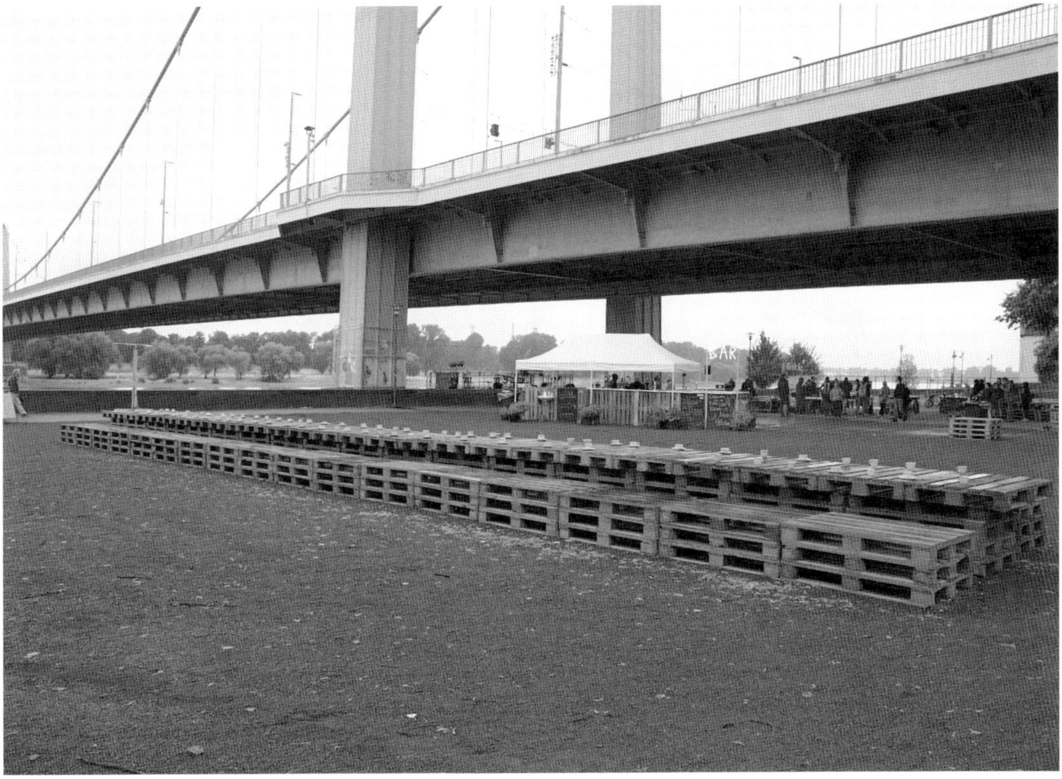

1.1.1

Our first idea—to lift the village, like in a museum on a socle—is received with big applause in the meeting of the elderly men. But that maybe shows more the despair of the villagers than our ingenious convincing. The proposal to explain this idea to Kofi Annan with a local dinner is accepted very enthusiastically. An elderly woman starts to list immediately what she would offer Kofi Annan for dinner, together with our students.

"Make Fufu not War" is printed on the T-shirt which our student Lukas bought in Ghana. We will try this in our next semester.

7. The Comfort Society

Festival der Regionen, Marchtrenk
July 1–9, 2017 / sun, heat, rain shower

All space&designSTRATEGISTS meet in the small Austrian town Marchtrenk in an attempt to research local conditions, which seem to be characterized by new dimensions of comfort.

Finally we arrive in Marchtrenk, where the region's summer festival took place. Urbanization there, like in every city, reached a new dimension. In performative urbanism the students not only try to discover the city of Marchtrenk in an acupunctural way, but also in a performative reality. We enter this practice deeply, in that we not only use the toothbrushes of the inhabitants and discover the lonely socks in the washbasket, but we even suck the bacteria out of their dirty carpet. We hawk with our baldachin, or ceremonial canopy, through the streets. We collect old television sets, out-of-date medicine, (and good luck charms). We take photos of every house, every fence, and categorize them. We look for black-and-white pictures, interview the garden gnomes, and research the identity based on the ringtones of the door. We take literally the first step in a new life.

8. Conclusion and Discussion

The cell phones of the Ghanese are the same as those of the residents of Marchtrenk, Cologne, or Linz. We agree with Henri Lefebvre's theory that urbanization of the city and of the countryside is the same, as he writes in his book *Production of Space*. Maybe we want even to push it one step further and place it on the globalized world. The haircuts, the clothes, they are the same in a European city as in an African village. Only the amount of lonely socks differs in Europe from Africa. What does this mean for our future? How will our life look? How will our society function? We are practiced in performative urbanism; we can even improvise it. We will practice some more to make possible, as well in our university, the near and far, exclusion and integration, heterogeneity and homogeneity, anonymity and community in the future.

The task for next semester is to design our life at university, and to not cooperate with all the problems in the world, so please clean drinking water, good

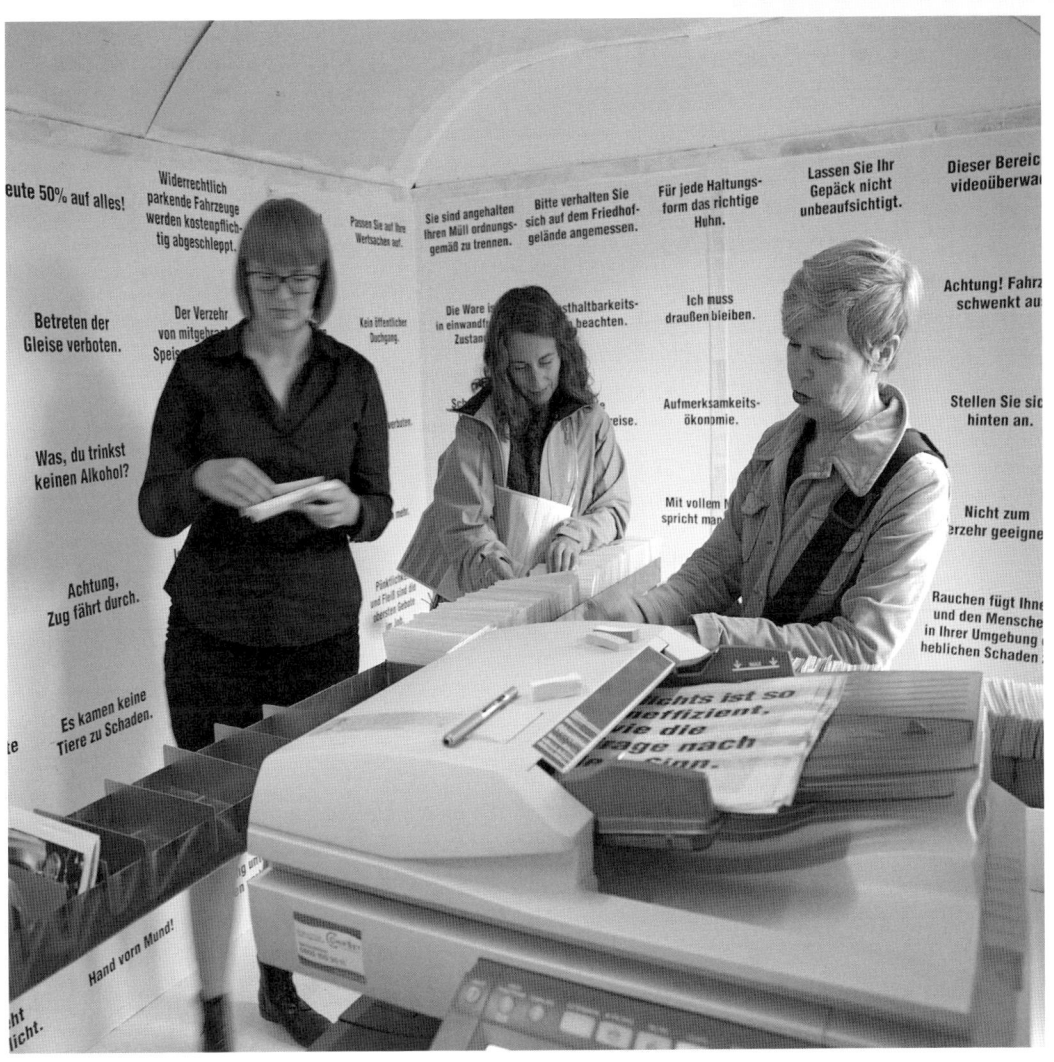

1.1.1

Figure 6: The Embassy,
© space&designSTRATEGIES

sanitation, healthy food, printers without dirty ink, clothes not made by modern (child) slaves, no nuclear power, no plastic waste (not in our blood either), and so on ... How does a university function in a broad welfare economy? We will watch and observe this from our Bay Watch (the learning theme) in the next semester. If you are around, you are welcome to visit us!

Rural Places
and Centralities

Stefan Rettich

Do you know the third-largest city in Germany, the city that covers the largest area in the republic after the two big city-states of Berlin (891 square kilometers) and Hamburg (755 square kilometers)? It is the small town of Gardelegen in the Altmark. Since January 1, 2011, this small town has been offering its roughly 24,000 residents a surface area of 632 square kilometers divided up into forty-nine districts, and Gardelegen is no exception. Möckern (523 square kilometers) and Zerbst (467 square kilometers) in Saxony-Anhalt are the fourth- and fifth-largest cities; they are followed by Wittstock/Dosse (420 square kilometers) in Brandenburg. Cologne, with a mere 405 square kilometers, lags far behind in seventh place (Statistisches Bundesamt 2017).

These figures testify to the dynamic process of contraction taking place in rural areas and the need to redefine centers and their peripheries, which includes adapting administrative structures. How to do so, and by what method, remains an open question. Saxony-Anhalt has chosen an approach that can be called fiscal regional development, since it is not based on the logic of planning spaces, but instead pursues the goal of creating particularly efficient administrative structures adapted to demographics. The state was rearranged in two stages. First, the number of districts was reduced from twenty-one to eleven in the course of a large-scale administrative reform in 2007 (Land Sachsen-Anhalt 2007, pp. 25–27). The independent cities of Magdeburg, Halle, and Dessau-Rosslau, were retained, the latter through fusion. In the course of a reorganization of municipal territory in 2011, the number of municipalities was reduced from 1,033 to today's 218 (Statistisches Landesamt Sachsen-Anhalt 2017), which led to such unusual phenomena as the creation of large, unified municipalities on the order of Gardelegen. As yet, no verified concepts or empirical values have evolved regarding the future organization of public services in such extensive communities with population densities of less than fifty residents per square kilometer. However, this development is posing a distinct challenge to the system based on Central Place Theory. The mesh size in the web of cities is now too large to allow getting back to business as usual. Is there a piece missing from the system in rural areas? And can large municipalities fill this vacuum?

For particularly sparsely inhabited areas like the Altmark, Jürgen Aring has developed a model for large municipalities that follows a dual principle of guaranteed

1.1.2

and self-responsible areas, referring to practices in the thinly populated areas of Sweden. According to this model, not everything should be considered equal everywhere, but instead there should be lower standards of public services in self-responsible areas, offset by more individual freedom, fewer regulations, lower taxes, and decentralized technologies (Aring 2010, pp. 764–777). Those who are uncomfortable with this sort of involuntary confrontation can always take advantage of the comfort zones in the guaranteed areas. Of course, this would require a change in Section 72 of Germany's Basic Law and its stipulation of the equality of living conditions. Besides, the value of these large municipalities would have to be bolstered by expanding the subsidiarity principle. In the Altmark, Aring sees a purely mathematical potential for five to six such large municipalities corresponding to a mid-central metropolitan area, with the perspective of having them possibly replace the rural districts in time; they would be a form of independent large-scale city-states, workaday regions with the most important segments of public services and the facilities of a midsize administrative center (*Mittelzentrum*). This is precisely the weak point of the district reform decreed by Saxony-Anhalt, since it does not provide for any programs or upward revaluation of the large municipalities, as shown by the example of Gardelegen. This consolidated municipality with its huge area is designated merely as an administrative subcenter (*Unterzentrum*) with a few of the functions of a midsize administrative center. Parts of what Aring developed as a model in the course of the IBA Urban Redevelopment in Saxony-Anhalt have now become reality. Among the key empirical results of the 2017 Regional Planning Report was that the state, in view of diminishing public funds, is increasingly pulling back and concentrating on its function of ensuring provision, thereby increasing the importance of the co-production of mixed actor networks in the provision of major segments of public services (BBSR 2017, p. 131).

Changes in the Midsized Administrative Centers

Challenges to the centrality model, on which the Central Place Theory (CPT) is based, are coming at ever-shorter intervals. While criticism in the nineteen-nineties focused on relocating functions in the agglomerations surrounding big cities in the course of the controversy regarding urban sprawl (Sieverts 1997, pp. 38–40), the tried-and-true model of recent German regional planning has been questioned, especially in the context of demographic change and public services in rural areas, and, in some German states, has even been adapted. This took regional planning into unknown territory. As regional disparities intensify, the discussion is focusing particularly on the treatment of midsized administrative centers, whose tasks have changed so greatly that the original public management models have to be further developed. This is especially evident in the example of Hesse. This state is affected by growth and contraction processes in equal measure. Especially in northern and eastern Hesse, many midsized rural administrative centers are diminishing, putting their status in the CPT on trial, while at the same time conditions in the Rhine-

Main region are changing to the benefit of big cities. Although even the smaller cities in this region are gaining in population, the importance of big cities in a functional respect is rising thanks to the boom in services, which goes far beyond the duties of traditional centrality organized by the state. The midsized administrative centers are losing importance and are in danger of becoming bedroom communities. In both cases—in the context of both shrinkage and growth—the CPT has no solutions for the geographically and functionally diverging initial conditions of the midsized administrative centers and their facilities (Oswalt et al. 2017).

Considering all this, the difference in the regional development models in recent use in different German states is significant. Starting from a homogeneous distribution of small and medium-sized towns, the state of Thuringia, for instance, does not classify any individual midsized administrative centers by their degree of centrality, but rather upgrades individual municipalities in strategic locations to a mid-central functional area. As primus inter pares among the midsized administrative centers, these areas are expected to take on additional public service tasks, including some of the functions of a regional center (*Oberzentrum*) (Freistaat Thüringen 2014). Furthermore, self-organized rural district and municipal area reforms are promoted by means of financial incentives.

Bavaria—which traditionally pays more attention to rural areas—is putting its trust in voluntary cooperation at the municipal level. Along with EU subsidies and heavy use of funds from the federal and state government program Kleine Städte und Kommunen (Small Towns and Municipalities), state funds are also being directed into promoting intercommunal collaborations, a practice that is proving to be extremely popular. The voluntary aspect appears to be an essential principle in this case. Integrierte ländliche Entwicklungskonzepte (ILEK; integrated rural development concepts) are being increasingly used as instruments to pursue a soft approach to regional planning.

These state-level initiatives aim primarily to reduce administration expenses by making adjustments to areas (enlargement) and to the organization of public service facilities (efficiency/collaboration), which not uncommonly meet with disapproval from municipalities and citizens fearing a devaluation of the specific area in which they live. Hence, more recent approaches are also of interest, such as the regional development strategy of Schleswig-Holstein, which pursues a process of participation and dialogue at the state level. A state-wide, bottom-up dialogue first produced a green paper with strategic guidelines, which is now being further developed in technical dialogues and is intended to result in a white book establishing the fundamentals of future regional planning (the Minister-President of the State of Schleswig-Holstein 2016).

From the Normative to the New Form of Centrality
In the discussion of Christaller's Central Place Theory, the type of centrality emphasized usually refers to an accumulation of major municipal functions. Alongside this

1.1.2

catalogue method of listing facilities for the exchange of central goods and services, however, Christaller also introduced the so-called telephone method for evaluating the significance of a place. By counting the number of telephone connections, he also took account of a place's virtual network of relationships to determine its significance in the geographical system (Christaller 1968, pp. 138–149). So it would be perfectly justifiable to question the normative definition of centrality in common use today and to understand and localize new forms of centrality, which, for instance, manifest through digitalization, and to develop new criteria for measuring and evaluating them.

In light of the above, it becomes clear how important broadband deployment is today to peripheral areas with regard to enhancing their importance and helping them catch up economically. The Internet of Things is also much more relevant in rural areas. In these areas, after all, this technology is not primarily a matter of convenience and individual optimization processes, as in cities, but rather a matter of essential public service issues: an online consultation can take the place of a long trip to see a doctor; Internet-based DRT (demand responsive transport) services make scheduled bus services unnecessary; garbage is picked up only when the trash can notifies the waste disposal contractor; and self-driving vehicle technology could bring improvement to all public service sectors. Barriers of geographical resistance and mobility pitfalls could be removed, and digital applications would help to form a wide variety of alliances that would aid in the co-production of public services and bring the city and the countryside closer together on the whole (Antonelli et al. 2017, pp. 42–45) (see figure 1).

Owing to the urgency of the problems we face, it can be assumed that the smart region will soon outrank the smart city. These realizations, as well as the willingness to invest in their implementation, are distinctly increasing in the political sphere. One of the core recommendations of the latest regional planning report, as well as the research needs indicated in it, underscores the potentials of digitalization with regard to public services. Not only must the broadband network be promoted, however, but also the ability of civil society to deal with the new possibilities since people in rural areas are often less digitally oriented (BBSR 2017, pp. 135–136).

Cultivated Landscape as Potential

The strongest potential of a rural region lies in its most innate aspect: the cultivated landscape.

Could not cultivated landscape serve as a support for regional planning, then? So far, the possibility of collaborations and the formation of city networks along the borders of rural areas has received little attention. Yet this is precisely where the need for action is greatest, as well as the potential for development and renewal. In this sense, an orientation to the historical cultivated landscape might well affect a positive future for the patterns of urban and community structure. Intensive regional networking could enable the emergence of new and efficient territorial

entities, rural republics, with regional value-added chains and specific cross-border geographical models. The region around the Harz, for instance, would have great potential. The central landscape zone defines the area and could give a new identity to the entire region in Saxony-Anhalt, as well as parts of Lower Saxony and Thuringia: the Republic of the Harz. A total of around 600,000 people live here, and it would be one of the most heavily populated areas in central Germany (Dolata and Rettich 2010, pp. 830–841) (see figure 2).

If it were networked, this region could be more efficiently organized and take over tasks of public services comparable to a regional center, albeit in a rural area. Apart from the defining cultivated landscape, the twenty-two midsized administrative centers and administrative subcenters in the Harz do, in fact, exhibit a large number of endogenous economic potentials, a variety of educational opportunities, and potentials for networking. For instance, it would take little to convert the current infrastructure into a 300-kilometer-long road and rail ring around the area's entire circumference, linked by specific hubs to other midsized administrative centers and regional centers. The natural potential of the Harz has been used to obtain energy from hydropower since

Figure 1: Digitalization minimizes barriers of geographical resistance and promotes cooperation between urban and rural areas, © T. Rustemeyer

1.1.2

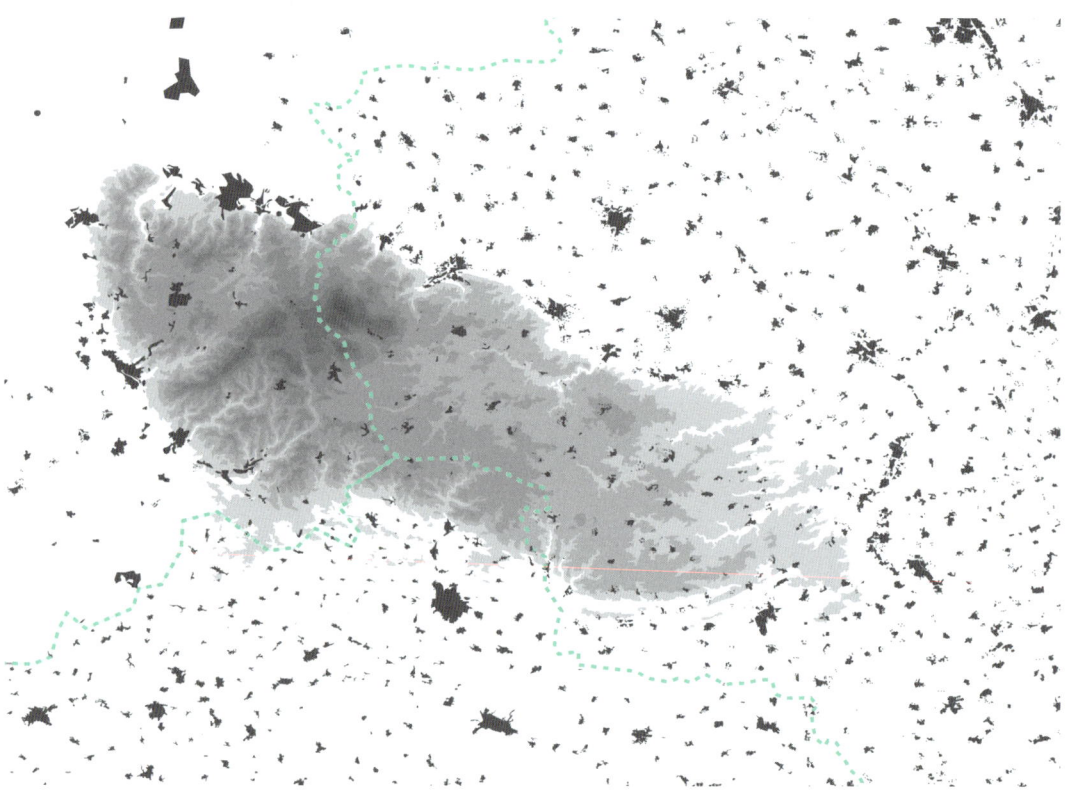

Figure 2: The Harz, showing
state borders, © K. Dolata/S. Rettich

time immemorial. Nature as a source of renewable energy could increase by adding wind energy and biomass. Using natural resources for tourism on the one hand and energy on the other need not be a contradiction and is already the status quo in the Harz (where dams for power generation also create artificial lakes that attract tourists). Industrial landscape is already widely understood to be a cultural sphere, as shown by the UNESCO World Heritage Site of the Oberharzer Wasserwirtschaft (Upper Harz Water Management). In the future, the new Republic of the Harz could further expand its synergies. The proximity to agriculture in the northern Harz (Börde) and the use of the cultivated area of the Mansfeld Land for wind power are of particular importance in this context. A third area of occupation in the Harz involves the healthcare industry and rehabilitation centers. Tradition and more recent specializations could be deepened and a common marketing system developed incorporating both institutional organizations and private commercial networks (see figure 3).

Republic of the Harz—a Governance Model

One key topic is the question of administration and governance structures in rural republics, especially in the Republic of the Harz, which would extend across three German states. Would a new component have to be added to the Central Place system? That is, could the future Republic of the Harz be a major central region, with its own budget independent of the states, discharging its duties of financing and organizing public services on its own, or should the governance model of this network of towns be structured rather informally, as is the case in German metropolitan regions? For the final exhibition at the IBA Urban Redevelopment, the more speculative, albeit equally realistic, version was chosen, since it would hardly be possible to cope with the profound changes in rural areas using Christaller's system of 1933—it was the picture of the system of cities and settlements existing in Germany in the wake of the great growth phase of industrialization and therefore appears poorly suited to the geographical polarization and contraction processes on a regional scale facing us today and in the future (see figure 4).

The idea of developing the Harz across borders as a unified cultivated and urban landscape has now left the paper stage behind and been taken up by the region's heads of administration. The Ein Harz (One Harz) initiative came into being in 2015, and now counts more than forty cities and municipalities, associations, companies, and institutions of higher education among its members, as well as five administrative districts, whose borders touch the Harz.

There are now plans to found Ein Harz GmbH under the umbrella of the Harz Regional Association in late 2017, with the aim of deepening regional ties and advancing common developments (Volksstimme 2017).

Europe of Regions

Europe's current crisis is increasingly becoming a crisis of nation-states, and one which will intensify as integration within the European Union progresses. As soon

1.1.2

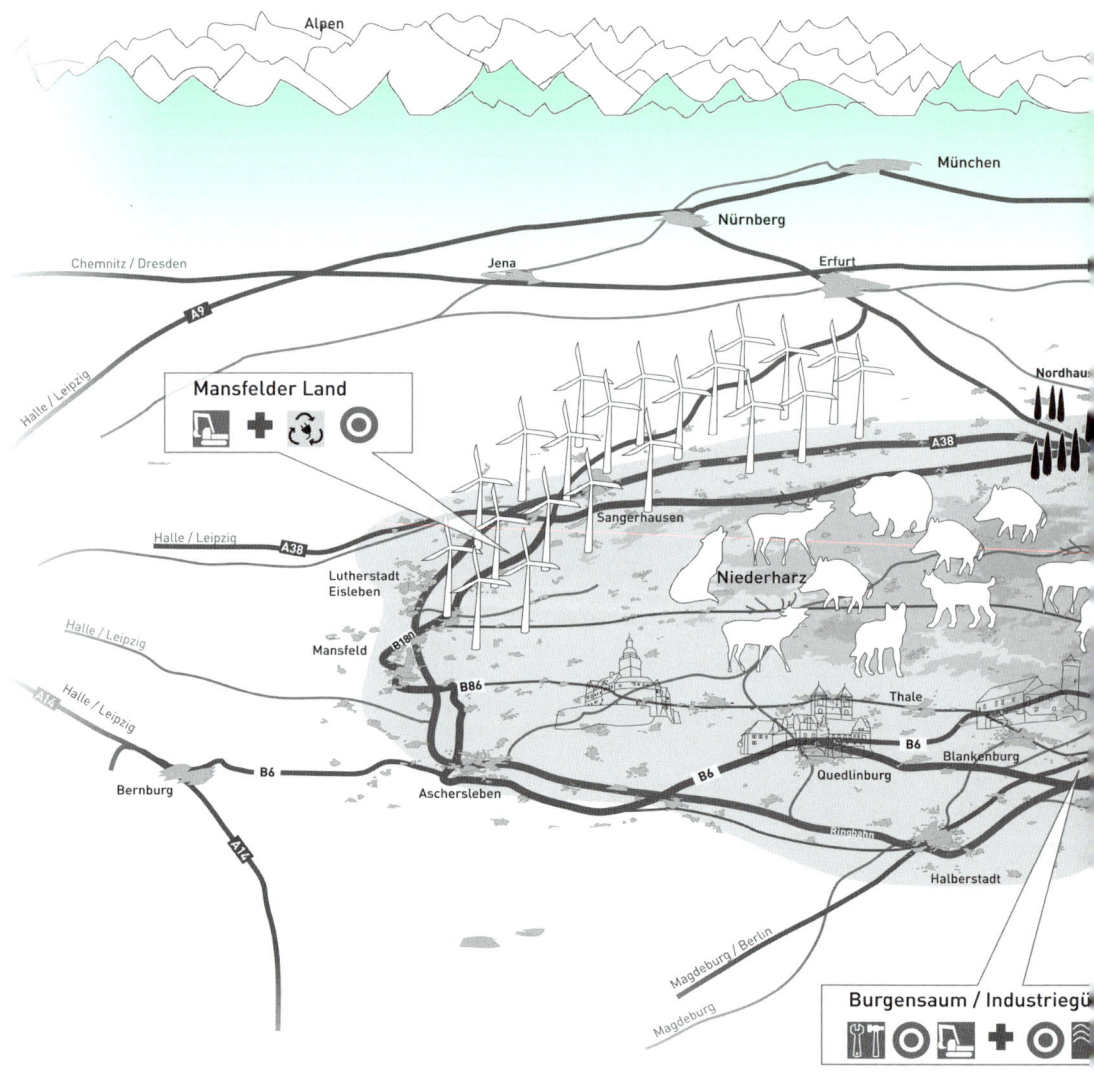

Alpen

München

Nürnberg

Chemnitz / Dresden

Jena

Erfurt

A9

Halle / Leipzig

Nordhaus

Mansfelder Land

A38

Halle / Leipzig

A38

Sangerhausen

Lutherstadt
Eisleben

Niederharz

Halle / Leipzig

B180

Mansfeld

Thale

B86

A14

Halle / Leipzig

B86

B6

Blankenburg

Bernburg

B6

Quedlinburg

Ascherleben

B6

Ringbahn

A14

Halberstadt

Magdeburg / Berlin

Magdeburg

Burgensaum / Industriegü

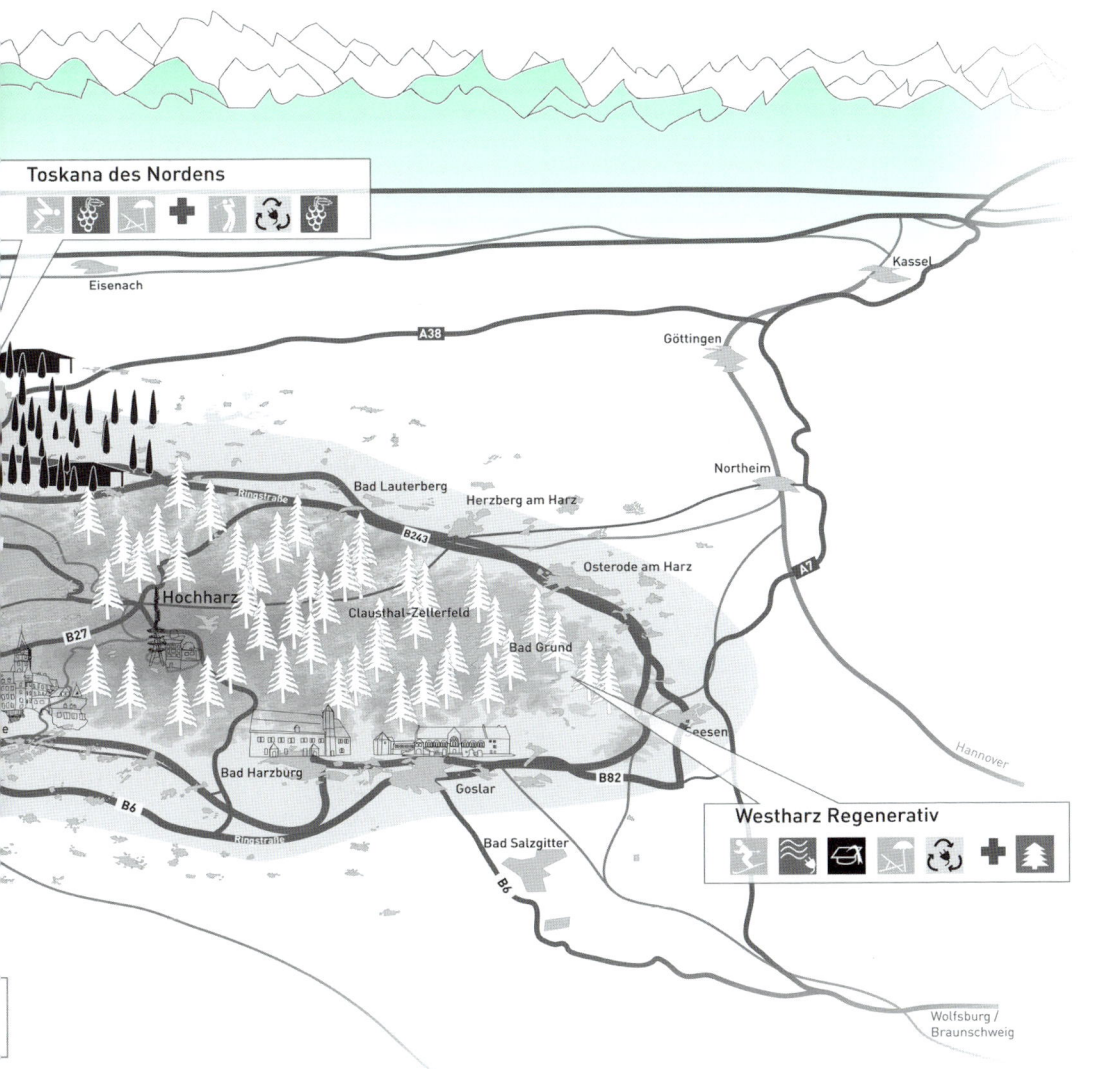

Figure 3: Republic of the Harz,
© K. Dolata/S. Rettich

Figure 4: Goodbye to the Central Place system, © S. Rettich

as the borders within Europe further dissolve, the notion of a nation-state founded on boundaries and sovereignty will become obsolete. Other political and regional reference structures will take its place. The efforts of Lombardy, Venetia, Catalonia, Scotland, or South Tyrol at attaining autonomy are harbingers of potential political and geographical structures in Europe. Ulrike Guérot is already developing a utopia in regard to the historical cultural regions of Europe and demanding a European republic consisting of regions rather than nation-states. She counters the fear of petty regionalism and the formation of identity-based zones by affirming that enhancing their political status will directly benefit the regions and their economies (Guérot 2017, pp. 148–151). Heightened autonomous action at the local level was also the plea put forth by Jürgen Aring. Giving the regions their own financial framework and allowing them to make independent decisions on how to use their funds will also strengthen decisions based on grass-roots democracy and political participation, forcing back extremist tendencies.

It is important for us urban and regional planners not to leave the field of discourse on rural areas and regional development in Europe to political scientists and geographers, and to ensure that space in itself is perceived as an argument.

References

Antonelli, C., F. Bentlin, A. Million, and S. Rettich (2017). *Die neo-europäische Stadt—Ein Manifest der Generation Y für eine neue Leipzig Charta*. Berlin.

Aring, J. (2010). "Gleichwertige Lebensverhältnisse—Invers frontiers—Selbstverantwortungsräume." Ministerium f. Landesentwicklung u. Verkehr Sachsen-Anhalt / conception P. Oswalt and E. Mittmann, ed. *IBA Stadtumbau Sachsen-Anhalt—Weniger ist Zukunft*. Berlin: pp. 764–777.

BBSR (2017). *Raumordnungsbericht 2017—Daseinsvorsorge sichern*. Bonn.

Christaller, W. (1968). *Die zentralen Orte in Süddeutschland* (Reprografischer Nachdruck der 1. Auflage, 1933, Jena). Darmstadt.

Der Ministerpräsident des Landes Schleswig-Holstein, ed. (2016). *Grünbuch Landesentwicklungsstrategie Schleswig-Holstein 2030*. Kiel.

Dolata, K. and S. Rettich (2010). "Republic of Harz." Ministerium f. Landesentwicklung u. Verkehr Sachsen-Anhalt / conception P. Oswalt and E. Mittmann, ed. *IBA Stadtumbau Sachsen-Anhalt—Weniger ist Zukunft*. Berlin: pp. 830–841.

Freistaat Thüringen / Ministerium für Bau, Landesentwicklung und Verkehr (2014). *Landesentwicklungsplan Thüringen 2025*. Erfurt.

Guérot, U. (2017). "Die europäischen Kulturregionen: Einheit in Vielfalt." *Arch+*. 228: pp. 148–151.

Land Sachsen-Anhalt (2007). *Leitbild der Gemeindegebietsreform Sachsen-Anhalt*.

Melhose, I. and T. Weisenburger (2017). "Große Pläne für 2017." *Volksstimme vom 25.2.2017*. Magdeburg/Halberstadt.

Oswalt, P., S. Rettich, and F. Roost (2017). *Vorbereitungspapier einer Tagung zu Mittelzentren in 2018*. Kassel.

Sieverts, T. (1997). *Zwischenstadt—Zwischen Ort und Welt, Raum und Zeit, Stadt und Land*. Braunschweig.

Statistisches Bundesamt (2017). "Städte in Deutschland nach Fläche und Bevölkerung auf Grundlage des ZENSUS 2011." Accessed July 15, 2017. www.destatis.de/DE/ZahlenFakten/LaenderRegionen/Regionales/Gemeindeverzeichnis/Administrativ/Aktuell/05Staedte.html.

Statistisches Landesamt Sachsen-Anhalt. Accessed October 20, 2017. www.stala.sachsen-anhalt.de/gk/fms/fms110113.htm.

1.1.2

Locate: A Translocal Perspective

Jonas König/Kai Vöckler

There is no need to locate something that holds a firm place. Locating responds to movements, flows, and ambiguity. It is an effort to establish relations, an attempt "to fix it." The double meaning is suggestive: it points to the ongoing prevalence of a mindset in which stability and locally grounded relations are perceived as the norm. Only recently, as the dominant narrative in urbanism suggests, has the attachment to locality and place evaporated in the light of acceleration, digitalization, and globalization (Smith 2000).

Not surprisingly, this narrative of the nonplace is rife with contradictions. Yet the increasing mobility of persons, objects, and ideas has sweeping effects. Places do not vanish, but they are increasingly interconnected; different relational spaces overlap at one place. Scholars have deployed the notion of translocality to conceptualize these changes in spatial ordering. The very changes, however, continue to challenge those who research, inhabit, and plan urban spaces. Three examples from Prishtina, the capital of Kosovo, but also a "translocal capital" (Vöckler and König 2016), illustrate novel necessities for (self-)locating.

Locating Research: Either Here or There?

Research on translocality often refers to the headquarter economies of the global city or to immigrant neighborhoods. This focus, however, overshadows a basic insight: translocality represents connections between concrete locations. While the global economy constitutes an ephemeral space of flows, migration relates tangible places to each other. There is no arrival city without a departure city. Migration as a sociospatial practice transforms both cities.

With close to 40 percent of the Kosovo population living abroad, Prishtina is the national hub of emigration. The city is not only directly affected by the exodus of inhabitants, but there is

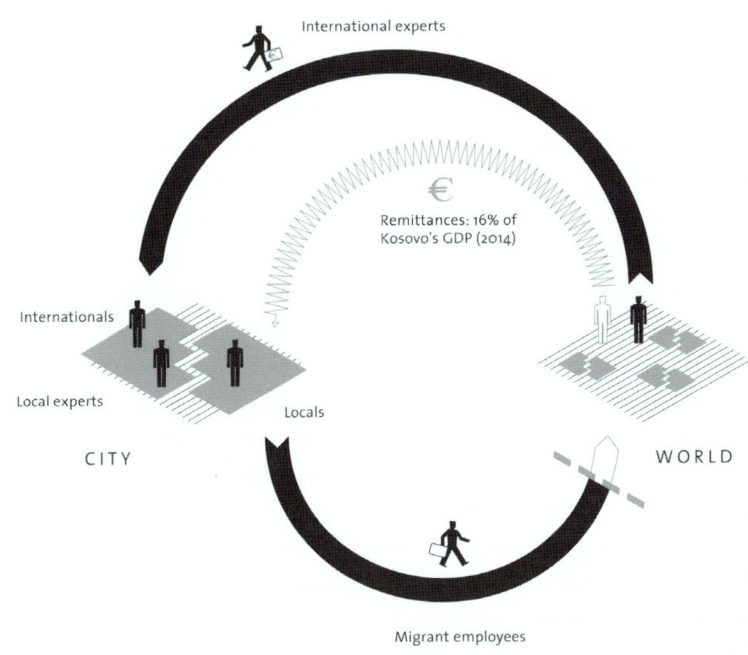

International experts

Remittances: 16% of Kosovo's GDP (2014)

Internationals

Local experts

Locals

CITY

WORLD

Migrant employees

also a continuous inflow from people who consider the city as a stopover. A specific infrastructure and an economy of emigration has emerged. Moreover, emigration is often temporary. The circular movement of people, the transfer of remittances, and the diffusion of cultural content materialize in the cityscape (Vöckler 2008), yet they are hardly researched. To grasp translocal spaces, urban studies would need to simultaneously study different places. For pragmatic reasons alone, research tends to be located here, not there.

Locating Inhabitants: Neither Here nor There?

Translocality is usually conceptualized as positive, transmitting the boundaries of territories and communities. For migrants, however, living in multiple spaces implies severe tensions (Waldinger 2015), as it notoriously conflicts with the nation-state and its spatial logic based on external delineation and internal homogenization (Held 2005). Tendencies of denationalization notwithstanding (Mau 2007), translocality confronts migrants with questions of identity and belonging.

A social practice to balance this struggle is straightforward: building oneself a "home" (Lopez 2015). Prishtina's cityscape is

1.1.3

significantly shaped by construction activities that are financed with emigrants' remittances and that aim to generate fixed points within translocal spaces. Yet, standing empty for most parts of the year (if used at all), these structures are problematic. While their functionality is mainly symbolic, migrant houses conflict with other spatial configurations and needs. The overlap of different translocalized spaces also challenges established concepts of urban planning.

Locating Plans: Here and There?

The example of Prishtina also epitomizes the translocality of urban planning as a professional field. A broad range of international NGOs and development agencies works in the city and supplements local actors. Together, they generate a relational space that obviously is not detached from the city, yet top-down approaches prevail where contextualization would be needed (Vöckler 2008). It remains an open question on how to involve actors like Prishtina's absent, but present diaspora in urban development processes—and to adapt to a context that itself is highly translocalized.

Figure 2: Remittances have significantly contributed to Prishtina's recent construction boom. Yet, a large portion is used for second homes, © Jonas König

Today, translocality is the norm rather than the exception. Urban professionals themselves have become translocal just like the fields in which they operate. Yet it remains a challenge to develop concepts, methods, and tools that allow binaries between here and there to be left behind.

1.1.3

References

Held, G. (2005). *Territorium und Großstadt*. Wiesbaden.

Lopez, S. (2015). *The Remittance Landscape*. Chicago.

Mau, S. (2007). *Transnationale Vergesellschaftung*. Frankfurt.

Smith, M.P. (2000). *Translocal Urbanism*. New Jersey.

Vöckler, K. (2008). *Prishtina is Everywhere*. Amsterdam.

Vöckler, K. and J. König (2017). "Prishtina. A Translocal Capital?" *MONU* 25: pp. 16–21.

Waldinger, R. (2015). *The Cross-Border Connection*. Cambridge, MA.

I Am Where You Are Not: On Concrete Action in Real Places

Markus Ambach

The work that we have done over the last ten years through the project platform MAP situates itself largely beyond classical art landscapes, opting instead for the types of urban spaces that might be described as transition zones, pioneer territories, and research areas. The use of these spaces is not yet determined, but still actively negotiated by society. Located at the intersection of art, urbanism, city planning, and everyday culture, our work is often concerned with the border zone between disciplines. The public sphere—where society's various discourses overlap and are mapped out—therefore logically represents a field of action.

In the actual local work in city- and landscapes such as the environment of the A40 in the Ruhr district,[1] the Lohberg district in Dinslaken,[2] and Mönchengladbach's city center,[3] there is an increasing discrepancy between action in the political-economic sphere and the concrete situations one confronts on site. As we see politics and the market as well as individual behavior ever more oriented to abstract systems of value and virtual spheres of life, feedback from the reality of a location is often completely missed. Interest in the center's margins steadily declines and largely allows for the abandonment of the remaining real places. It is not only the Ruhr district, which seems to suffer a surplus of space following the coal and steel industry's decline; various other districts' rural regions also show signs of societal neglect.

While the peripheries are devalued, urban spaces of action are ever denser as speculative objects and pools of value. What is

[1] See www.b1a40.de.

[2] See www.choreografie-einerlandschaft.de.

[3] "Ein ahnungsloser Traum vom Park;" see www.markusambachprojekte.de.

called urban quality in some regions has been reduced to contentious investment capital in others. The real estate market exploits that which is currently called public as well as that which actually is public. What's more, following from the concept of speculative space, the free action of every individual is, in turn, tied into the space and thereby capitalized on. Owning space manifests as pure potential so that the less action is permitted to take place, the more capital is generated.

Analogously, the individual's life optimizes without much resistance. It is not only artists that are subject to the seductive dictates of a placeless globalism. The demand for career profiles that function worldwide is blindly accepted, imminently threatening vernacular difference. Everywhere and nowhere all at once—and yet always the same—everyone shoots around the globe disregarding the ecological, social, and political consequences.

This is the world of individuals that follows from the model of action within the domain of the political economy, increasingly visualized in networks and on the data highway. As with financial markets and markets of production, politics also seems to have lost its true objective. In regions like the Ruhr district, the political successors of the former power in the coal and steel industries already resemble a caste, free from the reality of place and life in the virtual realm of the market and calculated power.

Renaissance of the Real

Beyond all polemics, these radical divergences between the political value-economy and real, lived environment contain surprising potential, which can particularly be seen on a local level. It not only leads to a split of interests in virtual and real space, but also has a provocative, utopian potential. The proposition: we abandon the virtual world that they want and retain the real one for ourselves. With the political economy's progressive withdrawal from real space, there is already a pleasant disinterestedness on the side of markets and methods. While virtual value is contentiously fought over, real places fall into disuse and open up the surprising possibility of revaluation. Where the lines between life and politics, place and economy, market and man are drawn, there emerges a peripheral space of the real: a new, parallel, depolarized space of action of a simple, sensual character.

1.1.4

Totally Local

A part of this utopia can already be found in the capillaries of local behavioral patterns. At the deepest point of its political existence, the abandoned site is newly experienced and transformed by those who were never granted permission to possess it. The Ruhr district is a paradigmatic example of this. Beyond politics and economics, people reappropriate the forgotten sites (of earlier industrial manufacturing) by means of site-specific, context-dependent strategies of action. Whether in alternative life plans, individual conceptions of the everyday, microcommunities, or self-organized associations, a life forms in the spaces that capital and (electoral) politics abandon, unconsciously and site-specifically designed and organized as a parallel system.

Space versus Practice

To that end, locality and the culture of practice play a specific role. While on an economic level the dependence on space and activity constantly reconstitutes itself, action moves into the foreground in its absence. A culture of practice that is always reliant on action in exterior spaces and living through the direct transfer of their knowledge is, by definition, open to unrestricted entry. It develops in a place's locality and a landscape's specificity. In lieu of abstract values, it makes use of its aesthetic and sensible consistency. It operates in the spaces that offer themselves to it, rather those from which it is constantly excluded. It organizes itself according to the space's conditions, instead of subjugating itself to the space. It sees to the site's emancipation as a pure space of action that negates the value of ownership and, in opposition, designs a space of local operation with a newly designed sensual character.

I Am Where You Are Not

In the local operation of a culture of practice, there is a departure from the eternally unredeemed promise of financial markets and a tendency toward unique tactics and practices. Through the reappropriation of autonomous individual behavior, it establishes—even if unconsciously—a parallel society that calls for a separation of interests in virtual and real spaces, representations and being, capital and quality. Even if this is a red rag for state politics, the ripped thread between people and politics has long created a whole set of subcommunities that have settled in the forgotten reality of space. They refer to a poly-political field in which the culture of practice creates alternatives to the culture of space, which will be specified in the future.

Learning From ...
For me, these qualities make operations in concrete, local contexts attractive, even though this is not only due to their immediacy, intensity, and sensuousness. They also offer the possibility of collective learning processes, an active exchange of both personal and societal knowledge, as well as its continual transformation. In specific local structures, one can find spaces with active, open ne- ▶ 2.1.1
gotiation processes. This leads to new paths and societal forms, operating from the local to the global. Opposed to the callous conditions of the universalized market, including in art and culture, there is a detailed heterogeneous complexity of life and everyday culture that can be understood as starting with the place, moving to the landscape and the world, and back again. Work in this field is beyond established categories; instead, it is consistently characterized by context-based thinking. In order to do justice to its protagonists, this work requires personal presence, a clear commitment to the reality of a site, and long-standing engagement.

1.1.4

1.2. Processes

- **1** The Machine

- **2** Drivers of Planning Processes: About the Contradiction of Time Aspects in Urban Development

- **3** Participation: Instrument or Culture?

The Machine

Andreas Krauth, Teleinternetcafe

A text chat with four participants in the near future about the appearance of a so-called process-visualization machine, a communication tool to facilitate decision-making.

The four participants of the text chat are:

The architect:
The architect brought in the initial concept for a step-by-step transformation of "our site," an inner city district that is about to be transformed over the next few years. The process-oriented concept is about identifying threads of consensus between top-down requirements and bottom-up initiatives.

The administrator:
The administrator is a member of administrative staff of the city's urban planning department and responsible for providing decision templates for the transformation of "our site" to the city parliament.

The owner:
The owner is the landowner of "our site" and wants to sell or lease the area without investing any resources.

The artist:
The artist has been an interim user of an existing building on "our site" for many years and is interested in transforming the existing interim status into something long term. The exciting interim uses made the area well known in the city.

1.2.1

the architect: big news, co-space producers! i found out about a new machine. it could solve all our problems at once.

the owner: sounds great!

the artist: i'm curious.

the architect: it's a process-visualization machine. i had the opportunity to see a prototype of it in action just a few hours ago and think we can apply the machine to the process development of our site.

the administrator: can you describe that more precisely?

the architect: of course. i'm trying to be brief. i have just been to a former farm in southwest france where the prototype of the process-visualization machine was presented by its inventor.

the owner: the secret place...

the architect: to make things a little clearer: this machine is not just a box with a touchscreen or a simple app. it stands in the barn of this old farm, a huge device, so big that you have to climb a ladder to get anywhere. it is difficult to describe what i've seen because i've never seen anything like it.

the artist: sounds like the world machine of franz gsellmann.

the architect: yes, similar, but fully functional.

the artist: wow.

the architect: and it gets even better. the machine is able to visualize a sequence of complex spatiotemporal constellations (e.g. the gradual structural changes at our site) over any period of time, both retrospectively rewinding to real states in the past (e.g. to analyze them) as well as planning ahead into the future. the needs of different actors involved in the planning process can be fed in; for example, the need for low-cost workspaces for artists is just as important as the need for an efficient business concept. so you can create a clear and applicable basis of decision as far as possible in the future, such as whether it more promising for a specific user to preserve an existing building or build a new one, or perhaps better still to create soft interests like public space that offers a place for a chill-out, a chat, a coffee, or just for hanging out.

the owner: hard to believe. great!

the administrator: i will try to translate that for myself: you say there is a machine with which it is possible to simplify the development process of our site, the cooperative development of which we have all been working on for some time, by reinsuring us that the planning decisions we make can be implemented 1:1 later as long as we keep to the requests of this machine?

the artist: my understanding is more or less the same, although "realistic" in this case probably once again means "economic." every day i am implementing something "realistic" at our site. i'm part of the economy of it.

the owner: me too.

the artist: the machine… just to understand… in principle it is ==a balancing mediation between real circumstances, requirements to be fulfilled, long-term planning goals==…? 2.3.2 ▶

the owner: as already stated several times before: as long as it breaks even at the end, i am very interested in a content-driven development of my site, gladly with local actors, gladly with existing buildings. the good thing with this machine could be that it would save us some time and speed up the process.

the artist: well… it is not automatically about accelerating everything, it is rather about taking more time for some areas to look more closely, e.g. to identify "local heroes" and together with them let emerge a positive momentum for change; while in other areas develop projects more rapidly, e.g. to create urgently needed new housing.

the administrator: that's what we want.

the artist: actually i see this machine more as a kind of reinsurance not to make the wrong decisions.

1.2.1

the architect: the machine manages to mediate between all these interests, always aiming to determine the best deal for everyone, not only including the structure of the architect in the future visualization, but also existing programs, real actors and persons, planning requirements...

but the most fascinating thing about the whole thing is the following: the machine can not only calculate the project's multiple dimensions, but it can also vividly show the project to anyone in a 3D model, no matter what moment in time.

the owner: how?

the architect: the visualization part of the machine is a kind of 3D projector, which looks like a huge table with a metal arm. the table is a surface with a grid representing the site as the design area. the long arm holds about ten flexible fast moving tentacles with tubes, coils, and wires, on which small projectors are attached. that means the projection is not just a beamer projection but also a physically built model. solid, with a firm structure, which can be changed from one moment to the next with the projector. as if with a 3D printer, you could fast forward and rewind, zoom in and out and choose different alternatives during the rewinding.

the owner: amazing.

the architect: the machine is still very large and unwieldy, but the inventor believes with further revision it could become smaller and smaller.

the artist: but our transformation process is not just a redistribution of programs into appropriate building volumes, also it involves a lot of social dependencies and constellations.

the administrator: true.

the artist: the built environment needs to be right. but the chemistry between all those who are involved in the design of the space must fit too.

the owner: that's what i already learned.

the artist: for my part, i'm really happy to be part of the professional discourse. i got the chance to be engaged, to explore our site, and i got to understand the perspective of an urban planner.

the architect: glad to hear.

the artist: i can like always quote michel de certeau.

the owner: but please be brief about it today.

the artist: short, with my own words: a one-dimensional interpretation of space as the built edges does not fully represent the development process of our site. with our regular informal discussions, for example, in which strongly different interests meet, we constantly create new spaces through our emotional interaction.

the owner: results of our interaction?

the administrator: yes, for example, with the new spatial agency we set up we now have a person on site, whose position is something between a housekeeper, curator, 1:1 urban-planner, mediator, and an important voice to continuously advocate the concept. the result is a new professional field as a cross section of many specialist competencies, something like a "concept estate agent."

the owner: interesting point about the "concept estate agent." never seen it like that.

the artist: all of this is way more important than the building volumes to be built. the urban planner does not make a city alone; the entire urban population does so together.

the architect: a site like ours is only a momentary constellation of fixed points. space is produced when directions of future development, different velocities, and the variability of time are associated.

the owner: well said!

the artist: we want to shape the city in practice, instead of merely planning blocks with programs.

1.2.1

the architect: i don't really consider myself a "block-slider," but sometimes these blocks in a model help to stimulate the imagination and create a common base for discussion.

the architect: however, the machine can do a lot more than blocks...

the owner: the story continues...

the architect: the scale of the timeframe taken into consideration and the scale of the physical representation can be adjusted. the machine's visualization includes different scales at different speeds, and every decision, no matter what size, is individually adjustable, e.g. in a detailed section, to identify small-scale and short-term repair needs in a particular spot and to understand their long-term effects.

the administrator: this would help us a lot in public relations and politics, if we had a tool to make such complex processes comprehensible in an intuitive way.

the architect: or for example: a seemingly unimportant person making use of the machine's specific abilities at a certain time could give the decisive impulse for the whole. that person's inclusion in the process is therefore important. or the machine could show where the process might get stuck (e.g. a loafer in the administration).

the administrator: that does not refer to myself.

the architect: on the strategically long-term timeline, basic qualities can be defined, such as a basic framework that defines particularly important spatial edges, distinct public spaces or narrow alleys, enabling a lively mix of programs, and of different users and residents, etc.

the administrator: like a zoning plan.

the architect: yes, but not only facts that can be fixed by numbers, but also soft factors such as special characteristics of the site, its materiality, its traces of use, and tiny hidden qualities like the sun shining on the stairs where the bus driver likes to drink his coffee every morning. so everything that is needed for the development of an authentic neighborhood.

the owner: splendid!

the administrator: i would like to say that zoning law is not simply applicable with a yes-or-no attitude. in complex processes, the line of argumentation has to meet the rules in order to accomplish what is aimed for in terms of content.

the artist: "authentic neighborhood"... yesterday, i read an article that stated that the term "authenticity" should be used with caution. the point made in the article was that authenticity is the absence of mendacity. but this is a very vague concept that cannot withstand discussion or analysis. i wonder how the machine is able to make comprehensible decisions considering such soft factors. in the same way, because of this vagueness, it might be used for many contradictory purposes.

the architect: a genius loci is always running the risk of being misused for contradictory things.

the artist: we should not forget where the urge for authenticity and originality may lead us. we can also stand for the doubt and our own disagreement.

the administrator: now it becomes philosophical. back to the facts.

the owner: please!

the administrator: i will try to translate for myself the potential helpfulness of this process-visualization machine. the fact is, we have an inner-city area that will open up to the city for a new development. in a subarea, there are various intermediate users from the arts and cultural scene who have activated an already quite interesting space.

the artist: like me.

the administrator: the process-oriented concept by the architect strives to follow this existing profile, forming the starting point for a location-specific strategy. a rapid densification of some parts of the site relieves those areas with existing buildings that are already in use and thus acts as a valve for the development pressure for the entire site.

1.2.1

the owner: exactly.

the administrator: the idea is that speeds of development in the various subareas are controlled individually. this way, our common strategy provides for the possibility of a procedural transformation, which allows for atmospheric and programmatic diversity.

the architect: well, so far the theory.

the administrator: i'm always amazed that after an initial mutual distrust and intense clashes between all of those now communicating here on an equal footing (the administration, the local actors, the owner, the politicians and the architect), a new culture of discussion has emerged. this has made it possible for all parties to think in a similar direction and try to direct the process in this direction.

the artist: comment: this culture of discussion is the actual production of space.

the administrator: the process-visualization machine, described by the architect today, could help us to explain this complex project in a clear manner to a general public, and at the same time the machine would be able to provide support in risk assessments and strategic decisions. in this way, as a group with different individual interests, it could show us in detail various threads of consensus that could then be more easily decided on.

the artist: but how can we avoid becoming simply the machine's servants?

the artist: in the end, we could all be stressed out by the machine— deprived of any human freedom of decision—always being ready in time and not being allowed to make a mistake, so that everything will happen just as the machine has calculated it before?

the architect: the machine does not require you to follow a set path consistently. it is able to react continuously to changing conditions and to include them in future scenarios. it works like a navigation system suggesting an alternative route in the event of a violation of the calculated route in order to reach the same destination.

the owner: but the alternative route after a wrong turn still takes longer than the one originally suggested. so we are back at the question: who guarantees the implementation of the machine's suggestions?

the architect: the inventor is actually already experimenting with a kind of punishment system, which prompts any actors who do not comply with their calculated obligation to carry out the calculated actions by means of electric power shocks via their smartphone.

the artist: this is the dictatorship of the machines!

the artist: considering how complicated it was until we had our legitimacy to shape this process worked out. what is the legitimacy of the machine all of a sudden?

the administrator: do not exaggerate. we do not have to apply this punishment mechanism right away, but it would be worth trying the machine. the machine would make it possible for us to stop permanently arriving at the borders of our respective profession and to have to talk and judge things that we have very little idea about.

the artist: but isn't it great that, e.g., the owner deals directly with me as an artist? this is a discussion of values that would otherwise be omitted. the architect tinkering behind closed doors can not simply develop his ideal plan or his ideal rule and feed it into the machine, but he has to reassure himself by paying attention to the interests of the public. in conclusion we have arrived at the same point of the discussion: space can only be produced through our interaction as a society.

the architect: that's true, i am aware of and like to assume the role of the planner as an designing moderator and i prefer it to the architect with a genius solution.

the artist: but isn't it the same thing if we let everything be dictated by a machine? don't we need permanent self-doubt? can the machine doubt?

1.2.1

the architect: to a certain degree i can understand the doubt, even if my conclusion would be not to block the technical possibilities of the process-visualization machine. i think the advantages prevail.

the artist: i try to quote a wise sentence from bruno latour, which i think should apply to all of us, at least to me it does. in my own words: i am not a guru who shows the only possible way. i am experimenting with contradictions. my allies are skepticism, doubt, uncertainty, hesitation.

the administrator: philosophical again...

the owner: i'm getting hungry...

the architect: i also think it leads too far now and one does not exclude the other. after all, it is also about the prototypical character of this machine, which would fit very well with our experimental development process.

the administrator: you always talk about prototypes. when would the machine be ready?

the architect: according to the inventor's opinion, a relatively reliable test operation could take place in approximately ten years. of course, on the assumption that the development of the machine is a source of interest and that the inventor has a sufficient budget for its further development.

the owner: so we were just talking about something hypothetical?

the administrator: ten years... half of us will be retired.

the artist: i'm against this nazi-machine anyway.

the architect: oh dear! godwin's law...

the administrator: when i finally try to translate for myself: as a group, we mainly agree with the positive aspects of the presented process-visualization machine. due to the long preordering time and the difficulty of calculating a cost-benefit ratio, a decision in favor of the use of the machine does not appear to be meaningful at the moment...

the owner: we should not preclude this too fast.

the artist: it finally stopped raining.

the owner: i'm hungry. what time is it?
the artist: let's check out the new café at the corner. you can sit in the sun.

the owner: why not.

the artist: meet there in 10 minutes?

the owner: deal!

the administrator: who writes the summary minutes?

the architect: just checked our chat history. confused discussion today.

1.2.1

Drivers of Planning Processes: About the Contradiction of Time Aspects in Urban Development

Yvonne Siegmund

"There is something new to be created here. This is supposed to be a creative quarter, developing a momentum; and on the other hand the handbrake is constantly pulled. It's like sitting in a high-speed Porsche—you could get started— but someone is always pulling the handbrake. You just bounce a bit."

A temporary user in the Labor

"I feel like we in the Labor are a very small cog, because we spin so fast yet simply don't move much. If we were a bit more substantial, then we could become a larger cog and wouldn't have to move so franticly."

Another temporary user

Do both statements contradict each other? They do, and they don't. But first things first...

In the further development of the Kreativquartier an der Dachauer Straße (Creative Quarter on Dachauer Straße), Munich's planning pursues a strategy in which the time factor plays a decisive role. While three out of four areas are being planned relatively quickly, the development of the Labor— officially called Kreativlabor (Creative Laboratory)—leaves much time for deceleration. This quarter, a five-hectare area owned by the city, is being developed and improvised through a nonqualified zoning plan and §34 of the Baugesetzbuch (BauGB). Planning and usage take place simultaneously. Maintaining the substance of old buildings and local characteristics means establishing flexible temporary use concepts that may provide new momentum for the entire district. This strategy is just as useful as it is paradoxical: on the one hand, the short-term nature of functions extends towards the makeshift solutions; on the other hand, this requires complying with necessary short-term fire protection measures and leasing space as quickly as possible. Not every planning phase therefore runs at an even pace.

The perception of the local users is similar. From their perspective, the processes are described as both hectic and slow. With metaphors of a gear wheel that is far too small and a sloweddown Porsche, both try to underline the inefficiency of these processes. Their options for action have been severely restricted with regard to their own planning time. From their point of view, they can't create sustainable projects under precarious conditions. Although it is contrary to the implicit logic of interim uses, it is the indefinite and short intervals of extension that destabilizes temporary users in terms of planning their security and action options. They are literally on "slipping slopes" (Rosa 2005, p. 190). And interestingly, fragmentation, instability, and insecurity are usually mentioned in the context of accelerated principles. Therefore, not only is the speed of development crucial, but also speed must be understood in the context of its intended period.

Nevertheless, the Munich example is a courageous experiment, but not an isolated case. This simultaneous planning and development mechanism counts among other international initiatives that try to protect their spaces from global accelerating forces by strengthening local characteristics and qualities through successive steering. The most famous among them are called Cittàslow and Slow Urbanism. Some try to create stability by slowing down in a dynamic, uncertain, and "unleashed" world (Harvey 1990); others try to speed up processes. The research project Rapid Planning, for example, develops infrastructural basics to deal with the explosive growth in megacities. And even the lengthy construction law offers opportunities to speed up formal processes through the application of the "accelerated procedure" (§§ 13a and 13b BauGB) or temporary special arrangements for "express buildings" (§246 BauGB). But speed has a downside. "Hamburg is Building Express Apartments in Slow Motion," said a recent headline in the *Hamburger Abendblatt*.

1.2.2

Perceived speeds in the Labor

Perceived planning periods in the Labor

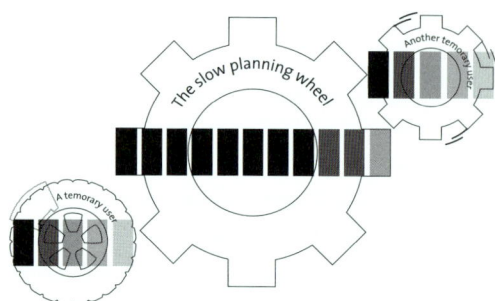

We are well acquainted with more prominent and large-scale projects in Hamburg, Berlin, and Stuttgart, all which suffer(ed) under unbridled acceleration that led to the halt of construction. It might sound trivial, but faster planning does not necessarily mean it can be developed faster.

We recall the two quotes at the beginning of this text. They show that dealing with time cannot be controlled through an objective measure. Whether fast or slow, a forced synchronization involves desynchronization and the potential for conflict, which is reflected in inadequate time and cost plans or developments that don't fit with the urban character. Goals and strategies, planning phases and periods of use, local practices and perceptions are not part of a universal speed: points in time, terms of planning or building phases, as well as local rhythms are also urban drivers. Therefore, many aspects of time are driving, steering and braking, stretching and shortening the planning processes, giving impulses and orientation.

The consequences of deaccelerated or accelerated (planned) actions are complex and sociospatial, functionally shaping in nature, and contributing "in themselves a time-changing quality" (Rosa 2005, p. 52). As a result, in a time-space-actor relationship, further discrepancies and dissonances are raised, whose causes and modes of action must be investigated in order to formulate appropriate spatiotemporal strategies according to the planning task.

Figure 1: The idea of a slow development of Munich's Kreativquartier and its reality—multiple and contradictory perceptions of time, © Yvonne Siegmund

References

Harvey, D. (1990). *The Condition of Postmodernity: An Enquiry into the Origins of Cultural Change.* Cambridge, MA.

Rosa, H. (2005). *Beschleunigung: Die Veränderungen der Zeitstrukturen in der Moderne.* Frankfurt am Main.

Participation: Instrument or Culture?

Hannes Rockenbauch

Among planners and politicians, it is widely agreed that participation is simply necessary. So far, so good. As to the question why all this is needed, the answer that is almost invariably given is that citizens have local knowledge that, as experts of everyday life, they must introduce into planning to ensure that all information relevant to decision-making is available for planners and politicians. In doing so, participation becomes an instrument of information acquisition for decision-makers in the fields of politics and administration. In most places, practice and the legal situation demonstrate that this understanding of participation as a form of public hearing is the predominant one—but must this be so? Already in 1969, Sherry R. Arnstein, in his essay "A Ladder of Citizen Participation," had called this understanding of participation a form of tokenism. Regarding the question as to what actual decision-making power is earmarked for citizens in participation processes, opinions differ until today, and not only in Germany (Selle 2013, p. 69).

The demand for greater decision-making power for citizens in planning processes is confronted with numerous objections. Essentially, they usually consist of denying that the citizens' ability to take complex assessment-based decisions is in the public interest (Selle 2013, p. 350). In order to remedy these and other familiar objections, much is invested in participation procedures with a view to reshaping them, such as those concerning learning processes for citizens. However, hardly anyone talks about the shortcomings on the other side, that is, on the part of the institutionalized routines in planning and politics, even though the bulk of current planning and political practice is not participation-capable. There is much that remains to be learned by all concerned parties in this regard.

1.2.3

Greater decision-making power for citizens not only means that planners and politicians must learn to hand power over to citizens, but also that their own usual processes and structures, and hence the culture of planning and policy processes, must be reinvented as a whole. In this sense, taking a chance on more democracy requires the courage to rethink administration and policy.

The overriding goal of this rethink is the approach to develop policy and planning processes as solidary learning processes between citizens, planners, and politicians. The purpose of these learning processes is the prudent handling of the uncertainty inherent in every complex planning task with regard to what the future holds and should hold. For the design of these processes, three core criteria are suggested here.

1. If citizens are to become equal partners concerning questions of urban development, planning processes must become open, fair, and integrate processes of binding negotiation, assessment, and learning. For this to succeed in the first place, it doesn't suffice anymore to organize participation in separate antecedent, subsequent, or parallel processes with respect to the official administrative and political routines. Instead, politicians, planners, and citizens should be brought together from start to finish.

1.5.2 ▶

2. We know from organizational research that the sectorial and hierarchical administrative structure with its iterative processes—predominant in most administrations to this day—is especially well suited for handling simple, routine tasks such as the issuance of a building permit. However, when it comes to complex planning tasks, such hierarchical working methods, and even project groups, quickly reach their limits (Scholl 1994). For issues concerning urban and spatial development, work on problem-related, nonhierarchical, and simultaneous cooperation procedures in the form of so-called ad-hoc organizations with planners, politicians, and citizens is already being done in some places. Such a procedure was most recently tested within the framework of the process for developing a spatial model for Karlsruhe (see Neppl 2015, p. 40).

3. Planners and politicians cannot solve conflicts of values, they cannot fully do away with uncertainty concerning the future, and they cannot eliminate human fallibility. However, they can learn to prudently handle these aspects. It would be prudent, by way of precaution, to plan organizational and spatial interventions to be as error-friendly, flexible, and revisable as possible (Hubig 2007). While the idea of the "provisional"—the idea to not

preclude future options for action—is easier to comprehend in the constructional and spatial field, it seems all the more difficult to reconcile it with our current political culture. Who in the public political sphere would admit that his or her idea and decisions are merely provisional? Who would elect a politician who so openly handles his or her fallibility? Apart from these difficulties, a culture of the provisional would have the great advantage of defusing conflicts. If joint negotiation and weighing processes "merely" lead to provisional results, subordinated positions within the process would assume an important corrective function or that of a fallback option. Errors would become important experiences, which would make it possible to do better in future.

What is certain is that providing greater participation to citizens in planning and policy processes first of all requires enabling the necessary culture of participation understood as common learning process to grow within these processes.

References

Arnstein, S. R. (1969). "A Ladder Of Citizen Participation." *Journal of the American Planning Association.* 35.04: pp. 216–224.

Hubig, C. (2007). *Die Kunst des Möglichen II, Ethik der Technik als provisorische Moral.* Bielefeld.

Neppl, M. (2015). *Auf dem Weg zum Räumlichen Leitbild Karlsruhe.* Karlsruhe.

Selle, K. (2013). *Über Bürgerbeteiligung hinaus: Stadtentwicklung als Gemeinschaftsaufgabe?* Detmold.

Scholl, B. (1994). *Aktionsplanung: Zur Behandlung komplexer Schwerpunktaufgaben in der Raumplanung.* Zurich.

1.3. Structures

The Arch: A Socio-Circular Gate to Technology

ConstructLab

Today, I could stand in front of a quite colorful, spectacular arch of eight meters, made from plastic bricks. I could look up and see it covered in tiles that have curious patterns, traces of multinational drinks companies, and if I looked closely, I would find a little number engraved in each one of them. I could wander around the city, and if I watched attentively, I would spot traces here and there that somehow relate to this arch.

But I could not reconstruct what exactly I had here before me, if I did not go back to the invention made, the story told, which engaged many people and became an experience in the collective memory that is scattered now.

Back to the beginning—one year before now—ConstructLab was commissioned to activate a former mining area in Genk, Belgium, within the city development plans, which foresee the establishment of an alternative energy hub above the mining tunnels that were closed and flooded in the eighties. This vast industri-al wasteland awaits its rediscovery and the return of human activity, to which we responded by building a living support structure for a social and experimental laboratory. In order to investigate a new standard brick that would cover a vault construction, we had to engage and link all kinds of hands and minds, people who we tried to seduce by telling the story. We tell the story here, as it was originally written before the realization of the project (which was actually completed in October 2017); we have opted to keep the future-looking, anticipatory framework of the original essay as we want to convey both the draft nature of the project—that it was experimental and with an open outcome—and the draft nature of the text. What follows is therefore not a retrospective description, but an imaginative composition of future temporal and social contexts, sketched with the means of language that can create a collective vision, but leave space for personal interpretation at the same time.

1.3.1

A Living Support Structure

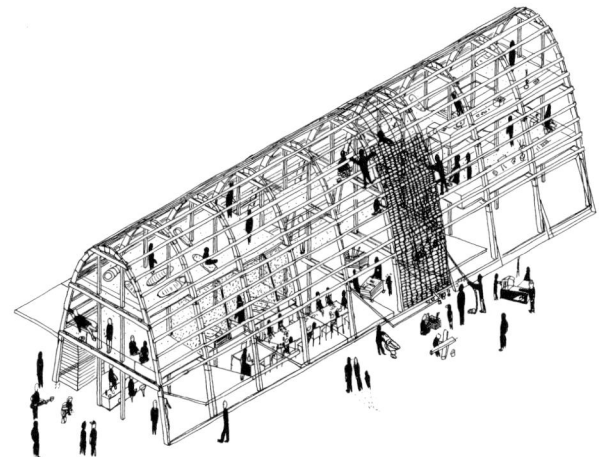

Figure 1 (p. 80): The Arch concept drawing, © ConstructLab
Figure 2: Isometric drawing of the Arch, © ConstructLab

The support structure is a building tool that stabilizes a construction during its installation. In the same sense it can be applied metaphorically as a social, artistic, and community-shaping tool to support and catalyze a first phase of appropriation.

In connection to the research activities already happening and to be established at Thorpark we propose an applied research laboratory that is situated somewhere between artistic experimentation and public research. It positions itself as a complementary approach to academic scientific research to deal with new technologies in an accessible and associative way.

Our built structure will be a place to share existing local knowledge and to learn new skills where instructors and learners can come from different fields of knowledge and social environments.

In order to accomplish a familiarity we will provide a vibrant, lively, convivial gathering place to share with neighbors, former miners, visitors, passers-by, and scientists from Thorpark. In the center of the activities are encounters, expression, and experimentation while the place will offer facilities for working theoretically and practically, eating and living together.

These moments will be captured in a tangible object, a generic brick that we will design and make together. The brick as a memory of our time together at Thorpark will be the building block for the new entrance gate to Thorpark, but also a new material that can enter into the existing Belgian brick market.

The Master-Builder and the Building Lodge

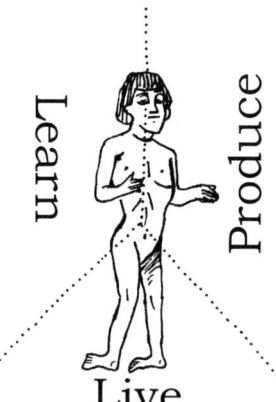

Figure 3: The Master-Builder,
© ConstructLab

The medieval occupation "master-builder" describes a fusion of different roles that does not exist anymore on modern construction sites. The master-builder not only led the construction, but also conceived the project, whether cathedral, palace, or fortress, and managed the construction. The master-builder switched between designing and building and therefore used his knowledge as an exceptionally skilled craftsman, often stonemason or carpenter. He led the building lodge—the store and workshop—where stone and wood were worked on. At the same time this space was also where the builders lived together, where a canteen fed the hungry workers, and knowledge and skills were exchanged. A construction site was a place of apprenticeship, which could well be worth a long journey to learn from a particularly skilled master-builder.

Materials and machines have changed, and building lodges are piled-up containers nowadays. Much more essential changes, however, are visible in the building process. On one hand, in the master-builder way, being universally responsible permitted an inclusive and intertwined procedure that considered all different disciplines while also anticipating unplanned outcomes. Due to the complexity of the task, certain aspects had to be defined later during the process. On the other hand it seems that knowledge in our society is not considered to arise from practical skills anymore, and we sometimes forget that we can learn from doing.

▶ 2.2.1   We experiment with building sites that are places of knowledge exchange and conviviality. In a first step we conceive places of production and furnish tools to then be able to produce a real construction site situation according to the local and concrete needs while staying adaptable throughout the process to unexpected turns.

ConstructLab is a hands-on, collaborative practice of designing and creating, which unites architects, artists, graphic and product designers, carpenters, and illustrators from different European countries. It has the goal that the construction site itself transforms city space into living space. This is where thoughts on the city and living in it are brought together.

The Craftsman of Plastic

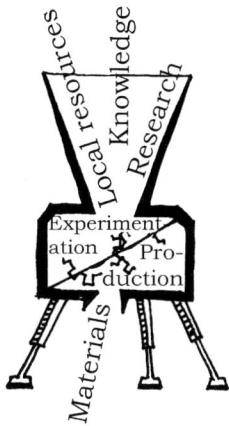

Figure 4: The Craftsman of Plastic, © ConstructLab

Recycling on an industrial scale is nothing new. However, the industrial processes have gaps in what could be a closed cycle of production, waste, and reproduction. Economic efficiency and productivity are the key terms that dictate to what degree materials and human power should be considered, exploited, or wasted. However, if we add factors such as learning outcomes, social encounters, and sustainability to this equation, new conditions make recycling interesting on a different scale. Deindustrializing this production process could make the recycling process a curious experiment for a wider public.

In the building lodge—with the wood, graphic, and plastic ateliers inside—the cycle would start by identifying and explaining the different kinds of waste and raw materials. The plastic would then be transformed into a new building material by using low-tech techniques with machines that will be partly designed and built by residents and researchers on site. In order to correspond to the scale of the systematic waste of plastic, we want to experiment with the production of a building material that can be repetitively reproduced and stacked, adapted and developed.

Plastic as a raw material can be treated in very specialized and efficient high-tech machines. But it can also, due to its low melting point, be transformed in plastic-specific, low-tech machines,

ovens, or presses. It does not only exist in surplus under the form of waste; it is also easy to treat and does not produce leftovers if handled well. It can—by treating it with the thoughtfulness and care given to handcrafts and through a mental shift that is produced by understanding the material better—gain worth without changing its materiality. In other words, we want to find the recipe to turn plastic into gold.

The project needs the skills of the people around—we can offer to involve former workers and miners and the ones that are yet to become craftsmen. The production process is participative and offers a perspective on how to self-make a building material that is normally made in an industrial process. The expertise and energy of the people of Genk has to be carefully collected in the preparation of the project, and then organized around local institutions and actors who share our interest to create learning spaces.

A Monument to Collective Effort and Gate to Empowerment

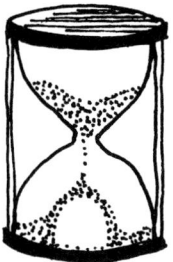

Figure 5: The Monument, © ConstructLab

The outcome could be a structure that symbolizes an entrance gate to the park and proposes a gathering and presentation place for the summer of 2017, while also forming a gate between past and future industry in the city.

The era of mining and the presence of the Ford company have given strong identities to the city of Genk. We intervene at a moment where the search for a new strong identity permits experimentation and a reflection on the vision of the future. The installation should document this time of development and is thus conceived as a transition object. However, we are cautious to make predictions of further evolutions of the city. A monument helps us to visualize the future by reading the alleged essence of the present. By representing a collective effort with the construction, the story of what can collectively be achieved becomes a possible reading of the spirit of the present. But also failure, evolution, dead-ends, and innovation are traced in the history of this production.

The arch, for the time it exists, will make us wonder if now could be a moment of a paradigm shift from the faith in efficiency and productivity to a smaller, transparent production in the city that incorporates deviation and allows change. In a reversed sense, its symbolic meaning in the first place serves its physical presence rather than the other way around.

Participation

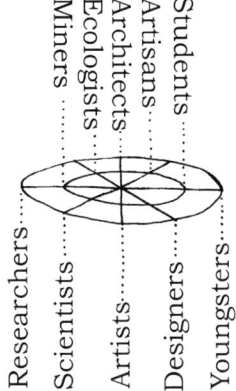

Figure 6: Participation, © ConstructLab

Our action focuses on popular education, creation, production, experimentation, and research. These themes are approached in different formats. The production should allow different levels of skill to open it up to a wide range of participants.

The planning of the summer program is partly set and partly open to spontaneous encounters and propositions from interested people. This flexibility, in combination with provided infrastructure (kitchen, sound system, projector, space, tools), can be interesting to many. In order to reach these potentially interested actors we have simple but efficient analog and digital communication tools to spread the word about a new vibrant space in the neighborhood and around the city. In a first residence in November the first bonds are made. Targeted groups include schools of practical and higher education, associations for sports and culture, artist residences, social centers, and Genk's many and diverse ethnic community houses, as well as the former mining community and researchers on site. Additionally, we invite international artists, designers, and researchers to hold residencies in the structure. They will be asked to propose public activities linked to their subject of research that address different groups, from children to students to elderly people.

Phase 1
Preparation

    Timing   Six months
    Agenda November–May

Description

First ConstructLab residency
(November 28–December 3)
On-site visits and getting to know the city and neighborhood.
Meetings with associations, institutions, potential collaborators,
and related project managers.

Second ConstructLab residency
(March 20–24)
Public presentations with institutions, associations, and neighbors
to launch the project and to follow up with contacts; meetings to
deepen and clarify collaboration. Communication via release of information for the public (poster, Facebook, website, flyers).

Goals

- Define a location; define a design; understand who are our
  administrative partners, invite potential collaborators to
  get to know them and make a first contact list; start a map
  of potential material partners; meet the first educational
  institutions; meet those responsible for Thorpark, etc.
- Provide the possibility for local actors to kick off initiatives
  related to and taking place within the to-be-built structure
  (with a good lead time).
- Spread the word about the project.

Phase 2
Building

    Timing   Three weeks
    Agenda May–June

Description

Building of the support structure (building lodge). With the ConstructLab team, organized local contributors, and more informal
local help we will create a typical vibrant ConstructLab construction site, including all needed facilities: dorms, kitchen, lavatories,

workshops. We arrive with a mobile workshop that will be used until the permanent workshop within the structure is installed.

Goals

- Build together; be present on site; involve local people; generate curiosity; create comfortable conditions.
- Initiate the temporary community that will grow over the summer.
- Gather knowledge, and start a database as a foundation for the material research, etc.

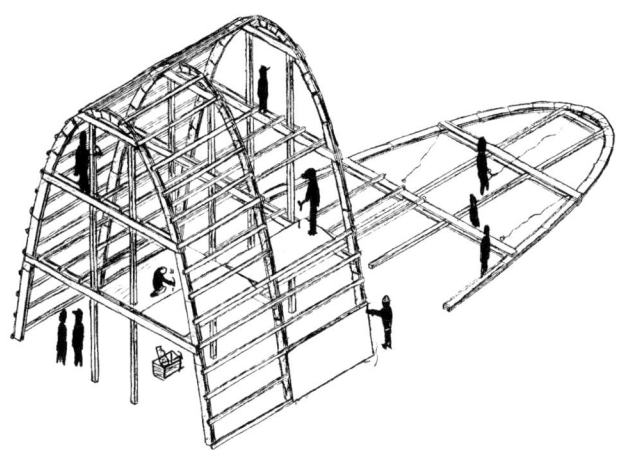

Figure 7: Phase 2 Building, © ConstructLab

Phase 3
Activation

Timing	Two months
Agenda	July–August

Description

The structure and site serve as a playful open laboratory, where programmed and spontaneous activities will activate the site during days and evenings. Residencies, workshops, and investigations will be complemented with cultural activities like theater performances, cinema projections, concerts, parties, dinners, open bar nights, discussions, etc. Two ConstructLab housekeepers live on site during this time to inhabit the space and to keep an overview over events, guests, maintenance, programming, planning, and communication. Planned residents are coming for a fixed period, proposing a research question and a workshop format as result of their stay. The focus will lie on machine-building and brick-making for the vault.

Goals

- Give space to the greatest number and diversity of people possible and through the proposed and self-growing activities to have people meet in this space who might not cross paths in everyday life.
- Create a valuable togetherness and vibrant atmosphere that can produce long-lasting energies and bonds.

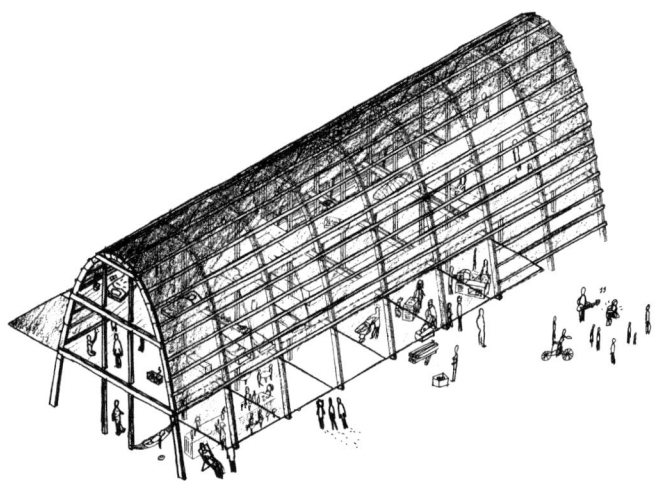

Figure 8: Phase 3 Activation,
© ConstructLab

Phase 4
Building Festival
    Timing   Two weeks
    Agenda   August

Description

To conclude the research phase we will propose a moment of collective building with students of architecture and design paired with the grown local network of participants and helpers. The grand gate is constructed with the building material developed on site. We organize a summer building festival to bring together a large team, composed of locals we met during the spring and summer and international participants.

The summer festival has a fee for the international participants; locals are free of charge.[1] It is accompanied by an educational and festive program to be developed with a local partner (e.g. school, art space).

1 Within the course of the project, it was decided to charge local participants half the fee to cover costs for the three meals, which the project budget could not cover.

Goals

- Get a lot of people together to build the arch in a festive and intense moment.
- Have all energies united before the end of the project.
- Produce a moment that can be remembered by the citizens of Genk.

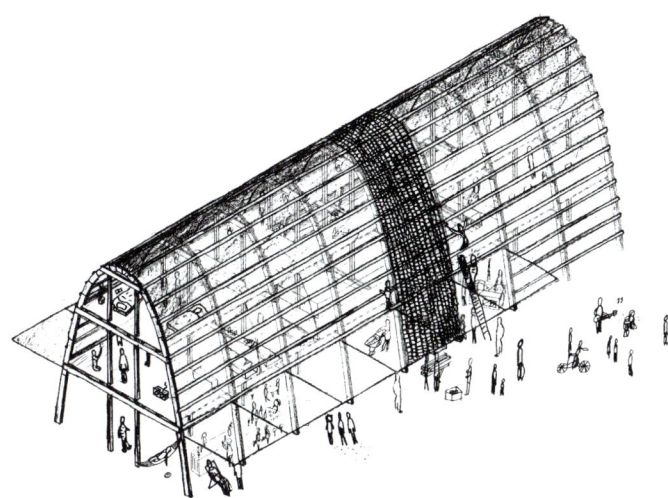

Figure 9: Phase 4 Building festival,
© ConstructLab

Phase 5
Handover Ceremony

Timing   One weekend
Agenda   October 1

Description

While the more important outcome of the project is an immaterial structure, some physical remains are also worth mentioning. The project will create firstly, a sculpture; secondly, a structure; thirdly, a process that can independently remain or move and have different time scales proper to themselves.

1.2.2 ◀

Achievements

- The symbolic entrance gate to the future Thorpark is meant to stay on site as the remains of the project, a monument of collective effort. If deconstructed, it can re-enter the material cycle.

- The structure constitutes the wood of the support structure, as well as cables, electronics, lamps, mattresses, sheets, towels, kitchen utensils, and many more things that are deconstructed and packed in September. While it cannot remain as a whole in Thorpark if not taken care of, this set can easily be moved to transform into a new shape or repeat the old shape in a new place to support dynamics in Genk, the region, or elsewhere.

- A new process of material production will be researched. This process will produce a know-how, machines, and very specific tools that will be for and from the people of Genk. It can be imagined that this process, including tools and machines, has a follow-up. It could be taken on by engaged participants of the project and stay in the neighborhood or even on site as a small factory using the transformed structure, serve in an already existing production place, be exhibited and thus continue to tell the story of the project, or be used as a starting point to serve further research.

Figure 10: Phase 5 Handover ceremony, © ConstructLab

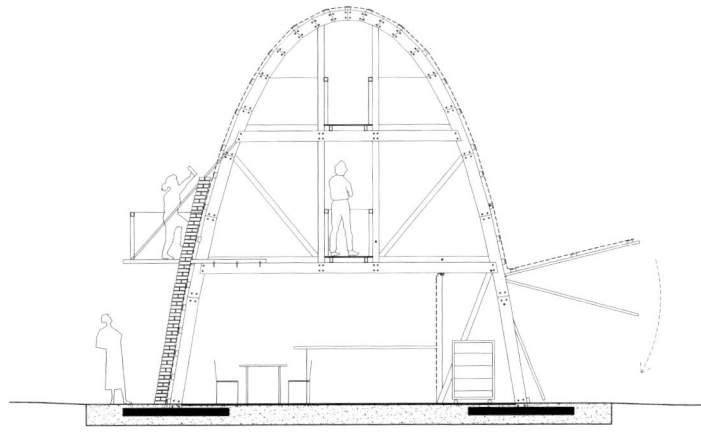

Figure 11: A section of the Arch,
© ConstructLab

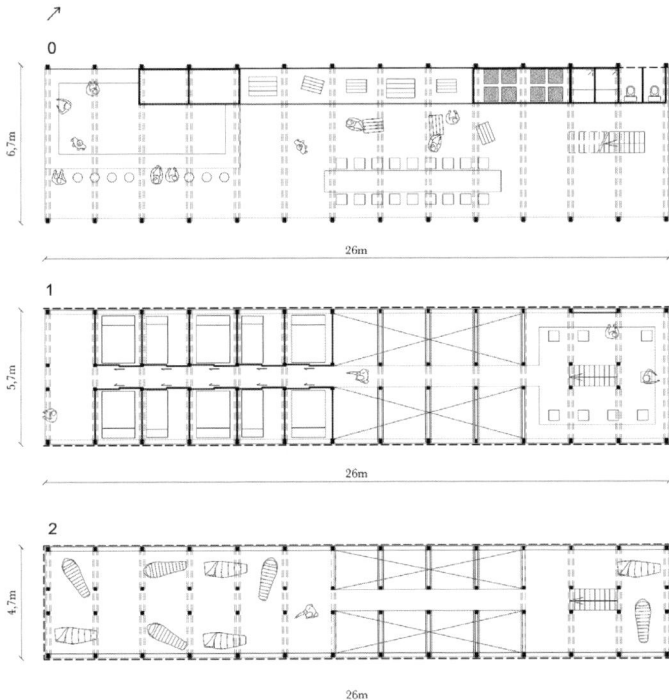

Figure 12: Plans of the Arch,
© ConstructLab

Facilities

Ground Floor

- kitchen for communal cooking
- public bar
- large eating-table
- storage for workshop material and machines
- flexible space for workshops and general atelier use
- storage of recycled material
- two showers
- two toilets

First Floor

- one studio space that can house up to six residents
- ten individual sleeping rooms
- terrace

Second Floor

- dormitory for up to twenty people

Figure 13: Monument to collective effort: the inaugurated entrance gate to Thorpark, from waste plastic bricks, covered from the inside with tiles produced by inhabitants and visitors in weekly workshops on site (the outside is used for solar tiles that supply the light circuit for illumination at night and result from collaborating with scientists of Thorpark), © ConstructLab

Figure 14 (p. 93): Living Support Structure enacted: the participants of the Arch building festival performing their acquired particular skills, © O.S.T. Collective

Urban Practice: The Form of the Informal

Markus Bader, raumlabor

Looking at the practice of raumlabor from the perspective of structure, it could be interesting to examine how raumlabor operates as a group and to look into the process design for the transition of Tempelhof airfield into a co-created public park. It would be interesting to also look at the recent urban school, an educational frame for city-making that happened 2016 in the Ruhr Valley, but as space here is limited, I recommend taking a look at the publication *Explorations in Urban Practice*. This text will present a series of descriptions, rather than proclaiming a hypothesis, challenging the reader with the form of a manifesto, or adopting the form of a how-to tutorial. I will present the two contexts raumlabor and Tempelhof Airport as case studies between the formal and informal.

Raumlabor's practice, since its beginning, sits between and interconnects a set of professional fields of work related to the city and space as a common interest. We have always been interested in transversal modes of looking at urban planning strategies with the eyes of an artist, bringing architectural strategies into the context of art, and creating spatial performances and performing spaces. How can we name this territory of interconnections between urban questions and spatial actions? Where it is not the architectural plan, but instead processes, design decisions, and spatial actions that are some of the tools at work? We suggest that this field of work, which emerged in many parallel practices in very different locations at the same time, could be called "urban practice." In this essay we can look at raumlabor as one possible example to test the term urban practice.

If we understand the city as an ongoing process, as a spatial frame and subject of negotiation, as an entity that is permanently co-produced and reshaped by all of our collective actions, we draw a dynamic understanding that includes qualities of plurality and simultaneity. The city has many dimensions. We like an approach to the city that embraces the complexity of this and is not looking for simple solutions. Urban practice, to our understanding, involves taking into account the social dimension, the spatial, the political, and maybe even the historical to form proposals for change and improvement. We also acknowledge that it can be super interesting to examine more closely what spatial practitioners or architects are actually doing, that the practice itself is interesting and can even be examined from a perspective of form.

From urbanism we take an understanding of space as a process and the politics related to that. From architecture we take a fundamental care for the quality of the space, its atmospheres, and its performance. We have sensitivity to the roles of the ones who take decisions and the ones affected by them. From art we take a fundamental curiosity to think across borders, a desire to express in any way that might seem suitable, subjectivity, and individual responsibility for each project. From theatre we might take the understanding of each spatial construction as an agreed frame for the people within to form it in the way it's perceived, following a common understanding of the protocol to act within the frame and present themselves.

Now that we evolved our architecture into urban practice, we might as well organize ourselves differently than an architectural office. The core of raumlabor has nine members, self-employed architects and artists. These members can be understood as the commoners, with the common entity raumlabor being the commons. This offers an interesting perspective, as it describes raumlabor both as a resource and as something to commit to and to take care of. Nevertheless, raumlabor's internal organization is highly informal and based on so-called soft forms, such as common interests, friendship, and trust. Between the raumlabor partners or commoners, there is very little specialization. Being part of raumlabor involves working on projects, presenting the common practice in workshops and lectures, as well as taking care of the shared work environment by looking after printers, going to get some new coffee, or making sure the dishwasher still works and the server is accessible. Taking care of raumlabor—a fluid entity, different in each member's head—involves its material and its immaterial sides. Raumlabor is a production of meaning, interpretations, positions, demands, and mutual affection. Not being restricted to a manifesto—as it was never written in 1999—raumlabor has been able to evolve fluidly in line with the interests of its members and meeting the challenges of the projects that are taken on. Obviously in this part of the text we understand structure as form, like the shape of an organization. I would reject that the term informal should be understood as the absence of form. In the contrary, exactly because of the informal way it's organized, raumlabor is generating a lot of form— nine members; one, two, or three of them working together on each project; ten to twenty projects in production at the same time. Raumlabor members tend to mix in different project teams, passing on the questions and expertise from one project to another through personal presence and involvement. The people carry the discussions from one group to another. This way of working allows us to focus on our interests and curiosity through project environments that are produced and experienced, and to avoid killing each other's proposals on an idea level before they had time to grow, be developed, and tested. Each raumlabor member has the freedom

1.5.2 ▶

1.3.2

and responsibility to decide if the work should be placed in the frame of raumlabor or not. There are no vetoes or any other mechanisms in the group that could stop a project team from pursuing their ambitions. This internal policy demands the trust of all members that work produced in raumlabor even without control will be done to the best quality possible. With most economic decisions being delegated to the project level—to responsibly manage available funds—and secondly to each individual, the discussions inside raumlabor itself can mainly focus on content and quality-related questions. Only recently, raumlabor adopted a ritual of scheduled group meetings every three months to discuss common objectives. Raumlabor as a commons taken care of and co-produced by its commoners involves both highly visible and invisible work, work with a social prestige and without, and work that supports output production and work that doesn't. Like this raumlabor is owned by everyone and no one at the same time and can never be sold.

On to Tempelhof

What if somebody who takes part in developing a place by bringing his or her ideas, imaginaries, and resources, and, therefore, investing life, time, and energy—basically somebody bringing his or her creative and social capital—is seen seen as an investor in the same way as somebody who brings economic capital? Wouldn't this wider understanding of the figure of the investor be a starting point for a more inclusive city-making, where civic initiatives find their places to develop their futures? Which types of processes and platforms would have to be developed for this understanding to be put into practice? Which are the tools needed to bridge the gaps between civic actors and politicians or representatives of the public administration? How can the very different languages and experiences in shaping the urban transformation be translated so that actors of the *Freie Szene* (free scene)[1] and planning professionals can work together in a common process?

◄ 1.2.3

Already in 2006 an understanding existed within Berlin's planning administration that the experiences gained by the actors of the Freie Szene in so-called temporary use projects and in various forms of self-organization could be a valuable resource for urban transformation contexts. Especially for those who are a little uncomfortable with the term participation, the publication of the book *Urban Pioneers* in 2007 offered some dramatic new ways

► 1.5.3

1 *Freie Szene* is a term used in Berlin for freelance artists and creatives across the disciplines who are not tied to an institutional form. They may collaborate and/or form coalitions on a temporary basis, but they act fundamentally differently than institutionally integrated artists.

of looking at these practices from a perspective of urban renewal and transformation—this remarkably in a publication funded by the very planning department of the city of Berlin, written by the studio Urban Catalyst.

Raumlabor together with Urban Catalyst and MBUP planners were invited in early 2007 to form a think tank for and with the planning department of Berlin to develop a strategy for the transformation of Tempelhof airport into a public park, to turn a technical infrastructure into a living piece of the urban fabric. The strategy looked at an activation and transformation through use, looking for ways to develop new protocols for collaborative city-making. How much guidance and reliable form is needed and how can we create a framework for nondetermined developments to foster? Could the public authorities as the owners of the site and initiators of the process, and the civic actors, bringing their social and creative capital to the very same process, work together on the future imaginaries? Could some of the experiences emerging from the fluid self-organization like raumlabor be scaled up to an urban level? Could we invent structures that would give all the participants in the process a robust framework to ensure that their investment was safe and respected?

As this text is written in 2018, looking back at an ambition of 2007, a rough outline of the events between then and now seems interesting. In the nineteen-nineties, the planning department orchestrated a master plan process. The chosen scheme aimed for new housing and industrial zones around the edges and a large public park in the center of the site called Sea of Grass (Wiesenmeer). The think tank worked for two years in 2007–8, concluding the work with the detailed recommendation handed over to administration and policymakers in December that year. Simultaneously, Astoc and BGMR were commissioned to update the nineteen-nineties-era master plan to 2008 conditions. The works of the think tank and the master plan update were not linked or synchronized. In addition to these parallel planning processes, Tempelhof repeatedly returned to the political debate. Accompanied by a large media campaign, a first referendum in April 2008 failed to get public approval for keeping the airport open indefinitely. Instead use of the airport stopped in October 2008. The Berlin government decided to communicate the updated master plan as Berlin's idea for Tempelhof's future. It promised large numbers of new flats, jobs, and the big park in its center. At the time, the real estate market in Berlin was relaxed, the financial crisis just unfolding, and real estate developments in a foreseeable future seemed a very abstract idea. With the airport remaining closed and its future uncertain, a public opinion grew that there are better ways of managing this public resource, which comprised a 300,000-square-meter building and a 360-acre site. In June 2009 around five thousand people demonstrated, calling for the opening of Tempelhofer Feld under the slogan "Have you ever squatted in an airport?" In May 2010 Tempelhofer Feld was finally opened to the public as a park enclosed by a fence with opening hours. It is since maintained by Grün Berlin GmbH, a company owned by the city of Berlin. In the same

1.2.2 ◀

1.3.2

year, Ines Rudolph, a partner in TX Architekten, was engaged to manage the urban pioneer process. Also in May 2010, raumlabor and many collaborators, partners, and friends inaugurated Tempelhofer Feld as a place for art with the international public art project The Knot. In late 2010 the department of urban planning formed a team to conceptualize an international building exhibition (IBA). The team consisted of seven independent experts, the author of this text being one of them. The team aimed to identify thresholds of paradigmatic change in city-making, and invent test sites for new urban policies. Under the headline IBA-Sofortstadt, strategies for civic city-making were to be developed and the Tempelhof process was hoped to have been adopted as IBA project; however, the IBA concept was politically undermined and finally stopped dead after the elections in 2011. At the same time, in spring 2011 the office Grossmax won a competition for the design of the Tempelhof. Simultaneously the first pioneer users started to inhabit Tempelhof. Amongst these is Allmende Kontor, a community garden project involving between 600 and 800 diverse people occupying 5,000 square meters of land, paying 5,000 euros per year. In the summer of 2012 raumlabor came back with The Great World Fair with artists spread out in self-designed World's Fair-style pavilions, offering open access overlaid over the public space. While initially around two hundred pioneer projects were expected, only around twenty—equipped with a temporary contract with Grün Berlin—were allowed to start running until 2013. The pioneers were located in themed areas, on land designated for future real estate development. In late 2013 the contracts were neither renewed nor revoked by Grün Berlin, pushing the urban pioneers with their entire social, economic, and creative investment into a very uncertain situation. The pioneer project of Arche Metropolis did not have its contract renewed and was asked to leave the area, adding to the pressure and frustration among the pioneer actors. With a referendum in May 2014, the people of Berlin vetoed the implementation of the master plan. A majority voted for the Tempelhof Law, fixing the status quo as unchangeable. After the very dynamic and controversial early years from 2010 to 2014, the four years since have been comparatively quiet. The pioneer process itself lingered on but was held back from growing, continuing at the small scale at which it had started. Tempelhof changed character, from a site of discussion about how (and for whom) to develop the city, to a vast inner city recreation area, a place to find distraction and joy.

Inscribed in this timeline are several appearances of raumlabor, aiming to contribute to the evolving imaginaries around Tempelhof's future. We assumed the roles of urban planners, artists, activists, policy advisers, and citizens. We gained intense experiences about how the city is made. The ambition of the think tank's strategy including the urban pioneer users was to radically turn around processes of urban invention and decision-making. Trusting the knowledge situated in citizens of Berlin around Tempelhofer Feld, the strategy was conceived as a framework with an open end. In almost direct contrast to the architectural design competition that produced imagery of the possible future, the urban pioneer process started

with an open call for people interested in running a piece of land in the center of town. The call asked for people with ideas, to come up with programs that could benefit the wider public. While our study advised mixing users with different ambitions, programs, audiences, scales, needs for resources, and skills in order to create something like a an urban humus, the pioneer users, instead, where located by theme. This problematic distance between the different pioneer users, both spatially and psychologically, undermined the aim of the process, which was to learn how to develop the city from its users and to acknowledge local expertise as equally important as the one of the professional planner for a consistent vision of the future. 1.4.1 ▶
Ultimately the process design refrained from proposing any fixed image but rather suggested ways of operating in order to keep the situated production of our future imaginaries going. The former head of Amsterdam's planning office, Jeroen Saris, gives us a rough outline of how to play such a process in time: he says five years are needed for maximum testing, inventing, involving, fostering growing dynamics between place, people, and ideas to create density of actors and activities as a base for drawing conclusions and learning. Only after five years can a slow process of consolidation and focusing be implemented, where long-term strategies and investments are carefully worked out and located.

But let's zoom out again. Tempelhof became the site of competing models of city-making. The traditional model involved a master plan, discussion at an expert level, and decision-making through competition juries or on a political level. The model suggested by the think tank proposed ideas, development, and testing in close collaboration between experts and civic actors, with mutual respect and eye-level decision-making. While most of Berlin's innovations have been created in environments similar to those suggested by the think tank, public policy on an urban level never really adopted this intelligence.

The years 2014–18 have been quiet on Tempelhofer Feld. In the neighboring area of Neukölln the opposite could be felt. With the roaring housing market a rapid gentrification process unfolded, including the dislocation of large portions of the original population through market mechanisms.

Many urban practitioners and people working in the Freie Szene are changing their tactics. Securing access to space has become an important topic of conversation, as well as a focus of many people's work. It could be described as looking for defensive strategies, binding energies, and accumulating creative capital, that ten years ago would have been invested in cultural projects open to the civic society. A general feeling of being under threat of being removed from the urban territory by the same market mechanisms observed in Neukölln creates pressure as a form, and more efficiency as both response and culture.

Reading the example of expertise shared and practices implied in Tempelhof, there is a new role of the public administration in city-making. To be inclusive, diverse, and democratic—that is, an open city—restrictive policies against market forces in relation to housing and small businesses are needed to create a hard edge

1.3.2

of common public interest reinforced by public administration. The same administration on the other hand can offer solid frameworks for very open processes in developing what the city wants to be in close collaboration with civic actors. This model would apply an attitude of competitiveness and restriction towards market forces and an attitude of care, trust, exchange, and eye-level negotiation towards the civic society, a model with a hard and soft edges strategically placed.

I hope that this text—without being too explicit—illustrates that the city is a result and a process at the same time, where informal strategies and formalized processes coincide, like hard and soft forms, like defined shapes and amorphous figures, inhabiting the same field. The recent debate about the urban commons can be read as the joining of people drawn to soft strategies. It is building a political and discursive repertoire to oppose the market-driven and rigid forms of city-making, to develop weapons for inclusive civic strategies. Even though urban transfor-

▶ 1.4.3 mation is an often slow and long-term process, it is important to understand that we can have an impact on its direction. When humans can change the climate of the planet, changing the trajectory of our living environments must be much easier. Working on alternatives to a straight-forward capitalist spatial regime is necessary. If we produce islands of otherness and different city-making, we create common places in space and time and thinking, sharing experiences on how to do it. There we can test and harden our tools while keeping the soft qualities with each other, respectfully negotiating and caring for the island and each other. This is where the future cities are being developed.

Verantwortung

Martin Wickel

Many parties participate in the creation of urban development: the investor who wants to develop a project; the neighbors who try to intervene; the general public that participates in the discussion; various authorities that represent public interest; NGOs; etc. At the center of all is the municipality. Looking at this picture the question may be raised: Who is responsible for urban development? Given the number of actors, can responsibility for urban development be shared?

Before, in this text, a complex term such as responsibility can be grasped, the author must disclose his starting point. This text is written by a legal scholar. And this text is not about responsibility, but about—in German—*Verantwortung*. This is not only a word, but also a complex concept that cannot always be fully translated. Hence, the attempt of a definition: *Verantwortung* (i.e., responsibility) is the attribution of a subject's obligation to an object "on the basis of a normative claim," according to Wikipedia (2017). Social norms can be of different origin. Here the focus lies on legal norms.

Searching for legal responsibility for urban development, one has to look at the law of urban development. So, what does responsibility mean in the context of urban development law? Who is in charge?

Looking at urban development law the answer is given by the Federal Building Code, which sets the major normative framework for urban development in Germany. Naturally, the Federal Building Code creates many responsibilities in the abovementioned sense. The term itself, however, is used very sparingly, only five times in more than 250 paragraphs. First, it is mentioned in section 1, subsection 5. There, it stands in the context of sustainable development and proclaims a responsibility towards future generations. The responsibility referred to here, however, seems to have a strong moral dimension rather than being an enforceable legal claim.

More relevant is section 2, subsection 1, which provides that land use planning falls within the responsibility of the municipalities. Here, the term is used primarily in the sense of a right, an

1·3·3

exclusive competence: the municipality determines its urban development. Interference by other state authorities is ruled out. It is common understanding among lawyers that this is only the concretization of the constitutional provision of article 28, subsection 2, of Grundgesetz (Basic Law). This provision gives municipalities the right to regulate all local affairs on their own responsibility. But this right is also an obligation, which becomes clear where the Federal Building Code regulates the cooperation with third parties. Section 11 shows, for instance, that the right to pursue urban development by the means of contracts with private parties does not release the municipality from its responsibility for urban development. The same is true for section 171f. Although the provision allows for site-related measures to be carried out under private responsibility, these measures must still be coordinated with the development goals of the municipality, which means that the municipality is still responsible for setting the framework.

The municipality is thus the central actor and carries the sole responsibility for its urban development. Is this finding surprising? Is the sole responsibility of the municipality not outdated and inappropriate given that all world talks about participatory planning and co-production of urban development? Should the responsibility for urban development be redistributed?

1.2.3 ◄

The answer is no. Participation is an important element in urban development. It creates identification with the development. It increases acceptance. It can improve the plans. And, those who participate take responsibility. But this is mainly responsibility for those interests they represent. Lawyers call it responsibility for one's own affairs. Those who do not participate and do not represent their interests cannot assert that they have not been heard. But this is not always true. Some interests are so important, or so obvious, or both that the municipality must address them on its own initiative. This is important because not all interests have the same access to decisions in urban development. The way and the intensity of their articulation may vary. Property normally finds easy access to decisions in the field of urban development. Its assignment is clear. Property owners are often in a good position to participate appropriately or to be represented by a representative. Other interests suffer from structural disadvantages. The environment cannot be attributed to anyone. With respect to social interests in many cases the persons concerned are not able to participate appropriately. This shows that the responsibility for urban development must rest with the municipality in the end. Urban

1.4.3 ►

development must serve the common good. Only the municipalities are obliged to pursue the common good in the first place.
Therefore, they must have the full responsibility for urban development.

Reference

"Verantwortung." *Wikipedia*. Accessed October 9, 2017. https://de.wikipedia.org/wiki
    /Verantwortung.

Swarm Architects

Martin Kohler

The swarm is a speculative metaphor for a form of collectivity and tactical strategy for architects and spatial activists.

In biology the swarm describes a fluid formation of individual members. Without a larger organization or hierarchy, the positions in space and time are highly coordinated and create a collective and ephemeral entity. To create swarms the individual has to follow three simple rules:

1. Move to the direction of the center of your surrounding swarm members.
2. Avoid collisions and move away if you get too close to any member.
3. Move roughly in the same direction as your neighbors.

Swarms don't have leaders as any member can initiate a collective movement. The swarm appears as a larger entity and, as such, can perform coordinated maneuvers. As a fluid formation, the swarm can break up into smaller groups or even disperse completely. This enables the swarm to penetrate boundaries impermeable for individuals of its size and makes it hard to attack. Other synergetic functions include the efficient use of resources for movement, increased sensitivity and attentiveness, and a larger range of actions beyond the capability of any single member. Applied as a speculative metaphor in architecture this might provide a mode of thinking for formations of experimental and socially engaged architects and spatial activists. The formation as a swarm offers a degree of freedom from conventional work structures and enables them to initiate nomadic or spontaneous projects, sometimes only loosely connected to the built environment on a scale competing with established practices and firms. The absence of hierarchical organization and comparable lack of mutual definitions and rules allows them to move faster and perhaps even shift their output into domains traditionally beyond the realm of architecture or design.

Established architecture firms are built around a strong signature typology, that is, at best, globally unique and competitive. Governments and financial investors favor these firms as they promise to secure investment, provide a calculable outcome, and deflect critique. The result is cities stuffed with Zaha Hadid, Frank Gehry, or Santiago Calatrava projects and alike. This architecture is politically and socially agnostic and deeply integrated into the market economy. At the same time young European architects have begun to challenge this custom. Collectives like InBetween Economies (Copenhagen), raumlabor (Berlin), or La Rivoluzione delle Seppie (Calabria) instead orient their practice around an often political objective. These spatial activists operate from the sidelines as facilitators, utilizing design not as an end in itself but as a means to pursue a specific aim. Social media platforms help collectives to promote themselves online—gathering huge numbers of followers and creating the capability to rally people around events—and to use networks to collaborate on a global level, enabling them to adopt alternative and entrepreneurial working methods that set them apart from established practice. This can prevent them from participating in most public tenders; and therefore, many of their works are without prior assignment.

Often only loosely connected and embedded in larger networks of sympathizers and supporters their behavior resembles some features of swarms. As with swarms none of the cited collectives has a fixed definition of who is and who is not part of the swarm. In their structure they resemble more breathing formations where individuals decide if they want to move within the swarm—and when they want to leave. Instead of having a founder or signature brand like the conventional architecture firms, these groups have a shared political agenda and a common toolset of   1.6.2 ▶
participative and interventionist architecture that forms the gravitational core connecting their members.

With the Pritzker Prize unexpectedly going to Chilean architect Alejandro Aravena, and the Turner Prize for Art to the London-based collective Assemble, architecture with a political agenda and interdisciplinary methods has gained enough visibility to influence the mainstream. Developed as swarms it may even bypass conventional planning procedures and surpass the mainstream.

1·3·4

1.4. Strategies

- **1** **The PlanBude Method: The Production of Desires as a New Mode of Urban Development**

- **2** **The Top Four Time Hacks**

- **3** **Longer Development Cycles, Please!**

- **4** **Money or Daydream: Difficulties and Changing Facets of Gaining Adequate Remuneration**

The PlanBude Method: The Production of Desires as a New Mode of Urban Development

PlanBude Hamburg talks to Daniela Brahm, ExRotaprint

PlanBude, a transdisciplinary office, is organizing the planning and participation for a 28,000-square-meter ensemble of houses in place of the former Esso-houses on the Reeperbahn in the St. Pauli area of Hamburg. The PlanBude idea was kicked off by an independent citizen's assembly in the FC St. Pauli ballroom. PlanBude now works under commission by the planning authority. In a unique planning process, PlanBude opened its doors at the construction site in the heart of St. Pauli and offered innovative tools that allowed complex contributions from everybody. PlanBude collected 2,300 wishes and designs in an open brief process. Eventually, politicians, planning authorities, and the private owners agreed to accept the PlanBude-developed "St. Pauli Code" from the neighborhood as a brief for the architectural competition and the ongoing planning process.

The following teammembers participated in the discussion: Margit Czenki (B1), Christoph Schäfer (B3), Renée Tribble (B4), and Lisa Marie Zander (B2). Daniela Brahm (I) moderated the discussion.

1.4.1

I: One important aspect for you seems to me to be the question of what your different occupations are?

B4: I'm actually an architect who is working in urban planning. And I've taught urban planning at HCU.

B1: We'd heard that Renée had worked in a planning office that was doing just this sort of tendering.

B4: I was able to bring along my knowledge of how to write a competition brief, how to talk with administrative bodies. Of course, this was practical because I always knew that if they wanted to keep to the timeline, they would now have to fill the jury, for instance. And then we suggested jury members. If you don't have a say in who's on the jury and the architect's offices, then you get a different result. You have to have a few in there who understand what's being done here.

B2: I was a neighbor and part of the St. Pauli do-it-yourself neighborhood meetings. The planning work group was founded—it had to do with the Esso-houses—and I thought I could add something here because I was studying architecture at that time. So, I come out of the movement with the aim of taking a part in shaping the city with the background of my own discipline.

I: And you are both artists?

B1: Yes, I am an artist. I always switch between political work, social work, and artistic work. So I always have an artistic aspiration.

B3: I am an artist. I studied it in a classical way. I've been interested in cities for a long time but wouldn't have thought of studying architecture. And then, relatively early on, I got my hands on these silver volumes from the Situationists. At the same time, I was interested in the participatory approaches to art from the early nineteen-seventies, especially Steven Willats, who basically started to develop tools, urban analyses. Not exactly to intervene in a hands-on way, however, but rather he was working on consciousness as a conceptual artist. I found it very interesting to transfer this into a context that is not top-down in a social democratic sense, but rather to appropriate the questionnaire and the investigation oneself.

I: A few of you are not here today. What do the others add to the group from their respective occupational backgrounds?

B1: Tina is the only one who was actually part of the Esso-houses initiative. She is a social worker and was at that time with the St. Pauli GWA (*Gemeinwesenarbeit*, or community work). It was important for the Esso-house tenants to have the opportunity to come back, and for us to be able to stay in contact.

B4: I always had the feeling that, because Tina did not come from an artistically creative field, it took us quite a while at first to be able to understand one another at all. The way of working is also different. For instance, she did a few things that were a bit simpler. She recommended we host a "planning coffee," rather than a "workshop" for the Esso-house tenants. Just little things that are important, though, in order not to lose contact.

I: You have to talk to different people in different languages.

B1: Then there's Volker, who is one of those who was here from the beginning. Later we brought in Patex, as well.

B4: Volker studied architecture and urbanism. Patex is a cultural scientist and a musician.

B1: At the beginning, Volker was important because he did not give the impression of coming from an initiative right away.

B2: The authorities knew that we also came from the movement and that we were part of the Netzwerk Recht auf Stadt (Right to City Network). And Volker was again a different face in the group.

I: With your different backgrounds and personalities, you soon made a point of setting yourselves up in a way that enabled you to use a variety of tactics. In social work, for instance, it is obvious that Tina speaks a different sort of language and therefore can come across as being more accessible. And Renée with her background as an architect has the knowledge of a planner, knows how things work, and in turn has a command of that language. Basically, this is a kind of guerilla tactic enabling you to offer something appropriate to anyone who might approach you in "hazardous situations."

B1: Right.

B3: When we talk about backgrounds, those are also predetermined breaking points. This works well in phases when everyone is curious about the others. But of course, there are also some routines that are not really reflected. In art, it is common for you to give reasons for what you do. You can't just fall back on a given vocabulary of concepts. You have to work to create your vocabulary. This is a kind of unwieldiness that gets into projects like these, but it also gives you the power of definition. I think

1.4.1

these points—where we discuss concepts, for instance—they are what give the finishing touches to a project. This may also be a point that gives you more opportunities, because you have defined things a bit more precisely, and thus you can assert yourself against the status quo, which tries to crush such projects everywhere. When you are facing people from the planning department, you sometimes get the impression that they are the embodiment of normativity. And when investors come in with their logic of optimization, Excel tables, and investments—when you want to stand your ground against arguments of this nature, then it is also really good if you have clearly defined what you want. And that is sort of the daily work of art, which doesn't do it in conflict with reality usually, but rather anywhere.

And I think that with planning, that is, with something that is largely immaterial to begin with, that it is extremely important to be clear about the concepts: what they mean, what you can accomplish with them.

B4: But I always found the slogan "Arm Your Desires" best of all, for instance, because it expresses in a simple way what it's really about. It has everything, like self-empowerment, trusting yourself, and it also conveys a sort of mild threat. As an urban planning office you can't go to an administration with such a slogan. Perhaps it is only in this sort of constellation that you can take such liberties. And it was also said of the administration that, yes, we need artistic means to do this.

B3: A government agency hires offices to do the work for them, which is actually a service. In this context, we benefited from the fact that art plays a role here, because art traditionally has exceptional rights in civil society. In art the promise of autonomy is fulfilled. Here there is a culturally acquired ability of dealing with it that is embedded pretty deeply in this society, that informal methods, which a more organized logic cannot deal with under normal circumstances, are somehow OK when it is art. Because people have a vague understanding in the back of their minds that art somehow sets its own rules. This is what artists always do; otherwise it's not art.

I: Art brings a certain carte blanche to the process. It also lets the administration breathe a sigh of relief because it senses that exceptional circumstances prevail and that this is also a good thing. Above all, though, you have marked a very important point. The fact is, there is a private owner, so you could not "change the world." But then to get involved anyway, and to ask what you can do to get what is most appropriate out of the given situation, what makes most sense for the people and the neighborhood. For me, this is the most important point.

B1: You rarely get so far without protest. But then to get the hang of how to really make something new out of the situation, where you yourself can learn a lot while also creating whole new conditions, this is what I find most exciting about the whole thing.

B3: In our contract negotiations with the district authorities, this could also have been something where a normal office would have been put under quite a bit of pressure to sign a contract quickly. This cost us a month of negotiations. This is, of course, a crucial point in guaranteeing this independence. And there's another thing: At that time, we had tested the place with a little threat—to organize a parallel production of desires there. We did not have the commission yet and we knew that if we wanted to, we could start a parallel planning process here with a normal special use permit, even without money. And we had made that clear. That would have delegitimized their whole process. And keeping this knowledge in mind was important. It's a kind of knowledge that's important for others to know, because this kind of thing is not done often enough.

I: You made a distinct threat that, "We're going to go on even without you."

B1: No, we really would have done it. We would then have done the PlanBude process on a smaller scale. And the results would have been even more catchy, more than from any office. You can be sure of that.

B3: It is above all a question of legitimacy. The way these planning procedures usually run is not very democratically legitimized, not like a well-organized survey would be. This is in fact a very sharp sword that initiatives can put to very good use.

B1: But then you also have to do it.

I: Right, you have to do it. But it is not self-evident that you will accomplish it better than a commissioned office. You bring along this commitment. By having really widespread participation with more than 2,300 contributions in four-and-a-half months—then you can't say that just some sixty-odd people took part—and then your legitimacy has become really enormous.

B3: This is a whole different thing than just planning with five names. Definitely.

I: If you look at the entire construction process, you see that the participation process you initiated took place within a period that was right at the beginning. Maybe this would be a good time to look back at it. What did you do, exactly? Everything seems such a matter of course, the night cards, the clay models, the Lego models, the forms for different age and language groups to fill out. Did you try them out beforehand? Or did you draw on your experiences?

B4: We had the containers from August onward, and were only able to start the process itself in October. In the summer, we discussed this quite a bit, particularly the questionnaire. There were very different opinions of what it should be able to

1.4.1

achieve, how it should look, what we were allowed to ask at all and how, and what we could record. At this point, we had already discussed all these topics like, what is this really all about, and such. The clay and Lego models, they came in relatively late. Then it was a question of how we could clearly depict something like this.

I: You yourselves worked your way into the subject while developing the questionnaire.

B1: First we had to agree on the questions. We didn't know one another very well yet. The slogan "Crack the St. Pauli Code" came first—and then came the definition. Afterwards.

I: First a slogan—and then you further refined the actual content?

B1: Right. And then, how do we explain it?

B4: At some point we had "Think St. Pauli into the Future." Maybe that was also the quality, the fact that we really did grapple with one another over such fundamental issues. Every word was important. In that way, we developed this common approach and gained an understanding of ourselves as a group.

B2: We were sitting around at your place with a wall full of little index cards with the topics we wanted to deal with and which topics would be handled with which tools.

I: What were those issues?

B4: "At the petrol station, you and me," "Roof Landscapes 2.0," "What goes into the cellar?" and so forth. These topics were then actually developed. Of course, there were also blank cards without any topics already printed on them. I really do think that Park Fiction was an important experience, of course, as well as a resource of knowledge to go on with. But the heat map, that was something we sort of picked out of other already existing tools. And we only developed the Reeperbahn Panorama in the course of the process.

B1: From the very start, we said that we were doing a production of desires. We were not doing an interrogation. And then we had these examples from Park Fiction, where you ask about situations rather than doing a survey. More like, where have you always felt good and what was the reason? Creating situations, asking about situations. You take this detour with the production of desires by leaving it entirely open and talking about situations.

I: This concept of "production of desires" sounds rather like swimming free of an obstruction. Those taking part are supposed to feel free. Were there any guide rails for what they were supposed to produce—maybe in the form of drawings and models—that you could use to navigate? The clay models, for instance?

B2: In the negotiations with the district authorities, we clearly stated that we were not using any specifications from the city or the owner of the property as a basis for the process. Of course, the city then feared that a park would be planned. But we did not share this fear.

B3: We told them at least once that we were dealing with it. But not that we accept it as a guideline.

B4: That was pretty important to the district. It was relatively clear to me, the way we would work, it would not matter whether there were 24,000 or 27,000 square meters—nobody can imagine that sort of thing anyway. We wanted first to get to the bottom of it all. That was also what we called the utopian surplus. Guide rails of this kind do not help at all. They put a framework up there on top. And we are working down here.

B2: We were also able to achieve many other statements with the clay model. That was the case with all the tools.

B1: For us, the guide rail was actually something rather different. The people had been taken out of the houses. And they wanted to come back. That was the main topic. Everybody knew this. That is why a park here was never an issue. Instead, the people wanted to come back. And St. Pauli is a place where displacement is happening. Many people have to move to the edge of town. That is why one demand from the neighborhood was that if at all, then something has to be built for the people here, for the neighborhood. That was more like a guide rail that nobody forced upon us, but it came out of the situation of the neighborhood and not from city officials.

I: Participation is always a bit tricky ... who is participating? What I'm mainly interested in are the people who do not take part, or who are difficult to reach. How did you handle that?

B3: One thing is key, and that is to start from everyday life. You have to be in the place. That was a conflict at first. And that is perhaps the most important tool, that the container is standing on the Reeperbahn, at the corner of everyday street and tourist avenue, so to speak. As a place in everyday life where people pass by. That you are here, that you are open, approachable. And that sometimes you just have a

1.4.1

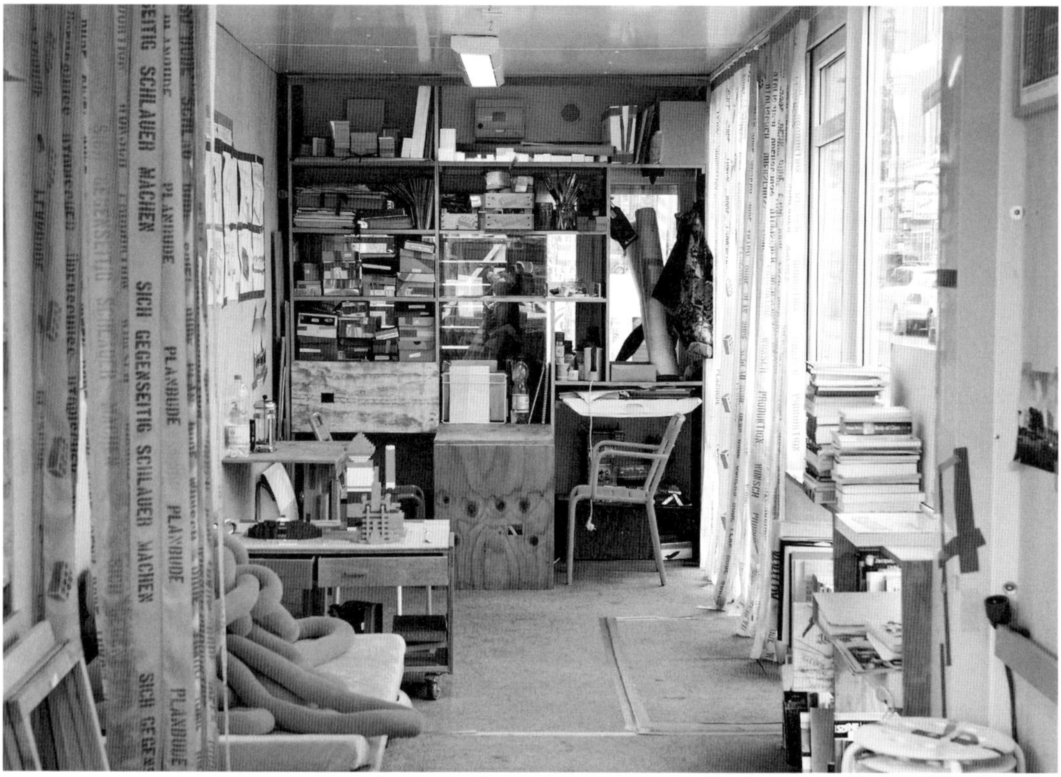
PLANBUDE
SICH GEGENSEITIG SCHLAUER MACHEN

ALDI

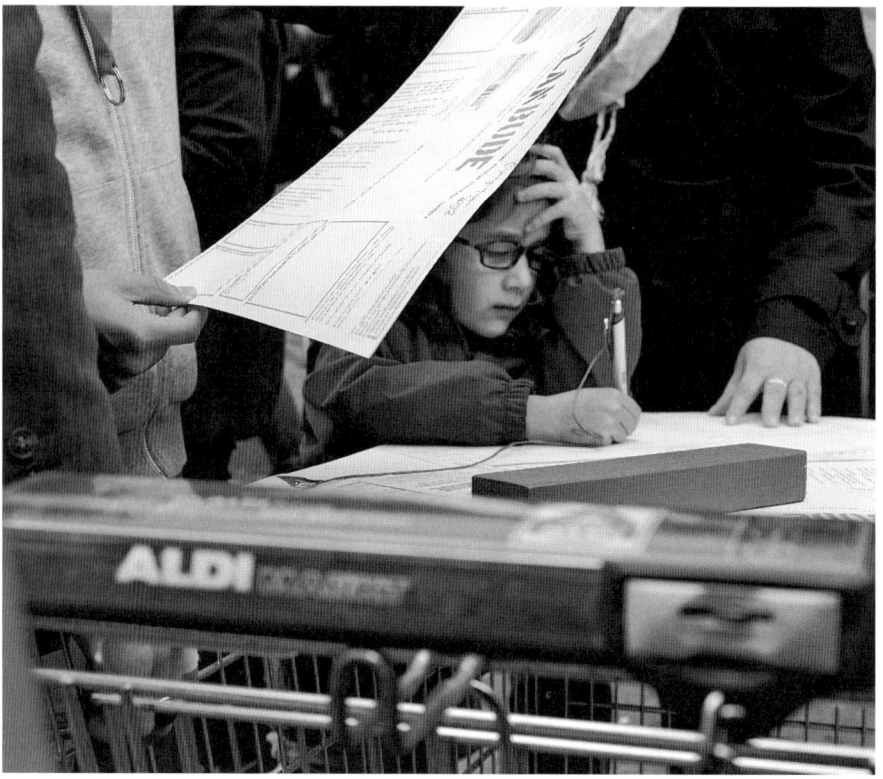

Figure 1 (p. 114): Be there: the PlanBude containers are in the middle of public space, are visible and open to all, © Frank Egel

Figure 2 (p. 114): The questionnaire: turn it, turn it upside down. Questions that get to the bottom of the matter, © Jörg Holst

Figure 3: Tactical furniture: the street as a planning office, © PlanBude Hamburg, Margit Czenki

Figure 4: PlanBude tools: produce wishes, formulate future ideas, © PlanBude Hamburg, Margit Czenki

1.4.1

talk with people. You might talk to someone about something or other four times over, and not until the fifth time do they come in.

I: So you were yourselves the people on site?

B3: Yes. Plus a crew of about six to ten planbuddies (supporting members of the PlanBude team), who all had different backgrounds. Every day there was a different language here.

I: I think there are quite a few people who think, "Nobody listens to me anyhow," who don't actually realize that their opinion is in fact welcome.

B3: We immediately—even before we had the commission—bagged a course with St. Pauli School for fourth grade and ninth and tenth grades. It's a mixed school and this mix was then here, as well. The effect is classic. You could also reproduce it. But the attitude to it cannot be reproduced; you have to learn it. And that is described as complicity. There has to be something that hooks up with everyday life and trusts everyday life to have the stronger imaginative power than investor logic. For me, it's a question of belief. And that is also something that can very well transcend ideologies and religions, divisions in society.

And the second thing was the tour through the pubs. We sought out different pubs for each workshop. And then we went piggyback with the "Buy Buy St. Pauli" movie, the documentary about of the Esso-houses, through all these taverns like Tippel 2, and we always had our planning tools with us. But it was more important to have to expose yourself to a situation where your own language is in the minority. You can't make bossy announcements in a pub. It's other people's home zone. And just to go in already changes something in your viewpoint. It has a corrective effect, because you're standing on someone else's territory. And with an attitude of solidarity or complicity in the end.

I: How was the participation of neighbors with migrant backgrounds? What's the situation with this issue here in St. Pauli? What has been your experience?

B1: If you define migrant as not so far away, there were lots of people here. Mostly you don't notice any more. The way we are, we don't ponder things like, "Where is he from?" That is why the statements on this topic are not so precise, because we don't divide it up like that. We only related it to language.

B2: Back to the people who otherwise do not get to be heard so well. This coming from the neighborhood and really always being on site or meeting at the supermarket. It was also totally important to reach certain people that way. And really, this being on site and then not at all any more. That the person sees you because you are otherwise at the container and then at Aldi. That has also been a special feature of PlanBude from the very beginning.

I: I think this kind of commitment is especially important—"We ourselves come from the hood and now we're doing this project." There's a lot of passion in there ... and that means you can't just repeat a project like this one. If we consider art, this really does resemble an artwork; it is specific and succeeds in the present moment. If someone wanted to repeat it somewhere else, you'd again need people who are just as committed. Now city planners may be tempted to think they could take the same course of action as PlanBude. What is often underestimated is that it only works with people who take the process in hand. I think it is very important to see that this personal engagement is not a service.

Certainly, you have already been asked whether you would do something like this again. We also get this question a lot. Would you do another project after this one? How would you do it?

B3: Yes, we would.

B1: We could have done this in a different form somewhere else, as well. For instance, we learned how to speak with people. People you don't otherwise get together with. You can learn that, if you are genuinely interested in other people. It could be my neighbor, and you don't think you're teaching them anything or have a different function. But really just a feeling of being the same.

B2: To take that seriously, and to take people seriously. To have a different understanding of what your own role in society is or in the neighborhood. Or just how a city develops and can develop. That is important. And you can apply that elsewhere, too.

I: You undertook this intensive participation process, you developed tools, evaluated the results, framed the concepts. You did the "translation work." So now I would like to ask about the expectations you aroused with this process and which, I assume, could not be fulfilled in all cases. You take on a responsibility toward the people and the neighborhood, that's important. Especially when you're on site, you put yourself within reach and you keep getting accosted. You would also have to communicate whenever certain desires are not achievable. You have to insist that people show understanding and help give thought to the problems at hand. This is where I see the great value of local work, that meetings and the subsequent actions are always under negotiation, right up to the end.

1.3.3 ◄

1.4.1

B3: This is an interesting moment: who is shirking responsibility, where, and when? This has nothing to do with transparence. Nor with democracy, either. It has more to do with this verse by Schiller, "Und setzest du nicht dein Leben ein, so soll dir nichts gewonnen sein" (roughly: if you don't put your life on the line, you shouldn't win anything). This counts for a lot in human communities. This kind of accountability, responsibility, and fighting this through, even if it gets you beat up, that's what matters.

B4: That could also maybe have to do with the way you communicate with people as a person. You notice pretty quickly whether somebody's intentions are sincere or not. And as long as nobody is willing to take it on, you won't do anything yourself either. In processes like this, these people in the background are usually much more important than you might think. And they are often the ones that get portrayed the least.

B3: On the other hand, the administration plays a role in the end. That is where things like this are portrayed. It's just not as easy to reproduce as a silly communi- cation kit with five colored cards to write down your ideas on what you need to know about participation and moderation. Maybe we should take a different look at all that, this question of reproducible or not reproducible. Because that idea about the personality is a good point, that then either needs it or not.

B4: And this experience—that you can actually only get by being part of the pro- cess and that you often take along to the next project—is a knowledge that often is given less value in the theoretical scientific discourse. How do you include your sub- jective knowledge and experience in research methodology?

▶ 1.6.2 **B3:** Basically, we too are in a situation where we would have to pass on such pro- cesses. Where we would in fact have to teach this sort of thing and pretty quickly train some people, who would then be able to take over doing this sort of thing? Masters studies, or institutes related to art, or architecture universities. This should be done much more often. Other actors will have to come along. Other forms of collectivity and applicability will have to be invented. The time for this is ripe, and the potential is there. That would be the other side of constancy, to have this sort of thing differently installed in training programs.

The Top Four Time Hacks

Lukasz Lendzinski/Peter Weigand, umschichten

Within the scope of the symposium Disziplinäre Grenzgänge, Studio umschichten from Stuttgart was invited to report from its practice. Using the framework of time, four projects were explicitly illuminated. Umschichten is working at the interface of art, architecture, and urban development; and they use the power of temporality to materialize a state of exception, a secret desire, or a problem, and thus initiate mental processes and discourses about spatial futures and programs. Their artistic practice is based on a careful use of materials and an approach that is strongly contextualized on site. It is about reacting in the process, an attending reacting, a reinterpretation of found circumstances and framework conditions. The processes and states of the transition are examined in the material as well as on site.

The Time-Window Trick *(Pop-up!, 2008)*

At the gates of Stuttgart's main railway station, behind the UFA Palace, the Stuttgart Pop-Up!—a platform for local residents and culture-makers—was created in an open building process. In a temporary construction, with components borrowed by a manufacturer, a platform was erected on a wasteland in the heart of Stuttgart, which served as a meeting place within the neighborhood as a stage and venue (see figure 1).

By means of a time-window trick—the purposeful shifting of the public view to the sheer event of time—an open construction and reconstruction process was made possible before and after the official opening of the project. Restricting the observation period and applying for an extra short time window in the middle of the overall process led to a relief for the authorities, to the approval of the project, and to the possibility of open planning and construction. The reconstruction and dismantling of the platform was an important part of the project and was open to people of all disciplines who were willing to cooperate. Together with the local residents, the building and the passing of a building and a community around this structure could be thematized and tested (see figure 2).

1.4.2

Figure 1: Pop-up!, © umschichten

Figure 2: Diagram Pop-up!,
© umschichten

Diagram

In comparison, there are two uniaxial diagrams: a time bar shows various events that follow each other and are more or less equally intense. In the Time-Window Trick the focus is on the one event while the other events are in a fog, or blurry.

The Time-Is-Money Trick *(Temporary Wall, 2011)*

Umschichten borrowed metal waste that had been pressed into cubes from the company Daimler-Benz, indulging in the material fetish for shiny, robust materials with a recognition value in the Wagenhalle Stuttgart. The cubes of residual metal, which were re-melted and further processed after the loan, were built into a temporary space installation, the Temporary Wall (see figure 3).

Figure 3: Temporary Wall,
© umschichten

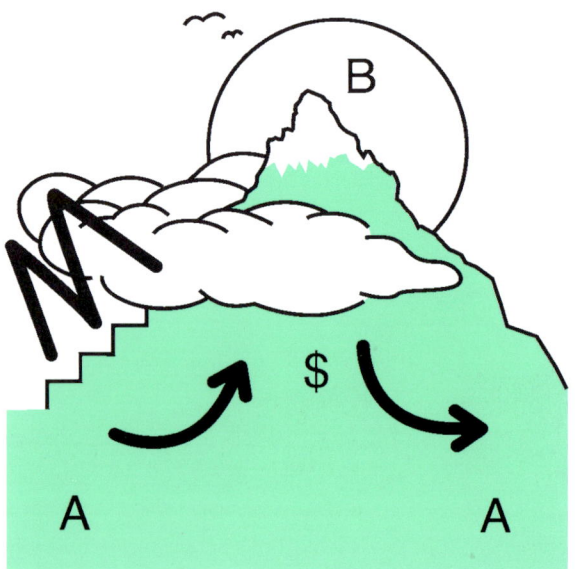

Figure 4: Diagram, Temporary Wall,
© umschichten
Figure 5 (p. 123): 72-Hour Urban Action,
© Mor Arkadir

The material used for the installation was thus charged with the factor of limited time, or limited power of disposition. The metal cubes were borrowed from Daimler-Benz as the pure metal value of the cubes would have excluded permanent acquisition. This material-time correlation shifts the ownership conditions of the material for a certain time. The temporary, free-of-charge ownership, however, led to a careful handling of the material; the entire installation needed to be able to be quickly deconstructed by simple mechanical measures (see figure 4).

The deliberate working with temporal transience, both in terms of the material and of its possession, had a considerable effect on the project. At the same time, this approach questioned traditional behavioral patterns in the use of materials, the concept of sustainability, and the relationship between individual actors in the context of building processes.

The Action Trick *(72-Hour Urban Action, 2012)*
About a hundred people from all over the world and different disciplines were invited for a short period to Stuttgart to realize ten small construction projects at ten different locations in a set time frame. Materials and tools were provided for this purpose. The participants had to develop a construction solution for a place assigned to them by lot within 72 hours. So an intensive contention of spaces in Stuttgart took place, by both locals and foreigners, and resulted in versatile installations in public spaces (see figure 5).

Planning and construction processes are usually subject to a slow and sticky procedure. This changed in the process of 72-Hour Urban Action. In the run-up, the organization of the (construction) festival and the application for the use of different locations were managed without a clear idea of what would ultimately be created. The other and important phases of the project were then carried out completely in the period of 72 hours. The design, the static approval, the supply of materials, and the construction were carried out within this set time frame.

The compression of processes and time sequences over a very narrow period of time results in a rapid process sequence and is in sharp contrast to the inertia of conventional planning processes. This compression of the various phases led to a powerful ignition, a bang-effect, that is much more dynamic compared to the average stress curve of conventional design processes (see figure 6).

Diagram
There are two graphs in which the x-axis marks the time course on which classic planning events are placed and the y-axis indicates the degree of stress. In the ordinary planning process, the stress curve is more or less constant; during the 72-Hour Urban Action, it is steadily ascending up to the explosive moment.

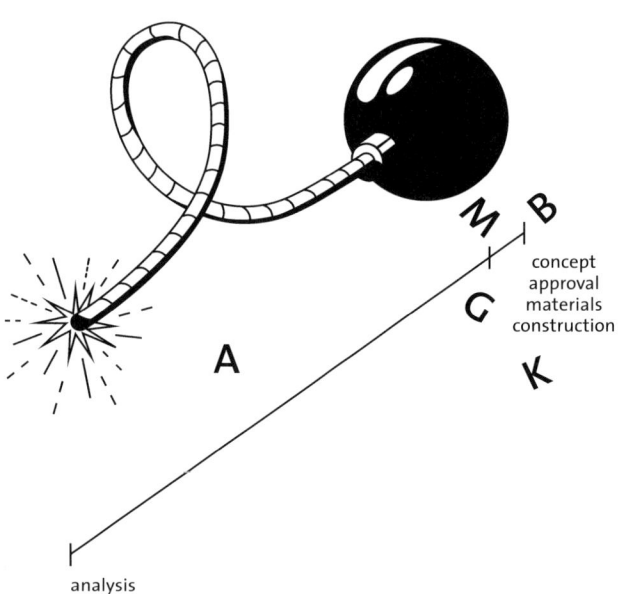

Figure 6: Diagram, 72-Hour Urban Action, © Mor Arkadir

The Dismantling-Is-Also-Nice Trick *(Super Bob—Rückbau Royale, 2012)*

As a counterpart to the classical museum, the Open Museum was built on the plateau of the contemporary gallery, the Galerie der Gegenwart. Initiated by the Baltic-Raw group, a temporary space was created for alternative, low-threshold culture.

As part of the project Rückbau Royale, umschichten redeveloped the dismantling of the Open Museum as another independent part of the project. Surprisingly, in the course of this process, an installation in the public space—a bobsleigh track for adults—evolved which was not previously planned nor did anyone expect it (see figure 7).

Figure 7: Rückbau Royale, © umschichten

1.4.2

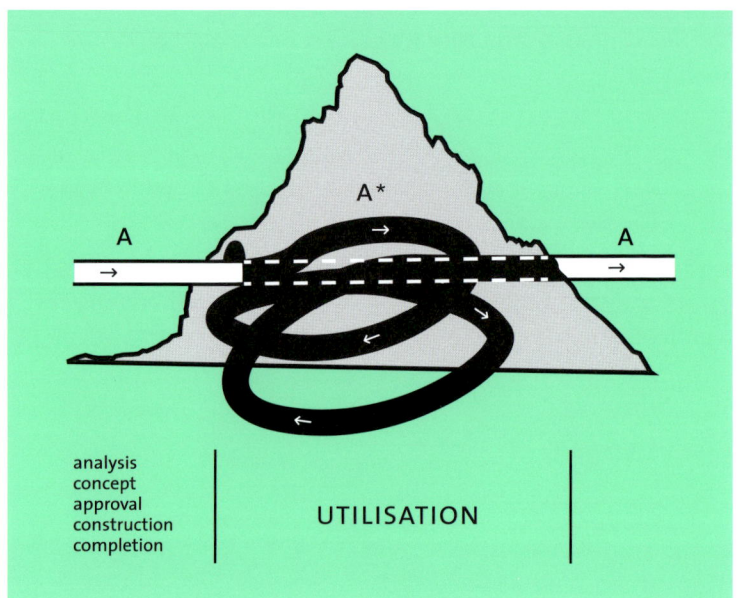

Figure 8: Diagram, Rückbau Royale, © umschichten

The reconstruction process is a process that is usually neglected and perceived as a necessary evil rather than an opportunity. As a result of the deceleration and thus expansion of this process, an enigmatic tension could arise that led to an unexpected event; the linear and usually dull process of dismantling had undergone a dramatic turn.

The slowing down of processes and the twisting of usually stringent sequences serves as a strategic tool to pay tribute to the ever-recurring emergence and passing, instead of purely product-fixed and result-oriented action. With this trick the dismantling was raised for a week to a sublime process. Parallels to the Kinskian screw are not to be pointed out here (see figure 8).

Diagram

There are two diagrams in which the y-axis represents the stress level, and the x-axis represents the time (t). In the first diagram, a long, straight-line diagram shows an ordinary reconstruction process; and, in turn, the second diagram shows a process that rotates like a helix with an explosive moment.

Longer Development Cycles, Please!

Frauke Burgdorff

Discussion of the future of the city and the city of the future is being encouraged at all levels as if there is no tomorrow. The German Federal Research Ministry and the Federal Construction Ministry are constantly awarding new contracts. The city of tomorrow and the city of the day after are coming to the fore. Heads are spinning around third-party funding at universities, and even in regional and municipal practice, a great deal of thought is currently going into drafts for 2030 and beyond.

What the future will bring is coming closer and reaching us in ever-shorter cycles. A new technological innovation is coming to market every two years. It takes about four years for a new way of doing business to leave its mark on the city—most recently Industry 4.0, and the sharing economy shortly before that. Take Airbnb, for instance. The company was founded nine years ago in California and is now a key factor influencing the housing market in Europe's high-influx cities.

Yet the length of the urban development cycle is the same as ever. There is no large, new piece of city to be had in fewer than twenty to thirty years. The Viennese lakeside town of Aspern was first designed in 1992, and the first phase of construction was completed twenty-five years later. The planning for HafenCity began in the early nineteen-nineties; the first zoning plan was ready with incredible speed a mere fourteen years later; the first phase of construction started after about twenty years. And the planning for the central train station in Stuttgart began in the mid-nineteen-nineties; the station is expected to be complete in less than ten years from now.

1·4·3

So does that mean that urban planning and urban development are not viable in the long term? Should the craft be left to the agile project developers in the smart city industry or the sharing economy? Launch a new city on the market every two years? Announce a new urban principle every four years? Or should we finally stop including every single interested party in the development of cities, delegate the task of weighing interests to state institutions, and return to the top-down principle so that the wheels can turn faster and the cities become engines of development rather than inhibitors? Haste is needed, after all. Climate change and global migration are posing immense challenges to our cities, and we must act now if we want to live to see the day after tomorrow.

But what do we really get from responding and anticipating? Does this make cities more sustainable, more stable?

In decades past, this has repeatedly led to rather bizarre discussions and blunders, and the fact that today's innovations are tomorrow's dinosaurs is a piece of wisdom that is all too painfully apparent in our cities. The social and technical repair and maintenance costs of oversized showcase projects in housing construction, or of the religious icons of international financial and cultural capital, are immense. Especially in recent decades, they have caused the most commonplace foundations of urban life—public services, with their infrastructure, schools, bridges, and hospitals—to be in some cases substantially weakened. Keeping up schools and repairing bridges was simply not politically attractive. Now, hastily installed stimulus plans, such as School 2020, are supposed to compensate for this neglect and once again create incentives to hurry up and make bad investments.

We should act to slow rather than fuel the cyclical fluctuations in the real estate industry and in housing construction. As recently as the first decade of this century, the experts among us were impressed by the shrinking cities and their aesthetic, and housing specialists were disillusioned by the meager rents and profits the markets were yielding. This uncertainty caused business cycles to become ever shorter, and international investment capital broke into the unstable markets like migratory locusts high on serotonin. All of us—the freelance planners and those in the public sector—made too little use of this phase because we thought we had to follow the market and do our planning with the wisdom of hindsight. What a delusion! Municipalities sold off their land and their housing companies; the state of North Rhine-Westphalia, its

LEG (regional development company). We all have to bear the fol-low-up costs, structurally and with our rents. And they will grow if we respond to the pressure on the housing market right now with a glut of land[1] or with misplaced tax incentives. Fortunately, there are also urban planners who are defending and pressing home the common good and the weighing of interests in this dynamic framework. The Soziale Bodennutzung (socially just land use) in Munich, the many other so-called building land resolutions, and the increasingly prevailing practice of concept-based contracting of public property hold out a hope.

These glimpses into the recent past show that the citizens of a city or a state, along with their political representatives and the administration, would do well to tackle their future confidently, prudently, and with a yen for complexity.

After all, the European city is made up of various forces that want to act within it and should be able to do so. The makers of a city's future are those who cement social bonds by organizing neighborhood associations or railway missions; those who inspire value creation in services, production, and trade; and those who advance cultural and social innovations. This explicitly does not include those who use clever investment models to profit from the limited supply of land as a commodity in ever-shorter cycles.

In order for the future-makers who contribute to the common good to have sufficient space, public authorities must not serve as sound amplifiers of the markets, but instead should weigh inter-ests and perform a countercyclical control function and, with a steady yet strong hand, give those who want to help shape this path a normative foundation, a constraining framework, and op-portunities to develop. Policymakers at all levels are being called upon to provide them with support.

1 Proponents hope that so-called trickle-down effects will apply, and that the new offerings will curb rent hikes at other locations. At present, however, there is not the least empirical basis for this assumption.

1.4.3

Money or Daydream: Difficulties and Changing Facets of Gaining Adequate Remuneration

Yvonne Werner

We have certain wishes and ideas how cities of tomorrow should look. Planners try to translate these ideas into reality and face not only city-specific but also practice-related challenges in their professional lives. They need a certain amount of idealism, ingenuity, and flexibility to assert themselves against inappropriate structures and traditional views.

Empty coffers in municipalities, a lack of creative will of private-sector builders, and the resulting standardized urban planning call for a rethink in urban design as well as for social problems and challenges. In this context new ways of thinking and planning processes are necessary and the demands are comprehensive: cooperation, openness to results, transdisciplinarity, flexibility, and the inclusion of local conditions. The design of these processes is difficult to reconcile with the formal structures in which they are embedded, making it more difficult for planners to generate a decent living.

For projects in Germany that are remunerated according to the fee scale for architects and engineers (HOAI), it becomes clear how inefficient the HOAI structure is with regard to the first three service stages: the first consultation, the preliminary design, and the construction drawings. These are rated too low, although these stages are particularly important to ensure the success of a project. Especially complex tasks have to be formulated explicitly at the beginning, but according to the established structure, actually fall into later stages. That means concession is only remunerated if the project is actually realized. Moreover, too little attention is paid in the HOAI to communicative tasks as it focuses on services that are necessary to build a building. Consulting services, the organization of a participation process, and its implementation in planning processes, however, cannot be considered detached from the basic services that are necessary to build a building. They must be integrated throughout the planning and construction process and in advance. In addition, a stronger evaluation of first three stages is necessary in order to counteract the fundamental problem of the underpaid design phase. The functional quality of the architecture depends to a large extent on the involvement of different actors and their considerations. A promotion or redefinition of the first three stages, or other solutions that allow early and continuous participation and analysis are necessary.

The limiting conditions remain for the time being. Until then, planners must continue to look for alternative ways to remunerate their practices. There are ways and means to overcome the discrepancy between the services required and their remuneration. Considering the practice, different approaches of acquisition, calculation, and remuneration can be identified.

Projects are not only acquired through direct and follow-up contracts and through successful participation in competitions—the self-initiation of projects is another possibility of acquisition. It requires skills in the field of project development and specialization in order to build up a network, negotiate an acceptable remuneration for the services, and necessary knowledge to recognize and assess potentials.

The problems of financing already begin with the calculation of costs, which requires a certain amount of experience in order to be able to assess—in the case of complex projects—which services are necessary and what their scope is. In principle, there are two models of cost calculation: the clients describe the order content and the office makes an offer or the client sets the budget and the office accordingly sets the project volume. This creates a

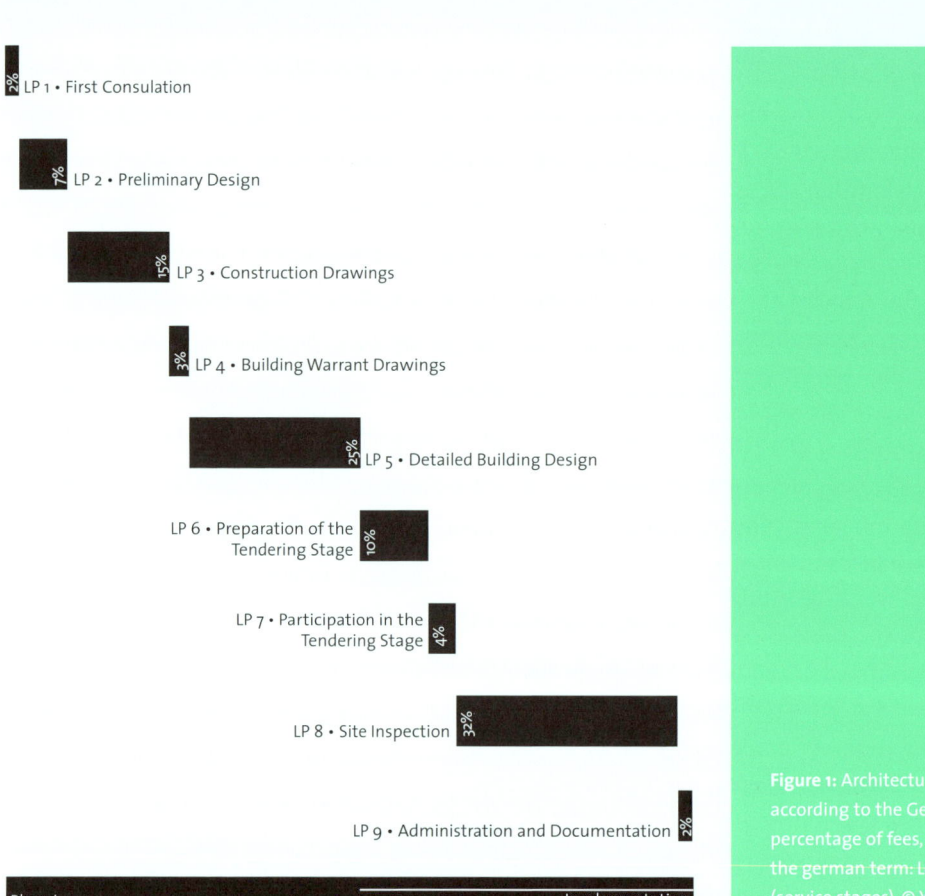

LP 1 • First Consulation 2%

LP 2 • Preliminary Design 7%

LP 3 • Construction Drawings 15%

LP 4 • Building Warrant Drawings 3%

LP 5 • Detailed Building Design 25%

LP 6 • Preparation of the Tendering Stage 10%

LP 7 • Participation in the Tendering Stage 4%

LP 8 • Site Inspection 32%

LP 9 • Administration and Documentation 2%

Planning   Implementation

Figure 1: Architectural services according to the German HOAI and percentage of fees, LP stands for the german term: Leistungsphase (service stages), © Yvonne Werner

paradox, because with an open-ended and flexible way of working it is not easy to predict the costs. In addition, for projects where the public sector is the contracting authority, it is difficult to make an offer that is well thought out and as accurate as possible as agreed project budgets cannot be easily adapted to the public procurement directives.

Another problem arises when services are provided due to the complex task and elaborate processes at the beginning of the project or during self-generation of the projects that are not provided for by the HOAI. There are various ways to achieve a (partial) compensation of the extra effort. Services rendered in the process earlier than provided will be charged later. However, this procedure is unsecured because it only works if the project is realized. If the project does not materialize, the concessions remain unpaid. Additional services can be contractually agreed and thus be rewarded— urban design projects in particular have room for negotiation—since only a leaflet is required as an orientation for the performance and remuneration of drafts and is not further specified in the HOAI.

In addition to formal conditions, logistical characteristics of architectural/planning offices in terms of self-image, external representation, work efficiency, willingness to financially compromise, and degree of flexibility logically contribute to the generation of income. Content-convincing projects, a suitable office organization, and good networking are necessary to succeed. To do this, the planners must know their competencies and possible achievements and be clear about what exactly is the product they offer. This profile development makes it possible to make specific demands on cooperation and remuneration for concrete services and competences. This task is difficult to implement, especially in work fields that are less standardized and permit less repeatability.

Projects are usually only implemented with highly elaborate and participatory processes if local circumstances or the political situation permit. Only few clients understand that costly processes not only prove their worth but also can pay off in exceptional cases in the long term. Only a greater acceptance of the procedures and the understanding that these are not nice add-ons but form an important basis for planning within complex mixed situations give rise to the hope for a formal integration of the changes and a more appropriate reward. Also, a rethinking of academic training in the planning disciplines must take place. Planners need additional skills in project development, networking, and transdisciplinary ways of working and controlling participation. Designers, you need a knack for the difficult balancing act between innovation and efficiency!

1.4.4

1.5. Competencies

- 1 Dripping: Unclosing Spaces by means of a Festival

- 2 " ... confidere necesse est ... "

- 3 Collective Self-Organization and the Making of the Urban: A Self-Empowering Practice of Subversive Potential

Dripping: Unclosing Spaces by means of a Festival

Dorothee Halbrock/Julia Jost/
Julia Lerch-Zajączkowska,
Hallo Festspiele/Schaltzentrale
Translation by Tina Steiger

On Cracks and Density

The term "competence" means, besides responsibility or ability, also portability or, in a geological context, "the resistance of a rock against either erosion or deformation" (Fossen 2010, p. 430). Equally, the attributes of portability and resistance refer to the rigidity of an object and, therefore, its density. The particles of a solid demonstrate densely allied and sorted atoms, blocking together into a solid. By its composition, solids impede a permeation from the outside, hence resisting the possibility of any destabilization. In order to open a solid—which by its mere nature is inaccessible to outsiders or to a congeneric public due to it being in private ownership—the materiality of water is most conducive. Water penetrates the smallest of cracks and crevices, its molecular polarity allows for it to be a cohesive compound, and due to the collective action of its hydrogen bonds, water gravitates to its own kind.

These physical properties inspired the initiators of the Hallo Festspiele, who had previous experience in temporary festival productions, when they started to address the question of the lack of spaces, or rather, the lack of more public spaces in the city. In 2014 a group of cultural and artistic producers from Hamburg were first brought together to develop a concept that could transform temporary cultural use to something longer term. This group was

1.5.1

Figure 1: Hallo Festspiele 2015,
© Daniel Kalinke

composed of a number of individuals from a broad spectrum of disciplines, including the performance collective cobratheater.cobra, the Golden Pudel Club, and the Hanseatische Materialverwaltung.

Stable and Fluid like Glass: Developing Mobile and Transparent Strategies for Settling In

With the idea of an artistic opening of space, the name "Hallo Festspiele" was introduced, which was, on the one hand, welcoming; and, on the other hand, appropriating a reference to the glamour of elite cultural institutions, such as Salzburger Festspiele, Bayreuther Festspiele, etc. Simultaneously, the idea for "Hallöchen" evolved as a series of events accompanying the Festspiele. These created a link between internal and external communication based on a concept of continuous invitations assuring a constant engagement of new people actively and regularly discussing, reflecting, and questioning the development process. With the Hallöchen, the group moved through well-known and familiar places, collecting people to join, such as in the Club Kraniche or the artist residence Vorwerkstift, among others.

The first edition of Hallo Festspiele was planned for late summer of 2014 at the so-called Kraftwerk Bille, the oldest, still-preserved electrical power plant in Hamburg's Hammerbrook borough, an area still heavily characterized by industrial vernacular,

Figure 2: Entrance area, Hallo Festspiele 2015, © Daniel Kalinke

but the owners of Kraftwerk Bille suddenly canceled and the event didn't take place. We continued to search for alternative spaces and sites until we were tipped off by city administrators that the ownership of the Kraftwerk Bille had changed hands. It now belonged to MIB Coloured Fields GmbH, a company that already owned the Baumwollspinnerei in Leipzig, as well as having developed the former AEG site in Nuremberg, allowing for both a mixture of subcultural uses and commercial rental spaces.

That is when the initiators of the Festspiele came into contact with MIB. The company was keen on giving them an audience, as they considered temporary use as being important to the activation of real estate in order to increase the intellectual worth of the property. The first Hallöchen took place in May of 2015 in the inner courtyard of the Kraftwerk Bille, offering the first opportunity to invite a public to the site and suggesting possibilities for what could be created in the future. Cobratheater.cobra staged a time travel event and, together with visitors, built a medieval village from clay and branches, all but giving an ironic gesture to prevalent festival stereotypes.

Reverse Glass Painting: Constantly Infiltrating
Together, content and modes of working were generated, and in July 2015 a nonprofit association was founded called Viele Grüße

1.5.1

Figure 3: Collage of the process: Hallo
Festspiele, Schaltzentrale, and Viele
Grüße von e.V., © Stephanie Wunderlich

von—Verein zur Förderung raumöffnender Kultur e.V. (Many Greetings From—Association for the Cultural and Artistic Reactivation of Space). The focus was on expanding the collaborating group and developing an open and process-oriented event, which would put the first foot in the door of opening the Kraftwerk Bille to the public.

In September 2015, the inaugural Hallo Festspiele kicked off with a week-long collaborative and collective site development. The organizing team invited new guests to take part in shaping the festival's spaces by making use of building materials harvested in the surrounding neighborhood together with architects from umschichten and Stararchitekten. At the same time, the waterfront areas, which had been sites of the first year's Festspiele, were used for self-organized concerts, games, and performances. Despite cloudbursts and rain showers, the entire event, which was completely funded by the collaborators themselves, concluded on sound financial footing.

By collecting materials from the neighboring businesses, we made first contact with the surroundings, inviting those working close by to take part or visit the Festspiele. In this respect, the industrial nature of the surrounding borough came to be reflected in the materials used at Kraftwerk Bille. By going door-to-door, we were able to personally invite all of the relatively small number of residents living in the surrounding neighborhood.

After the first festival, the Hallo Festspiele team received a comparably large grant from the City of Hamburg for the following year. For the first time, this allowed a comprehensive exploration of the vicinity of the Kraftwerk Bille and research into projects in other places, such as Schauspielhaus in Hamburg, Les Grands Voisins in France, and Plataforma Trafaria in Portugal. The Hallöchen series continued in the surrounding neighborhood, with the intention that they functioned both as a platform for inviting new people, as well as a collector of knowledge about the spaces and places in pursuit of developing a long-term vision. In that way, we could personally introduce ourselves to the surrounding neighbors and become familiar with their contexts in order to together discuss ideas for how parts of the Kraftwerk Bille—or the entire site—could be brought back to public use. These "neighborhood-Hallöchen" took place in the vicinity of Kraftwerk Bille, at places such as the trucker's diner, a shipping cellar, an old neighborhood pub, and the Rowing Club Bille. Together with the expanding network of experts of the surrounding environment (Rowing Club Bille, artists' houses, refugee shelters), coupled with the knowledge that east Hamburg would undergo major changes in light of the city's master plan Stromaufwärts an Elbe und Bille (Upstream Developments along the Rivers Elbe and Bille), which was presented to the public in 2014, the idea for an experimental neighborhood bureau—a space intertwining the arts and urban development—was born. What came to be known as the Schaltzentrale was meant as a meeting space for the neighborhood, and especially residents of the newly placed refugee housing facilities, in order to partake in the development of the Kraftwerk Bille (see figure 4).

1.5.1

Figure 4: First encounter Schaltzentrale
(May 2016), © Daniel Kalinke

The Leak Bursts ...

... and the water seeped in. We allowed the onset of a flood, eliciting the transformational power of water into establishments. Time and again, we communicated to the municipality as well as the owner that our intention for the temporary Hallo Festspiele was to establish a long-term public use for the at-the-time vast halls of Kraftwerk Bille. It became about convincing the owners to allow temporary access to the vast halls for the purpose of researching for the Festspiele and the accompanying Hallöchen. The owners were immediately willing to open the spaces for temporary use; therefore, our strategy was—and remains—to initiate temporary uses in order to establish and make long-term uses conceivable. Over time and with the experience of collaborating with our Viele Grüße von e.V. Association, we established a relationship of trust with the owners so that they offered access to a space in the front house of the ensemble in the spring of 2016. It was not the expansive, 2,000-square-meter Kesselhalle, around which the initial design had been developed, but the 230-square-meter, partly unheated office space, which was charming, but in need of restoration. This space (unlike the other building complexes of Kraftwerk Bille under historical protection) was marked for demolition, and offered to the association as a temporary use (see figure 5).

We applied the concept of the Schaltzentrale to the spaces and rooms offered to us, and agreed upon a rent-free lease, in which the Viele Grüße von Association would merely cover the utility costs. In the late summer of 2016, the second Festspiele was, amongst other events, used to activate the Schaltzentrale for the first time. The inventory of the Festspiele was assembled so that it could subsequently be used for the Schaltzentrale and nearly every night there were roundtable talks with different participants in order to discuss future concepts for the space.

Simultaneously the inner spaces of the Kraftwerk Bille were activated with self-developed theater pieces, music, performances, and installations by architecture groups from across Europe. Many of the participants came together from previous exchange projects in France and Portugal, which had taken place throughout the year and addressed similar themes (like the conversion of a former hospital in Paris or an old prison in Lisbon). The Hallo Festspiele 2016 was a grand celebration, with great efforts by a team that worked almost exclusively on a voluntary basis.

From Scratch yet Inside

So the competence of Hallo Festspiele, as a construct, initially materialized contrary to its definition, rather as responsibility or qualification. During the origins of the Hallo Festspiele, artists, researchers, and autodidacts of many disciplines and niches came together to realize the events, often finding themselves taking on actions and responsibilities in previously unknown areas. These thirty to fifty collaborators therefore constantly had to fill gaps in competences, caused by the temporally and

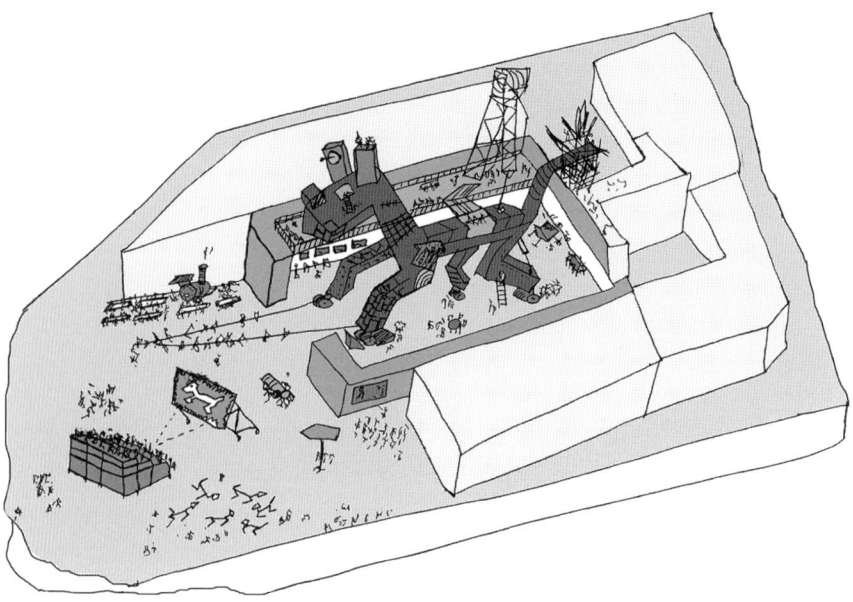

Figure 5: Trojan Dog in the so-called Kesselhalle at Kraftwerk Bille, © Lukasz Lendzinski (umschichten)/ Julia Lerch-Zajączkowska

financially limited capacities of the festival framework. The vast team, which had initially seeped through the cracks and crevices of the building like water, evaporated to a smaller group of about ten people. The intuitive, but yet not concrete, ideal of a working mode and its associated output was not possible in the large group format, and gave way to the necessity of logistics.

Therefore, in the winter of 2016 the remaining active members decided to change the organizing structure, transforming the spiraling collective into a group with clearer responsibilities. Equally, the opportunity of having a stable space at our disposal would be used to achieve the participatory initiatives that had always formed the foundation of Hallo in the long term, rather than limiting them to the week of the Festspiele. The content of Hallo Festspiele would be tightened, allowing for artistic spatial research, rather than putting all artistic content up for discussion to the entire group.

In the winter of 2016–17 the Schaltzentrale again started from scratch, lacking financial support and with a heavily reduced group of people, in unrenovated spaces. By means of small activations (like, for example, an improvised café, which was open for a few hours a day), spaces were opened to the public, along with courtyard parties, in which future possible uses were sketched and informal meetings with the wider neighborhood congregated, continuously experimenting and establishing desired programs. Simultaneously, various grant proposals were (and will continue to be) written, which led to the helpful news in the spring that the Schaltzentrale—as a place of encounters as well as the artistically developed concept for the Hallo Festspiele—will receive public subsidies. For the latter, the emphasis is placed on researching the auditory perception of the spaces of Kraftwerk Bille throughout 2017, having been granted financial support from the municipal and federal government.

The Schaltzentrale currently considers itself an experimental and artistic neighborhood bureau. The impressive spaces of the entire site will be made accessible to the interested public through continuous residences, talks, discussions, performances, celebrations, exhibitions, public construction sites, and performative tours; while the rooms of the Schaltzentrale offer a regular space for all kinds of exchanges. It offers a meeting place for residents and those working nearby, a working and exhibition space, and a platform for discussions about alternative forms of urban development, specifically in regards to the development of so-called Hamburg-East, at the focal point of the municipal master plan Stromaufwärts an Elbe und Bille.

Doing Laps

We have found a place for common working and being, with the establishment of the first perpetual performance at Kraftwerk Bille from which we have agency—a base in which the everyday encounters offer opportunities for new and completely different relationships, especially with the surrounding actors. It is a type of institutionalization, offering a hub of networks and having a reputation to be taken seriously within the wider urban development discourse.

In order to remain agile, it is important for us to consider, assess, and question the Hallo Festspiel every year. After Hallo Festspiele activated the outer areas in 2015, the expansive halls in 2016, and the various floors in 2017, we will move onto the water in 2018. With the support of and in cooperation with experts and marine professionals we want to test the river Bille as a space of possibilities and experimentation. We will explore what an alternative wharf could look like on the quay wall of the Kraftwerk Bille and what activities and actions could be possible, and research the potential and the meaning of water as and for public space.

1.5.1

Reference

Fossen, H. (2010). *Structural Geology.* Cambridge, UK.

"… confidere necesse est …"

Michael Koch

The Fact Is

When you go outside the borders of your discipline, go out exploring new urban spheres of work and go after solutions beyond formal certainties, you have to be able to trust: in the meaningfulness of what you are doing and in the integrity of the actors you are dealing with.

The Rise of the Informal

Starting in the nineteen-seventies, *Instandbesetzungen* (urban homesteading with renovation)—in practice, occupying houses to prevent their impending demolition—became widespread. The occupier's own work often helped breathe new life into houses that had already been written off. Toleration of the occupying renovators was followed by renegotiated leasing contracts. They represented a venture into uncharted regulatory terrain. It was in this political context that the IBA Berlin (1979–1987) developed and qualified its strategies of "careful urban renewal." The new orientation toward seeing existing buildings as building stock was not only a paradigm shift, but also a response of planning concepts to economic crisis and less certain growth. Following German reunification, the "guardhouses" in Leipzig continued this strategy of situational user agreements when the "perforated city" was under discussion as a guiding principle for Leipzig in view of the uncertain outlook for development.

"Change without growth" then became a leitmotif of the IBA Emscher Park (1989–1999), "incrementalism with perspective" (Karl Ganser) the apposite method, and "interim use" a new topos of urban development concepts. If development prospects were uncertain or transitional arrangements were necessary, temporary user agreements were negotiated for plots and buildings. Both IBAs functioned as midwives of informal planning and at the same time signaled a *Planungsdämmerung* (twilight of planning). Formal planning was reaching its limits. An occasional laissez-faire attitude toward the occupiers and an acceptance of a time limitation on the experimental use—and thus also acceptance of a definitive eviction date—often proved to be a challenge for all involved. The gaps now opening up in formal regulatory possibilities had to be bridged over with mutual trust, and new agreement possibilities had to be sought.

Trust is undoubtedly an important characteristic for any sort of interpersonal relationship. But does not "having to trust" also place a burden upon it, and all the more when the relationship is between actors in informal planning processes?

Trust or Control

Traditional, formalized urban planning also needs trust—trust in the correctness and aptness of normative requirements and sovereign law. Adherence to norms and rules of formal planning, however, can be verified through formalized procedures; trust can be replaced by control. Rules that are followed then point to a successful weighing and balancing of interests, as well as, in the end, to the correctness and fairness of the planning decisions that are made.

If we compare planning law and planning culture in Germany and Switzerland, we discover a stronger situational and grassroots, democratic legal formalization and concretization of planning requirements in Switzerland. This means that detailed regulations are the result of concrete negotiation processes between various actors on site. The common will formed in these negotiations strengthens trust in the correctness of the planning decisions being made and in the rules derived from them. This culturally anchored, grassroots, democratic decision-making process has been in practice for decades and is founded on a deep feeling of collective responsibility.

New fields of work for the co-operative and co-productive   2.5 ▶
changing and shaping of cities today often range far outside the respective formalized planning routines and instruments, and thus lack this promised certainty and dependability. The give-and-take in the necessary negotiation processes challenges the trust potential of everyone involved.

Business partners must be able to trust one another. The dictionary defines trust as "... being firmly convinced of the reliability, dependability of a person or thing ..." Fake news has shaken our trust in the truthfulness of news and challenges us to exert control. Here trust as a "mechanism for reducing complexity" (Niklas Luhmann) reaches its limits and provokes an examination of the related narrative.

Looking for Perspectives

Informal planning processes are undertakings fraught with conceptual, regulatory, and instrumental uncertainties. As a special sort of experimental and situational format, however, they also harbor a large potential for identification. Genius loci and *Eigenlogik* (inherent logic) (Martina Löw) give rise to stories anchored in social spaces. These can nurture the trust needed to navigate the informal archipelago of uncertainty.

Trust must not only be put into informal planning processes, but these very processes must also create spaces and opportunities for building trust. In this way, informal processes can become places from which to take the leap into "new terrains" of civil society. Trust "as an intermediary state between knowing and not knowing" (Georg Simmel) thus becomes capable of being experienced as an active characteristic pointing to the future.

When Georg Franck postulates the "urban commons," or when the "commons" are repeatedly invoked in the discourse related to urban planning, then this means that the traditional social negotiation processes on individual use and the use of common or public goods is being discussed as a possible reference for future regulatory processes in our urban societies. This smacks strongly of the utopian idea of free agreement as the regulatory mode for a nonviolent, anarchistic society. The actions of the Situationist International in the nineteen-seventies were redolent of this idea. Today, situational deregulation of obstructive bylaws followed by a re-regulation negotiated and agreed on site could be a worthwhile perspective for solving concrete urban problems.

The Fact Is

You just can't get by without trust.

Collective Self-Organization and the Making of the Urban: A Self-Empowering Practice of Subversive Potential

Melanie Giza

Nowadays we face a capitalism that is unleashed by neoliberal politics and tends to push capitalistic exploitation of cities over the edge. Cities seem to have become resources, products, and means of production all at once. In his book *Rebel Cities*, David Harvey states, "[...] the never-ending need to dispose of overaccumulating capital [is] driving towards endless and sprawling urban growth no matter what the social, environmental, or political consequences" (Harvey 2012, p. xvi). Indeed, capitalist logic of exploitation sets frameworks for urban development. On the basis of paradigms of urban planning one can see the linkage between capitalist accumulation, absorption, and the making of the urban, such as functional separation and the rise of the suburbs in Fordism, which we intriguingly call an economic miracle. Those who consider themselves experts in urban development, especially in the era of neoliberalism, need to reflect on the powerful impact of "a disgusting mess of a globalizing, urbanizing capital run amok" (Harvey 2012, p. xvi).

In the past, crises of accumulation have often led to bloody conflicts of power. According to Hannah Arendt, legitimacy to rule and therefore power rises from the collective will of the following (Arendt 1970). In my PhD thesis I research the practice of self-organization as an empowerment strategy with a potentially subversive character against a capitalistically driven making of the urban. Since the well-developed capitalistic societies that we are dealing with might have turned the subversion of today into a promising business idea by tomorrow, there might be doubts regarding the effectivity of subversion. Nevertheless, a practice generally seems to be subversive if it, for instance by a process of infiltration, twists certain unreasonable relations around. Subversion needs to be separated from opposition or denial because it is rather conspirative, well known in terms of anti-state expression but usually does not enforce societal dropout. Subversion offers a variety of practices like sabotage or vandalism that are linked to legal issues as well. However, one can tell by the hype regarding guerilla tactics that subversion tends to be endangered of becoming tomorrow's new conformism.

In the conflict of capitalist exploitation, I would like to point out the empowering potential of self-organization in rather small, consensus-based, collectively structured, and solidly acting units for a rather autonomous making of the urban. I once strolled around my field of research, a neighborhood in Leipzig, when I discovered a graffiti displaying the 1968-based slogan, "Bildet Banden!" (Form gangs!). According to the concept of power by Arendt (Arendt 1970), I interpreted the slogan as a political message and therefore a demand of acting collectively. By the number of noncommercial, collectively run locations and residential projects with often social, cultural, hedonistic, or even political approaches in the neighborhood it appeared to me that self-organization must have become a seemingly common practice with a strong impact on communitarization. The rising social network and infrastructure between these spots create what I like to describe as the emergence of a scene (Haunss 2004) in my research. When it comes to people's motivation for self-organizing, I noticed quite a political shift in my field of research over the years.

In a former shrinking city like Leipzig, with a lack of inhabitants and a nonexistent housing market, the roots of self-organization seemed to be located rather in a lack of infrastructure and probably a greater freedom, whereas nowadays and assumingly due to urban growth and rising economic pressure, social inclusion and the preservation of noncommercial spaces seem to become more relevant. However, the number of self-organized collective properties withdrawn from the local housing market, especially in my field of research but not just in Leipzig, is an interesting example of self-organization being successfully applied. Private property is the basic feature of capitalist societies and the housing market is usually at the center of speculative transactions. Despite that, self-organized collective property fundamentally refuses improvements of one's stock of capital. It even reveals its potentially subversive character when levering out common mechanisms of the housing market in one of the most relevant hotspots for capitalist urban-making. Furthermore, self-organization can be used as a political tool for self-empowering as it usually strives for greater autonomy as it seems to enable a rather emancipated process of the urban-making against capitalist exploitation.

1.5.3

References

Harvey, D. (2012). *Rebel Cities: From the Right to the City to the Urban Revolution.* London.

Arendt, H. (1970). *On Violence.* Orlando.

Haunss, S. (2004). *Identität in Bewegung. Prozesse kollektiver Identität bei den Autonomen und in der Schwulenbewegung.* Bürgergesellschaft und Demokratie 19. Wiesbaden.

1.6. Authorships

Who Is the Author?

Michael Obrist, feld72

Exkursus: Law Makers[1]

In 2007 a man called Gilberto Kassab with one law changed the perception of the public space and the possibilities of architecture in a city of eleven million people (twenty million in the greater metropolitan area). The mayor of São Paulo with the Lei Cidade Limpa (the Law for the Clean City) redefined the rule of advertisement in public space, and in fact, he banned it. Empty billboards have become the fragile remains of a formerly overexposed city, but it is in the night when the main difference between the present and the past is evident:

No memories of Times Square, no global competition against Tokyo's Ginza, no evocation of *Blade Runner*. A city where light has just been reduced again to illuminate and not to communicate. A city full of beauty farms and cosmetic surgery, but no billboards with seduction through advertisement of the perfect female body in public space anymore. As director (and educated architect) Fernando Meirelles (*City of God*) stated, for the first time he can see the city without having to *read* it.

As our perception is focused on recognizing those things that are new and added to our visual field faster than those that are removed, it becomes a surreal experience going through São Paulo at night. A city walk with phantom pains. The biggest urban agglomeration of South America has become one of Italo Calvino's *Invisible Cities*, where one defining and exaggerated element creates a specific city. São Paulo's naked architecture.

Architettura é (soltanto) Architettura, Aldo Rossi?

It was billboards and a sign system that created a new impulse to architectural theory, when Venturi, Scott Brown, and Izenour in 1979 learned from Las Vegas, and it was just a little law in 2007, that made the decorated shed impossible in the most prestigious Brazilian urban area of 1,500 square kilometers.

But some parts of the advertisement industry tried to find alternative ways. An informal system has emerged: people hired for

1 In this text the author enters in a dialogue with himself, revisiting thoughts published in 2013 in his essay "Trojan Horses and Other Social Animals" (L. Feireiss, ed., *Space Matters Chronicles*, Vienna 2013, pp. 108–119) which he further develops in the context of this book.

1.6.1

carrying advertisements on movable signboards and even on their clothes are popping out on different parts of the streets, flexible enough to react to police presence and to customers' behaviors. The informal and the illegal formed a strong alliance. It's the body that now becomes the last frontier, the remaining moving spatial element for advertisement free of restrictions.

A new architecture and new urban strategies will arise from this change of law. Who was the author of this new impossibility for one kind of architecture and the gate-opener for another kind of architecture?

Gilberto Kassab? The advertisement industry? Architects and urbanists? The capital or the people, just to name two of the most frequently used and in the end empty words for every reason of change?

Who is the author?

When feld72 was invited by curator Lilli Hollein as the Austrian contribution to the São Paulo Biennial in 2007, it was exactly those mechanisms that intrigued us and that we reflected with our installation and intervention on site. It is the relation of space and our contemporary society and those shifting borders between architecture, urbanism, art, and other disciplines that interest us and define our practice. To react to the complexity of our world, we have to redefine the *arsenal of architecture* and to enrich it with new tools, strategies, and tactics.

Changing Systems

The years at the beginning of the millennium saw the arrival of new architecture groups with enigmatic names in the city of Vienna—some only men, others only women, but mostly mixed groups: AWG-AllesWirdGut, Artec, Caramel, feld72, gaupenraub+/−, the Next Enterprise, Nonconform, Pool, querkraft, Rataplan, RAHM, just to name a few—where the most striking element was that there was no relation to the founder's name. The search for a name—which could sometimes be read as a program, but mostly remained quite cryptic—could be seen as a clear reference to the sixties and seventies, during which time Vienna saw the birth of groups with similar names, some of which later became very famous: Coop Himmelb(l)au, Haus-Rucker-Co (whose parts later transformed into Ortner&Ortner Baukunst and Zamp Kelp where the names of the founders are very clear and visible), Zünd-Up, Salz der Erde, etc.

As a clear distinction to former architecture studios such as MVRDV, and much earlier, the first boygroup of Italian architecture founded 1932—the highly influential BBPR— whose studio names were created by the initials of the team members' surnames, these new studios had no reference to surnames at all. And that was not only part of a funny way of representing oneself, but also reflected a representation of a new internal structure: they were all formed by equally represented partners, who perceived themselves more a collective or a bigger group entity than single individuals working together. In a certain way they were more like jazz combos with equally gifted and famous instrumental players than rock groups with a lead singer. Teamwork made official. A new collaborative spirit found its way in perceiving the profession of architecture already from the beginning as a collective work. The flexibility and adaptability of this structure were also a response to the changing economic conditions within the profession of architecture and enabled the structure to compete in different fields without leaving the core profession. A few of those groups similar to the ones founded in the seventies worked on the expanded fields of architecture and moved into transdisciplinarity. So the group name not only reflected a change in structure with the affirmation of teamwork with different skills as the professional approach of the studio, but also it indicated the possibility of operating in different fields related to architecture, the arts, and social space with a brand name which could be used in different fields as well.

The creation of the brand also created a new perception of authorship: the output of work generated in the studios was all labeled under one brand name, and it was not the celebration of the single genius celebrated in Ayn Rand's *Fountainhead*, but of a quite hidden collective approach. During the last decade one could observe very clearly the development of different organizational structures of those different studios and the positioning within the different disciplines through to today—some of those went clearly into the field of architecture; some studios remained in their crossover position; others found a career in the world of the arts. The brand remained—the structure changed.

The idea of the collective group labeled with a strong name was a particular phenomenon of the sixties and seventies, when the creation of these groups was a strategy of self-representation that derived from the youth culture with their first models of pop groups and were in opposition to the classical ego-orientated model of the (male) architect. Mostly, a name became a program: Archigram with their exploration of technology, infrastructure, and pop culture; or Superstudio and Archizoom in their tentative of going radical into *Superarchitettura*—"Superarchitettura is the architecture of superproduction, superconsumption, superinduction to consume, the supermarket, the superman, super gas," as they wrote in their radical manifesto for the homonymous exhibition in 1966 at Jolly2 in Pistoia. Ant Farm in California could not be understood without the idea of the hedonism of the hippie movement and their counterculture position to the American lifestyle. Ant Farm was not merely a studio, but was the search of a collective and hedonistic, holistic experience based on the rejection of traditional society models. Even in the name of one of the few still active groups formed in those decades the name became program: Coop Himmelb(l)au: a cooperative, which should be able to build structures similar to the blue sky. Paradoxically this collective over the years has transformed into a one-man-show of one of its founders, Wolf Prix, and is now one of the most famous examples of the phenomena of star architecture. Strongly under the influence and rediscovering of Situationism the nineties also saw rise of

1.6.1

collective groups such as FAT and muf in London, and Stalker in Rome, with their own specific agendas, but a strong will towards collectiveness and the expansion of the boundaries of the discipline. New urban phenomena and the following shift in the discipline of architecture created new opportunities and new reflections on the nature of the discipline and its possibilities, and maybe it was no coincidence that the collective raumlabor was founded in Berlin, and the architecture studio Complizen has one of its headquarters and main operation field in the shrinking city of Halle.

Architecture is a job of many. Although everybody knows about the complexity of big projects, which are just possible with a huge number of gifted architects, engineers, and specialists working together, the media search for the one big name behind it, maybe as a consequence of our strange human nature of questioning constantly if there is somebody behind the complexity of our world. It seems that the more exceptional—or artistic—the nature of the architectural work, the less journalists are satisfied with a company name; they are in search for the single genius. It is interesting that this happens in times where famous artists dealing with big structures like Olafur Eliasson, Jeff Koons, or Vito Acconci have developed large-scale studios with a number of collaborators, very similar to the old artist ateliers of the Renaissance and the Baroque periods—or to architecture studios of today—and in doing so, they generate a system of production where a single genius alone would not be able to create such an enormous variety and complexity of projects. This leads to key questions about authorship and the origin of work, which are fundamental for the economy of the art market.

Who is the author?

After a decade of discussing the death of the author in late-twentieth-century philosophy, it was paradoxically mainly the well-educated group of architecture and art critics with a clear insight into the background processes within the offices who have continued the affirmation of architecture as the work of the single genius with clear authorship. The rise of the star-system in architecture was a product of the media, and it took a while until the media recognized the presence of new tendencies in architecture that were based on completely different approaches and ways of representation than those of the usual suspects of the star system. It is also predictable that in order to make these phenomena easy comprehensible, a lot of simplification will take place in the communication process from sender to receiver of the message.

In some of these new approaches to the discipline the question of participation and involvement of potential users have become crucial. Not only do we find collaboration in the internal structure of these studios, but also in a bigger teamwork collaborating on an equal level with specialists of other disciplines, organized again sometimes in a similar way. To this complexity we have to add the participation process, and we find ourselves in a system of feedback and projection. It is less about the author of the final work, than to the initiator and developer of the rules of the game, on which these creative processes can now evolve. The output of the work becomes a possibility based on self-established rules. The authors might be more game developers.

As the architectural theoretician Kari Jormakka stated, "The architects of feld72 do not approach architecture in terms of established categories of function, form or kind, but rather ask what the city is capable of. (...) while it is certainly possible to appreciate architecture as one of the visual arts, or even study buildings semiotically as systems of signs, the interest in the work of feld72 lies elsewhere. In their performative design the focus is on how the built environment contributes to the construction of a lifeworld, i.e. how architecture partakes in the constitution and perpetuation of quotidian social relations through the interaction of the body with a structured environment."[2]

Buildings as performative instruments and generators of social space become sort of Trojan horses with inherent additional programs and platforms for possibilities that can surprise the users, let them rediscover the adventure and poetry in the everyday.

[It was the search for conceptual] platforms and open structures on which the users could build up and find their own way of interpretation—not a linear time setting for a performance, but the construction of a common ground based on increasing possibilities and an ontology of coincidences. Opening up choices. Creating responsibility.

2.6.1 ▶

As in most of the projects by feld72 in social space, different methods of participation played a fundamental rule. Participation is not a supply of services with an already known and predefined output, but a starting point for an open process and shared adventure. The expertise of the inhabitants as connoisseurs of their own surroundings is incorporated into the body of knowledge formed by the other experts, creating a broad understanding of place and social context.

Also in those social housing projects by feld72 where the possible future inhabitants were known, the methods of participation defined an environment, where already from the beginning they have taken responsibility. Through the whole process of participation a community has evolved, supported by their broad understanding of the design and space decisions that formed the different housing complexes. Sharing experiences to become part of one story.

2 Jormakka, K. (2008). "Theory and Design in the Fourth Machine Age." L. Hollien, ed. *Urbanism—For Sale*: feld72. Vienna/New York.

1.6.1

"A story is a little knot or complex of that species of connectedness which we call relevance. In the nineteen-sixties, students were fighting for *relevance*, and I would assume that any A is relevant to any B if both A and B are parts or components of the same *story*. Again we face connectedness at more than one level: First, connection between A and B by virtue of their being components in the same story. And then, connectedness between people in that all think in terms of stories."

(Gregory Bateson in "Mind and Nature")

If the process becomes too complex, authorship becomes unclear—or even not important at all.

For most of the studios involved in these kinds of works, it is more about the process than the final work, and the question of authorship becomes diffuse and of secondary importance. There lies a beauty in the (un)predictability of the process leading to new previously unthinkable solutions.

Authorship in that moment becomes important just for others. In crime stories there is always a crucial moment where things get too complex, and there is a need to bring order in chaos, and it is in these moments that someone says, "Follow the money!"

Law Makers—Again

Although authorship might become less important for the creators of a process or of the platforms and infrastructures on which certain open processes can find their way and expression, at the end of the day our working environment and professional system are defined by laws and responsibilities.

These are also reflected in the money flow. The ones with responsibility are paid or punished.

And although we might celebrate the new ways of working together, creating complexity and community, as long as we don't find a way to change also the legal framework, the question of authorship might be just a philosophical one, on which we all agree in the good times.

It is in the case when something unpredictably bad happens and the consequences have to be taken, that the state unfortunately has a clear answer to our question:

Who is the author?

The one(s) that go(es) into prison if something is going wrong.

References

Obrist, M. (2013). "Trojan Horses and Other Social Animals." L. Feireiss, ed. *Space Matters Chronicles*. Vienna/NewYork.

Jormakka, K. (2008). "Theory and Design in the fourth Machine Age." L. Hollein, *Urbanism—For Sale: feld72*. Vienna/New York.

Professionals of the Unplanned

Camilla Guadalupi

Introduction

In recent years, there has been an increasing interest in *urban tactics*, micro-spatial practices characterized by a do-it-yourself attitude, as means to shape and regenerate urban spaces (Boonstra and Boelens 2011; Douglas 2014; Iveson 2013; Oswalt et al. 2013). While a precise definition of the label urban tactics is problematic (Mould 2014), the generally recognized common features of the initiatives are a relatively short time horizon, a relatively small spatial scale, the mobilization of the locally available resources, and a kind of open-endedness (Brenner 2015). This trend has been studied from a great range of points of view: as an opportunity for a more livable and dynamic city (Oswalt et al. 2013); as an expression of the neoliberal character of contemporary urban policies (Mayer 2013; Mould 2014; Tonkiss 2013); or as a challenge to the role of the professionals engaged with spatial transformation (Awan et al. 2011; Miessen 2011; Petrescu and Petcou 2013). This last branch is the topic of interest of this contribution. Indeed, while urban tactics are often reduced to forms of citizen activism, their diffusion is pushing the unfolding of a growing body of professional realities. There is a new kind of urban expertise that is being constructed and whose toolkit includes the tactical appropriation of public space, the active engagement of local communities, and the acknowledgement of the social dimension of space. This new generation of subversive, socially minded, and politically motivated groups is experimenting with self-initiated projects, new forms of financing, and 1.4.4 ◀ alternative organizational structures, mostly in the form of multidisciplinary—and precarious—collectives. The analysis of these realities forces us to go beyond traditional dichotomies. Oppositions such as formal/informal or top-down/bottom-up are not helping to understand the ambivalent relationship between these practices and the official planning policies.

1.6.2

The first section aims at drawing a sketched portrait of these groups of professionals, elaborating on interviews with twelve different groups active in Europe. Taking the direct voices of such professionals as empirical material follows the claim of Jacobs and Merriman (2011) for listening more carefully to the practitioners, too often not enough consulted by the geographers of architecture,[1] and faces the opportunity to acknowledge them as epistemic partners (Douglas and Marcus 2008). It is a preliminary and incomplete description of these profiles, focusing on the conception of space that these practices are enacting.

The second section aims at exploring the complex politics of such way of acting, and it has the ambition to introduce the possibility of investigating these subjects assuming a poststructuralist perspective, a theoretical stream that is gaining increasing popularity within geography scholarships. This theoretical viewpoint overcomes the sharp dualism between resistance and complicity, diving into the ambiguity of these practices and avoiding the neoliberal co-optation paradigm, by which they could easily be targeted as examples of endorsement. It is argued that such an interpretation would "overestimate the coherence of 'the powerful' and the seamlessness with which 'order' is produced" (Massey in Sharp 2000, p. 280).

A Sketched Portrait of an Emerging Expertise

The urban professionals who are engaging themselves with urban tactics step over the "the self-defined boundaries of the profession [of architecture]" (Awan et al. 2011, p. 30), whose outputs are expected to be buildings or plans, and experiment with different ways to impact the physical and symbolic dimension of space. The diversity of the practices corresponds to a variety of people operating in the field with different skills, ideological and political premises, aims, and methods. This section deals with this emerging expertise elaborating on twelve semistructured interviews with groups active in Turin, Rome, Marseille, Brussels, and Lisbon. Given the absence of clear-cut definitions of such contemporary and blurred phenomena and the exploratory attitude of the interviews, the construction of the sample derives from a snowball-sampling methodology.

The great majority of the interviewees have a background in architecture, which is not surprising since architecture, among the other disciplines concerning space such as geography or urban planning, is the one with the strongest practical objective of

1 Geography of architecture is a sub-field of cultural geography dealing with the analysis of the built environment and its relationships with individuals and society. It encompasses a variety of approaches, going from cultural approaches aiming at underlining the symbolic dimension of buildings, passing through Marxist-inspired critiques of the role of architecture, to more recent developments inspired by pragmatism and STS studies focusing on the sociomaterial dimension of architectural practice and using nonrepresentational theory as a framework (for a brief historical overview see Lees 2001, Kraftl 2010, and Lorne 2017).

directly intervening in space. Furthermore, the economic crises following 2008 had a huge impact on the building industry, pushing many architects to look for alternative professional niches. When assessing the prominence of architecture as a background, it becomes clear why the main attempts to define these kinds of realities in the scientific literature come from scholars in the field of architecture: "spatial agency" (Awan et al. 2011), "crossbench practitioner" (Miessen 2011), or "transgressive practice" (Petrescu and Petcou 2013) are just some examples. The debate is thus mainly framed as a reflection on the changing role of the architect, even affirming that, "as a contemporary architect, one confronts the dilemma of a profession that no longer really exists" (Miessen 2011, p. 245). Nevertheless, there is no sense of belonging to a specific discipline emerging from the interviews. As one interviewee put it: "It could be a bit pretentious to say it is architecture; we build little things [...] maybe a sort of activation [...] we don't really know if we have a definition for what we do" (Morgane, member of Collectif Baya, Brussels, January 2017). Other responses included: "In the square I see myself as something between a social worker and an urbanist utopian thinker, something like this" (Tim, member of Toestand, Brussels, January 2017) and "Every member could answer a different thing [...] basically we do things we like [...]" (Stefano, member of Orizzontale, Rome, October 2016). When the participants were asked to give a definition of what they are doing, the majority could not define unproblematically their own work. Some felt that a new vocabulary or a redefinition of architecture would be needed to gain more credibility. "That would be a relief: to not feel delegitimized because you are not building a wall, but making an action [...]," one interviewee said, adding, "You say, this is architecture for me, I am shaping the space" (Serena, member of ATISuffix, Rome, October 2016). Others perceived the process of finding a definition as threatening, somehow closing new possibilities and forms of experimentation. For example, one interviewee said: "Then you can call it architecture, art, design, carpentry, product [...] we are not interested in being put into boxes" (Stefano, member of Orizzontale, Rome, October 2016).

This floating between disciplines resonates with the definition of relational planning approaches given by Tornaghi (2015) as outcomes of cross-fertilization between disciplines. This observation may support the hypothesis that this way of acting assumes a relational conception of space, a key idea that strongly influenced the contemporary debate on the city and the urban (Amin and Thrift 2002; Farías and Bender 2011; McFarlane 2011). It is argued here that these experiences could represent a bridge between practice and some of the latest theoretical findings in urban studies, and that the analysis of such collectives could help in exploring "where contemporary architectural practice converges and diverges from broader geographic research" (Lorne 2017, p. 277). Following Murdoch, who affirms that "planning 'performs' or 'enacts' spaces of different kinds" (2006, p. 132), it is suggested to develop further research investigating what kind of space is enacted by these practices.

1.6.2

These groups clearly shifted their objective from designing objects, fixed entities, or black boxes, to designing *things*, assemblages of heterogeneous entities (Storni 2015). In this context, the process appears much more important than the output. All the groups interviewed found it very hard to choose one of their projects as particularly representative of their approach because every project is different depending on the unique situation: "We do everything, from self-building to performances, and so we don't manage to have, we cannot have a unique output [...] an installation, a performance, a graphic product, a video ... it changes time by time depending on what we think could be the best means" (Maria, member of ATISuffix, Rome, October 2016).

They are all concerned with public space, with the uses and the practices on such spaces, but there is not a fixed receipt to intervene in such a becoming space. The acknowledgement of the ever-becoming feature of space and of the shared dimension of its production while downsizing their own role creates more common ground for all these experiences. Being related to public space does not mean to intervene just on formally public space, rather the publicness, still assuming a relational conception, is conceived "not as an attached attribute or a label, rather as a varying and relational way of being 'space'" (Tornaghi 2015, p. 25). Relating to the fluidity of space, one informant reported that "temporariness is a political choice" (Roberto, member of Orizzontale, Rome, October 2017), considering the importance given to the reversibility of the projects.

The temporal and often local aspect of the interventions unmasks some issues of efficacy and relevance of such practices. Furthermore, the precariousness of the practices is mirrored in the precariousness of the subjects. Anyway, while it would be possible to interpret such a trend as a response to the high rate of unemployment among young architects, none of the interviewees started such activity after trying without success to find a job in a traditional studio; the great majority started the activities while still students at the university. The difficulties in finding a stable job surely affect the life choices of the subjects involved, but in the interviews the collective was never presented as a fallback. As said above, a clear definition is missing, thus it is not yet part of a codified discourse; nevertheless, such groups inspire a strong sense of belonging among the participants and they constitute a means of identification. Even in the case in which it does not constitute a full-time job, "your brain is on it 24/24 hours" (Panagiotis, member of ATISuffix, Rome, October 2016). Another interviewee alluded to the impossibility of giving as much time as wanted to the collective "because at the end of the day you have to pay the rent" (Giulia, member of de:forma, Turin, October 2016).

Some reflections on the political potential of these experiences are proposed in the next section, given the ambiguous social model they imply, but also the mobilization in a progressive direction of affects and passions, aspects that play a central role in the field of politics (Mouffe 2000).

Entrepreneurial Urban Activism

The double-face essence of the practices, which are both transformative and ephemeral, is mirrored in the ambivalence of the actors enacting them. This ambiguity, mostly derived from their entrepreneurial attitude, makes these subjects hard to categorize. As precarious young professionals with a very small impact on urban dynamics they are of course not part of the ruling class, but as educated and mostly sophisticated professionals neither are they representative of deprived or dispossessed groups. On one side, this new generation of professionals is a expression of an attitude towards self-entrepreneurship, flexibilization of labor, and the provision of fragmented, quick, and low-cost interventions, often part of the neighborhood regeneration programs which are "such a hallmark of the roll-out neo-liberalizing city" (Mayer 2013, p. 8). On the other side, it is also true that the same experiences could be framed as a response to urban neoliberalism, whose logic, in the context of the so-called austerity urbanism, does not leave much space to the sociospatial self-consciousness of the professionals, who feel more and more de-powered in the institutionalized workplaces.

Informed by a Foucauldian relational conception of power, this paper argues that the investigation of these ambivalent figures of entrepreneurialized urban activism could contribute to overcome what Rose calls "the romantic quest for an anti-establishment politics" (2002, p. 397), representing a heckler within the resistance narrative. Without neglecting that these precarious practices are unavoidably imbued with the contemporary capitalism, their diffusion and eventual complicity with institutional policies question the metaphor of the margins and force these subjects not "to evade the *responsibilities* of power" (Massey in Sharp 2000, p. 285, emphasis in the text). Furthermore, they don't fit in the role of the "naïve," "uncritical," and "un-reflexive" actor met by the "critical," "reflexive," and "distanced" enquirer (Latour 2005). The choice of working, at least sometimes, within an institutional framework, with the ambivalences it implies, is taken consciously. As one interviewee put it: "We don't agree with the system, globally, how it works and so on. You can choose to stay out of it, but first of all it is very complicated to be out of it, really out of it [...] we decided to try to go in and try to change things by the inside [...] it's longer, it is sometimes really exhausting, because there are people in front of you that don't want to change anything [...] but we decided to try in this way" (Florent, member of collectif etc, Marseille, October 2016). Talking about this issue another interviewee said: "There is the risk to be exploited by the system that you are criticizing, to be used as a palliative" (Tiago, member of ateliermob, Lisbon, July 2017). And the frustration that this could represent is not hidden: "Personally I am a bit frustrated with our position in this project [...] They [the municipality] want to use us like puppets [...] I don't want to work like this" (Tim, member of Toestand, Brussels, January 2017).

Resisting the temptation of dismissing such experiences as functional to the business-as-usual means to frame such experiences not as examples of endorsement,

1.6.2

thus spaces of domination, but as expressions of agonistic arenas (Mouffe 1999), spaces of production in which an entanglement of power relations is performed. This move implies a reframing of the concept of neoliberal ideology and the role of critique. If ideology is not conceived as deception, but as the set of normative references characterizing an historical period, then the "inherent ambiguity of critique" (Boltanski and Chiapello 2007, p. 40) is evident and not surprising as it is always sharing these references with the system it is criticizing. This conception helps in softening the paradigm of neoliberal co-optation, which contributes to the disabling universal pessimism (Coutard and Guy 2007) denounced by some authors within the majority of urban studies scholarships. Instead of questioning whether these experiences are revolutionary or not, it is argued that it could be more fruitful to analyze which values and legitimation criteria are put into question by these practices, following the terminology of Boltanski and Chiapello (2007), in order to test their political potential and to draw the social project they imply. To understand the meaning of such a project, the work that needs to be done is to collect the critiques they are putting forward: against the shared consensus of participation, a conflictual and contested self-appropriation of space; against the capitalistic emphasis on functionality and efficiency, a recreational use of space; against the current hyperspecialization of knowledge and production, the idea of a multifaceted urban practitioner.

References

Amin, A. and N. Thrift (2002). *Cities: Reimagining the Urban.* Cambridge, UK.

Awan, N., T. Schneider and J. Till (2011). *Spatial Agency: Other Ways of Doing Architecture.* New York.

Boltanski, L. and E. Chiapello (2007). *The New Spirit of Capitalism.* London.

Boonstra, B. and L. Boelens (2011). "Self-Organization in Urban Development: Towards a New Perspective on Spatial Planning." *Urban Research & Practice* 4.2: pp. 99–122.

Brenner, N. (2015). "Is 'Tactical Urbanism' an Alternative to Neoliberal Urbanism?" post at MoMa. http://post.at.moma.org/content_items. /587-is-tactical-urbanism-an-alternative-to-neoliberal-urbanism

Coutard, O. and S. Guy (2007). "STS and the City: Politics and Practices of Hope." *Science, Technology, & Human Values* 32.6: pp. 713–734.

Douglas, G.C.C. (2014). "Do-It-Yourself Urban Design: The Social Practice of Informal 'Improvement' through Unauthorized Alteration: DO-IT-YOURSELF URBAN DESIGN." *City Community* 13.1: pp. 5–25.

Douglas, R. H. and G. E. Marcus (2008). "Para-Ethnography." L. M. Given, ed. *The SAGE Encyclopedia of Qualitative Research Methods.* Thousand Oaks, California.

Farías, I. and T. Bender, eds. (2011). *Urban Assemblages: How Actor-Network Theory Changes Urban Studies.* London.

Iveson, K. (2013). "Cities within the City: Do-It-Yourself Urbanism and the Right to the City." *International Journal of Urban and Regional Research* 37.3: pp. 941–956.

Jacobs, J. M. and P. Merriman (2011). "Practising architectures." *Social & Cultural Geography* 12.3: pp. 211–222.

Kraftl, P. (2010). "Geographies of Architecture: The Multiple Lives of Buildings." *Geography Compass* 4.5: pp. 402–15.

Latour, B. (2005). *Reassembling the Social: An Introduction to Actor-Network-Theory.* New York.

Lees, L. (2001). "Towards A Critical Geography of Architecture: The Case of an Ersatz Colosseum." *Ecumene* 8.1: pp. 51–86.

Lorne, C. (2017). "Spatial Agency and Practising Architecture beyond Buildings." *Social & Cultural Geography* 18.2: pp. 268–87.

Mayer, M. (2013). "First World Urban Activism: Beyond Austerity Urbanism and Creative City Politics." *City* 17.1: pp. 5–19.

McFarlane, C. (2011). "Assemblage and Critical Urbanism." *City* 15.2: pp. 204–224.

Miessen, M. (2011). *The Nightmare of Participation: Crossbench Praxis as a Mode of Criticality* Berlin.

Mouffe, C. (2000). "Politics and Passions." *Ethical Perspectives* 7.2: pp. 146–150.

Mould, O. (2014). "Tactical Urbanism: The New Vernacular of the Creative City." *Geography Compass* 8.8: pp. 529–539.

Murdoch, J. (2006). *Post-Structuralist Geography: A Guide to Relational Space.* London.

Oswalt, P., K. Overmeyer and P. Misselwitz, eds. (2013). *Urban Catalyst: The Power of Temporary Use* Berlin.

Petrescu, D. and C. Petcou (2013). "Tactics for a Transgressive Practice." *Architectural Design* 83.6: pp. 58–65.

Rose, M. (2002). "The Seductions of Resistance: Power, Politics, and a Performative Style of Systems." *Environment and Planning D: Society and Space* 20.4: pp. 383–400.

Sharp, J. P. (2000). *Entanglements of Power: Geographies of Domination/Resistance* London.

Storni, C. (2015). "Notes on ANT for Designers: Ontological, Methodological and Epistemological Turn in Collaborative Design." *CoDesign* 11: pp. 166–178.

Tonkiss, F. (2013). "Austerity Urbanism and the Makeshift City." City. 17.3: pp. 312–324. doi:10.1080/13604813.2013.795332.

Tornaghi, C. (2014). "Relational Ontology of Public Space and Action-Orientated Pedagogy in Action: Dilemmas of Professional Ethics and Social Justice." S. Knierbein and C. Tornaghi, eds. *Public Space and Relational Perspectives: New Challenges for Architecture and Planning.* New York.

1.6.2

Snøhetta: People Process Projects
An Introduction to Creative Work and Methodology—The Value of Architecture in Creating Community

Jette Cathrin Hopp, Snøhetta

Snøhetta's commitment to an integrated, transdisciplinary practice, including architecture, landscape, interior, and design, has few parallels within the industry. The quality and strength of identity provoked by our designs is achieved by incorporating deep research, transforming what are often obstructions into potentiality, and including the social and political environment in the creative process. Our work strives to enhance our sense of place, identity, and relationship to others and the physical spaces we inhabit, whether natural or human-made.

Our content-based approach is derived from long-standing Nordic traditions of humanistic values and we stand our social grounds. Our projects are not driven by style, but are genuinely born out of the premises embedded in every task, unfolding the singularity of every object, every design, and every result. They have equality and accessibility as primary drivers, evolving from a common ground of generosity.

At the heart of all Snøhetta's work is a commitment to shaping the built environment both in the service of humanism and the longevity of our planet. Our interdisciplinary design process ensures that our projects are both poetic and pragmatic, where high design works in conjunction with sustainable building performance. A commitment to social and environmental sustainability is key to success for public ownership of the built environment. Because of that, our projects involve extensive collaboration with clients, users, contractors, and other stakeholders. The collective design process results in a shared knowledge base, and a shared investment in the development. This in turn, will encourage all parties to take on the responsibility that is required to secure the ideas through later phases (see figure 1).

Snøhetta practices a self-defined transdisciplinary process in which different professionals—from architects to visual artists, philosophers to sociologists—exchange roles to explore differing perspectives without the prejudice of convention. Within our office, Snøhetta emphasizes an open exchange between roles and disciplines—architects, landscape architects, interior architects, and graphic designers collaborate in an integrated process, ensuring multiple voices are represented from the onset of the project. When working with clients or other stakeholders, this approach continues in a working method we have named "transpositioning" when we challenge clients to become architects and architects to become clients. When interested parties come together as equals, we create a place to mutually understand each other's objectives and interests.

Transpositioning promotes the positive benefits of moving out of one's comfort zone. It defies narrow-minded thinking and encourages holistic approaches. Snøhetta approaches design with the idea that creativity and innovation is not always the sole domain of the architect or the designer, but is a product and process of collaboration among all participants in a project. We believe that architecture and design also can allow creativity and innovation to emerge from within, resulting in an organic realization of a shared vision. Client, user, and internal office workshops drive our design process and can often produce the most exciting, useful, and fresh takes on a problem, giving way to a built project that can respond in kind (see figure 2).

1.6.3

Figure 1: Snøhetta
Oslo, Skur 39, © Marc Goodwin
Figure 2 (p. 167): Concept workshop,
© Snøhetta

One of our important tools in this process is what we call the "card game." Randomly divided into groups, all parties use a pre-configured set of picture cards to associate and discuss what qualities, goals, and visions each stakeholder has for the project, its people, and its process. Further the groups take their concept to our state-of-the-art workshop facilities and make a physical model or manifestation of their common idea. The game ends with the groups presenting their concepts, allowing everyone involved to get to know each other's ideas and further develop these through discussions (see figure 3).

We know that with well-conceived design we can help things run more fluidly, improve people's well-being, and make life more enjoyable. Every project is a unique expression of the ethos of its users, climate, and context. A built environment can be interpreted as a point of departure: it is where the architecture starts to communicate, the point from where it starts to interact with the public. The role of architecture in that sense is to create strong and sustainable identities for cities and communities.

The Clientless Architect: How Digital Platforms Are Changing the Relationship between Architects and Clients

Carlo Ratti

"I am sick of listening to clients talking about their tastes," burst out Luis Barragán, one of the most prominent architects of the past century.

It was the nineteen-forties, and Mexico's real estate sector had experienced several decades of sustained growth. Amid rapid urban expansion, Barragán had built a career designing successful but somewhat banal architecture. After years of working for difficult and unimaginative patrons, he reached a decisive moment: "I am quitting with all my clients. From now on, I am going to work for one client only: myself" (Zanco 2001, p. 17).

In the following years, Barragán designed only a handful of buildings, developing a characteristic style blending modernism with the earthy and colorful vernacular from his native Guadalajara. However, those few projects—including his own studio and a few private homes in Mexico City's El Pedregal neighborhood—

came to be known as some of the greatest architectural achievements of the time. In 1980, they won him the Pritzker Prize (the equivalent of a Nobel Prize for architecture), establishing him in the pantheon of twentieth-century architects.

Of course, Barragán had the luxury of approaching the practice of design on his own terms. He was financially stable, and could pay the bail for his aesthetic freedom. Without obligations to a client, he was bound only by the laws of physics and his own imagination—a rare freedom, bordering on fantasy for many architects today. However, Barragán's creative emancipation could become the norm for a young generation of creatives thanks to the introduction of new digital platforms.

Today, enterprising architects and designers are overcoming the financial hurdle with crowdfunding websites such as Kickstarter or Indiegogo. Instead of waiting to be approached by clients, architects can propose a project and seek a community of like-minded people to support it. Speculation can precede commissioning and contractual hurdles. In other words, digital platforms allow designers to start from an idea and coalesce a community of thought and interest around it.

1.4.4 ◄

It may seem far-fetched, but crowdfunding has already become very popular with consumer products. Online supporters can preorder one or more items, effectively footing the bill for product design, development, and production. Examples span a broad spectrum—from cars to clothing to "the coolest cooler." Jibo, a new type of social robot for the home designed by colleagues at MIT in Boston, raised over three million dollars on crowdfunding platforms. This, in turn, became a successful launching pad for raising venture capital and launching production.

Similar examples are now entering the space of architecture and planning. A few years ago, a trio of young artists and architects based in New York launched a Kickstarter campaign to fund a public project called +POOL. They proposed a whimsical, speculative, and technologically innovative design for a public swimming facility floating in the Hudson River. Over three thousand people invested in the project, receiving a commemorative tile, access to an opening party, and proud participation in what could become an iconic element of New York City.

Another example is the Luchtsingel, a pedestrian bridge in Rotterdam. The project would link three disconnected areas of the city, providing key accessibility for their economic development.

Luchtsingel has become known as one of the world's first public infrastructure projects paid (mostly) through online crowdfunding. Backers' names were engraved on bridge components, based on different tiers of engagement. Similarly, a private project in Germany, Weissenhaus, used online support to restore and expand a centuries-old estate near Hamburg. What is now a luxury resort was financed through one of Europe's largest crowdfunding campaigns, at over eight million dollars. Most importantly, the project is now inspiring a number of start-ups to bring crowdfunding into real estate.

Crowdfunding, of course, raises its own set of issues. When (or, if) a project achieves its goal, the creators are responsible for delivery. Even if it is simple to create a compelling video and quickly raise tremendous amounts of money, investment comes with obligations. Particularly in fields such as product design and architecture, there are a number of risks that can delay execution, and investors can quickly become vicious at any deviation from the original idea. Furthermore, crowdfunding mechanisms applied to buildings (as opposed to products) introduce an additional set of challenges. The basic premise of Kickstarter is that "backers" who invest in a project receive a reward ... but what is the reward for public architecture, other than name recognition or a commemorative plaque?

Regardless, crowdfunding platforms are maturing, and they could provide all of us—architects and designers—with a new tool to achieve unprecedented freedom. Instead of hunting for clients, we can turn our focus on hunting for ideas. Following in Luis Barragán's footsteps, perhaps one day we could all start "working for one client only: ourselves."

1.6.4

References

Zanco, F. (2001). *Luis Barragán: The Quiet Revolution*. Milan.
"+POOL, Tile by Tile by Family and PlayLab." *Kickstarter*. Accessed September 4, 2017. https://www.kickstarter.com/projects/694835844/pool-tile-by-tile.
Frearson, A. (2015). "Crowdfunded Luchtsingel Pedestrian Bridge Opens in Rotterdam." *Dezeen*, July 16. https://www.dezeen.com/2015/07/16/luchtsingel-elevated-pathways-bridges-rotterdam-cityscape-zus-architects/

TRANSFER: Education— Further Learning

2.1. Multiscale

- **1** There Is No Choice

- **2** From Airside to Airpark: Planning and Designing the Hybrid Potentials of City-Airports

- **3** Waterside: Crossing the Border between Land and Water

There Is No Choice

Christoph Heinemann

From 1924–26 Le Corbusier realized the Cité Frugès, his first large housing project in Pessac near Bordeaux, commissioned by a local manufacturer, Henry Frugès, as habitations for his workers and their families. Le Corbusier conceived the quarter as a garden city consisting of different terraced and freestanding typologies. The houses illustrate perfectly the elementary premises Le Corbusier defined for architecture (*Cinq points de l'architecture moderne*)—the concrete structure of the buildings allowing for an open floor plan and free articulation of the facades; the flat roofs to be used as terraces. Cité Frugès was a test bed for the further development of housing in modern architecture and mass housing in the twentieth century. The prototypical design is key to build effectively and at low cost—the whole concept starts from the desire to prevent class struggle by providing equal qualities and standards for all.

Yet the residents of Cité Frugès were overwhelmed by so much modernity and sensed that they might be the guinea pigs of some bigger scheme. In spite of the newly achieved comfort, the houses did not resemble what they thought a house should be and look like by their standards—neighbors already referred to the housing as the Moroccan quarter because of the flat roofs ... Thus the inhabitants started transforming the buildings according to their practical needs and tastes, adding gabled rooftops, resizing horizontal windows to common formats decorated with flower pots. This transformation process and its underlying motives are well documented and described in Philippe Boudon's socio-architectural study on Pessac, based in large part on interviews with the residents (Boudon 1969).

What is intriguing and to some seems a paradox is that Le Corbusier's basic design structurally provided the capacity for change, adaptability, and transformation—one could think that these houses were made for appropriation and adaption. Instead the common interpretation takes the transformations as evidence showing that the modern concept failed (if not calling it vandalism proper). Referring to Le Corbusier's later Radiant City, Jane Jacobs states, "Le Corbusier's Utopia was a condition of what he called maximum liberty, by which he seems to have meant not liberty to do anything much, but liberty from ordinary responsibility" (Jacobs 1961, p. 22). The inhabitant is incapacitated because everything is well planned and sufficiently provided; there is no need to actively interfere and spatially change living conditions.

2.1.1

Jane Jacobs also argues that Radiant City (and City Beautiful) were "primarily architectural design cults rather than cults of social reform" and that "modern city planning has been burdened since its beginnings by the unsuitable aim of converting cities into disciplined works of art" (Jacobs 1961, p. 375). This point is crucial to understand the misunderstanding. The interdiction to transform domestic space is not based on functional dogmas but rather on artistic ones. The work must be protected—not the constitution of space. Funnily enough, during the last decades the houses of Pessac have been bought by people who very much appreciate Le Corbusier's design and they are now restored to their old condition; in fact, any transformation has to follow this retroactive design brief now.

Relating to the Everyday

Traditionally the city's structure and its everyday architecture was planned and built based on a high degree of common sense and skills. Distinct exclusion allowed for coherent inclusion—the capacity to welcome different forms of use as well as to transform and change over time was thereby offered up to a certain, but sufficient, degree. The city's twentieth-century expansion, not only in surface but especially in performance, required special functional and social determinations for multiple and conflicting forms of use. This development resulted in a loss of coherence (of common sense or "ordinary responsibility" as mentioned above)—many possibilities to interfere directly with the built environment as an inhabitant and user were restricted.

With Modernism the scope of work of architects expanded into the production of everyday architecture—to the "field," as N. John Habraken calls it. Since then the built environment as a whole is considered as architecture and common architecture is designed based on academic premises and propositions. Top-down planning, even class-conscious or in advocacy, works with specific assignments on what would fit presumed modern forms of living. The involvement of architects and planners in the production of everyday architecture is based on top-down design approaches, for better or worse.

In his writings Habraken describes the whole problem, its interdependencies, and relations very clearly and takes the argument a step further than Jane Jacobs. In his first book, *Supports* (1972), Habraken elaborates on the problem of mass housing and its shortcomings. He introduces a distinction between support and infill—a basic, framing structure allows for individual fittings and thus enables appropriation and interaction with the built environment. This approach aims to re-establish what Habraken calls the "natural relationship" of the inhabitant to his habitation and to restore (design-) responsibility for the ordinary (interestingly a first step of this way of thinking may be discovered in Le Corbusier's Plan Obus for Algiers).

In his most recent publication, *Palladio's Children* (2005), a conclusion and summary of his years of experience and research, Habraken makes clear that top-down planning and thinking is closely linked to the discipline's self-conception. He argues that, at the latest since Palladio's series of villas outside of Venice (thus projects liberated from the urban context) and his widely published and acclaimed writings, the production of space and the transfer of knowledge is based on the Palladian example and is a matter restricted to peer-to-peer communication, not linked to common experience and practice anymore. Habraken shows that architects, contrary to their self-conception in defining architecture as an autonomous discipline, got more and more involved in providing the everyday environment and are deeply embedded in the field and its modes of production. He claims to embrace the fact of being a part of the ordinary production of space and to change the design approach (and thinking) to overcome obvious contradictions.

This reasoning demands relating to the common and the everyday. It initially asks for an architecture and urban structure conceived to allow for participation and appropriation. Urban fabrics as well as buildings thereby have to provide quite similar qualities—orders may be different but not the basic requirement (to support). Furthermore the relation to other disciplines is questioned by acknowledging a different position of the planner in the development process. The architect becomes an expert among and relating to others taking part in the production of everyday urban space. Both issues apply independent of scale.

Scales and Dimensions

And there is something more to this. The city can't be exclusive anymore. It is a place for everyone without exception. To establish a consistent connection between specific uses or typologies and different programs and forms of control, scale—understood as a criterion for the application of different competences and responsibilities or for spatial and social hierarchies—is no longer a valuable indicator. Planning can't relate on scale to develop a project. Coherence is achieved by linking multiple dimensions—options and actions. Many issues are at stake in a discourse of different actors in different situations: land policy, planning procedures, financial models, rights of ownership, tenancy and use, forms of use and lifestyles.

For over a century, planning (at least in Western societies) is programming urban space by attribution, through all scales from zoning to housing typologies. This way to manage the city is based on the belief that societal relations can be kept in balance by allocating determined spatial concepts to specific uses and user groups. Planning laws are needed to protect basic rights and planning security is key for the development of projects. At the same time providing planning security by itself leads to segregation and is often corrupted to mask speculation.

As a reaction to today's ubiquitous urbanity, the right to the city, *Le droit à la ville* (Lefebvre 1968), asks for equal access to all possibilities and qualities the city has to offer. The city can't be compartmentalized to provide specific environments for distinct groups or classes—at least not by assignment or, worse, prejudgment. If specific part-public spaces emerge, they should be the result of negotiation and action. Planning today is more about enabling stories to unfold (and designing a

2.1.1

building is the same as designing a city as it has to take into consideration equal premises). Integrative concepts have to involve local actors and global players, future users and inhabitants to enact urban diversity. To develop a (collective) story and to define common goals, networks have to form and specific choices have to be made to lay out a common path and ground.

Certainly disciplinary boundaries must be crossed to achieve process-oriented design; furthermore, participation is key to develop coherent projects. Planners and architects themselves have to become actors in these development processes, scouting options, negotiating programs, defining frameworks and decisive steps, situating buildings according to situational needs. This shift (or turn) asks for new ways to deal with planning, the production of space, and architecture—not the result or the determining plan has to be protected (not even as a work of art) but the process of planning and creating space, open to control by occupation and use.

Spaces of Negotiation

(In this sense) space is designed for negotiation or formed by negotiation. Herein lies a perhaps small but sometimes crucial distinction considering the relation of actors, experts, and users.

A structure can be designed to enable participation and as a space open for appropriation, to support negotiations and sustained transformation. To create and provide this capacity is a design task and, as mentioned above, this kind of brief is generally questioning the design approach to architecture. Thereby, in large parts, the conception of space remains in the field of expertise of the architects. The design is not independent of the development process and has to reflect, translate, and stage the specific needs and deeds formulated by actors and future users. A spatial concept allowing for conflicts and negotiation, partly undetermined and open for specific fittings, is created to reflect the respective situation and to host whatever action should take place. Still the planner/architect is not necessarily an involved actor, and he/she will be addressed as such.

Forming spaces by negotiation in turn might be essentially different. In this case the collaboration with actors and future users leads to a more direct and formal translation of claims and demands into spatial solutions. The architect should be a real actor in this development process; his/her field of expertise being limited and committed to certain intrinsic claims only, he/she could also just be a service provider completely dependent on the specific (design) brief given. Anyway, at a certain point in the process, the architect will be addressed as an expert, in general and whether he/she wants to or not. The main difference between the two options to implement participation may be that the first one delivers a spatial concept as a playground for action before the negotiation takes place, while the second one is merely a result of this process (which does not mean that it is necessarily inflexible afterwards).

Actor-Based Design and Participatory Planning

Didier Éribon describes a similar problematic as he refers to his position as a sociologist towards the problematic of class struggles and ways to overcome those (Éribon 2009, pp. 51–52):

"(...) People know that things are different elsewhere, but that elsewhere seems part of a far off and inaccessible universe. So much that people feel neither excluded from nor deprived of all sorts of things because they have no access to what, in those far off social realms, constitutes a self-evident norm. It's in the order of things, and there's nothing more to be said about it. No one thinks about how the order of things actually works, because to do so would require being able to see oneself from a different point of view, have a bird's eye view on one's own life and the lives of other people. Only if you actually manage to move from one side of the border to the other, as happened in my case, can you get out from under the implacable logic of all those things that go without saying in order to perceive the terrible injustice of this unequal distribution of prospects and possibilities. (...) And that is why any sociology or any philosophy that begins by placing at the center of its project 'the point of view of the actors' and the 'meaning they give to their actions' runs the risk of simply reproducing a shorthand version of the mystified relation that social agents maintain with their own practices and desires, and consequently does nothing more than serve to perpetuate the world as it currently stands—an ideology of justification (for the established order). (...) A theory's power and interest lie precisely in the fact that it doesn't consider it as sufficient simply to record the words that 'actors' say about their 'actions,' but that rather, it sets as a goal to allow both individuals and groups to see and to think differently about what they are and what they do, and then, perhaps, to change what they do and what they are. (...)"

Éribon argues that real progress can be made by analyzing complex interdependencies from a certain distance and that only this distance will allow to define new common goals and to take things a step further. Ultimately and related to the field of architecture this affects questions of expertise and cross-disciplinary work—all the more since architects particularly are trained to bundle different points of view and specific knowledge to forge a project. The field has widened in such a way that there is no doubt that they must embrace the whole complexity of project development to realize coherent designs. Expertise as understood so far has failed or at least must be adapted to reconnect with urban reality. To do so means to get involved. Then the question is—how to not lose the distance?

Éribon is concerned with society and societal progress as a whole—a big project. He is criticizing other experts from his field, actor-basing their research to formulate general answers to big issues. Transferring his argumentation at first glance seems to exclude the possibility of a progressive, actor-based design process. Maybe, and following this critique, the crucial point is less the distance allowing for the formulation of a common project than the size of the project—actually the

2.1.1

number of actors involved in relation to the main issues defined and the project being tangible enough to allow for all participants to stay focused on specific targets and overall objectives (scale matters after all!). Pursuing common societal goals today must, rather than may, take different and diverse forms.

A small, specific project can relate to larger claims and be a driving force to achieve general societal claims—you have to shorten the distance to hit the target. Interdisciplinary work and participation is only efficient if (societal as well as situational) premises are clearly named and defined; expertise then will be respected on all levels and among all participants as enhancing the collaborative process and serving the common project. This inclusiveness requires the exclusion of many options—to keep a process safe of corruption means to keep it as simple and straight as possible. To merge and successfully include different positions and various competences, the integrity of the project is key to stay on track from planning to realization. Consequently it would be wrong to institutionalize participatory planning processes by predefining a set of generic tools to organize them. What should be institutionalized is just the right to participate.

Diversity and Form

In the present urban condition a common project can only be specific and based on concrete action. Yet structural spatial approaches and the use of standards are not necessarily contradicting difference and diversity. Maybe it would be more appropriate to illustrate different ways to tackle this whole complex by a practical example:

For several years a project has evolved at Spielbudenplatz in Hamburg on the site of a former housing estate, named the Essohouses, after a legendary petrol station open 24/7. The plot had been sold to real estate developers without the city intervening and the inhabitants had been evicted from the existing buildings (after these had been declared structurally unfit). Resistance, initially formed to save the houses, paved the way for negotiations with borough and city about the future planning process. A collective of local actors, artists, and planners (PlanBude) was commissioned to organize a participatory process to collect wishes, ideas, and claims of the local inhabitants and actors. This resulted in the so-called St. Pauli Code, a listing of premises for the future programming and design of the city block: diversity, adaptability, originality—a mix of clubs and commerce integrating existing

Figure 1: NL Architects and BeL's proposal for urban design: different houses and identities for specific user groups. Control is embodied and diversity is pictured,
© NL Architects + BeL

2.1.1

local venues and start-ups from the neighborhood, apartments for rent only, with a high percentage of subsidized housing. The brief for the following urban design competition is the result of a close cooperation between the developer and Plan-Bude and was, in itself, a remarkable step (Planbude 2018).

In particular, the entries of BeL & NL Architects and Lacaton & Vassal quite obviously showed ways of dealing with the brief. Lacaton & Vassal's project is basically operating with one typology or rather a structural system offering different functional and climatic zones and most of all space. Only a few differentiations respond to specific programmatic requirements or formulate thresholds. The facades are designed and organized according to practical and technical needs and thus are not celebrating or differentiating between public and private spaces. Indoors or outdoors—it is up to the user to become visible, to claim space, to stage diversity. The architecture is enabling but not securing the expressionism postulated as a major feature by the code.

On the contrary BeL & NL answer the brief by dividing the block into several distinct houses, thus creating visible, different units and identities for the specific user groups. Control is embodied and diversity is pictured. The buildings, formally differing in style and particularly in height, are specialized to such an extent that functional and economic aspects are neglected, which, as an overall result (on the scale of the city block), allows for a specific building economy balancing the claims of the developer and the local actors. The formal picture is not only credible according to the code but its heterogeneity is also a decisive factor compensating possible losses on both sides—commercial space on one hand, subsidized space on the other.

It is true that choice can kill a movement and it may be an appropriate explanation to why this entry was the winning project. It is quite clear that this project can only be successful if the balance is kept during the whole planning process and that it will depend on continuous coordination and the commitment of all participants. Lacaton & Vassal's project depends on trust into the future development allowing for the appropriation of spaces—thus on basic common sense that is evidently missing sometimes. BeL & NL's project is leaving little room for options, it states what has been achieved and thus secures the status to go further on from there. This diminishes flexibilities, at high risk, but is credible to this point. The common project is tangible now and who can predict what the future holds?

References

Boudon, P. (1969). *Pessac de Le Corbusier: 1927–1967 Étude socio-architecturale*. Paris.

Éribon, D. (2013). *Returning to Reims*. Los Angeles; *first published 2009. Retour à Reims*. Paris.

Habraken, N. J. (1972). *Supports—An Alternative to Mass Housing*. London; first published 1961. *De dragers en de mensen—Het einde van de massawoningbouw*. Amsterdam.

Habraken, N. J. (2005). *Palladio's Children*. London.

Jacobs, J. (1961). *The Death and Life of Great American Cities*. New York.

"St. Pauli Code." PlanBude, accessed January 15, 2018. http://planbude.de/st-pauli-code.

"And the Winner is: NL-Architects and BEL- Architekten!" PlanBude, accessed January 15, 2018. http://planbude.de/and-the-winner-is-nl-architects.

2.1.1

From Airside to Airpark: Planning and Designing the Hybrid Potentials of City-Airports

Rainer Johann

Transforming Airports Creates New Concepts

Since the nineteen-nineties, airports worldwide have expanded and transformed dramatically, as have the city-regions that host them. Architects describe the phenomenon of changing airports as one where that they have become like a new city quarter, city center, or even an "Airport-City" in the city-region (Koolhaas 1995; Güller Güller 2003).

Cultural geographers and landscape architects, however, discover the same object of transition as a special kind of "landscape" (Cosgrove 1999; Dümpelmann, Waldheim 2016). Cosgrove goes so far as to compare airports with an English garden in the city-region. Airport planners, meanwhile, tend to understand an airport in strictly infrastructural terms, dividing it into the *airside*—the runways and landing strips and the airport perimeter—and the *landside*—most parts of the terminals, that is, the infrastructural link to the city-region. These provoking concepts of airport-as city-quarter and airport-as-landscape imply that airports today are in fact much more than just monofunctional infrastructure for air traffic (Mensen 2013, p. 275). But how can these ideas be ex-plained—particularly the concept of airport as garden—and can one understand them?

Airport and Its Airside as Landscape?

The concept of "airport as landscape" and a comparison with an English garden features a broad variety of visual, economical, quantitative, ecological, geographic, and design-based elements and arguments (Cosgrove 1999, pp. 221–232). From a bird's eye view, the airport, its runways, and its green spaces seem much more similar to such landscape parks than to urban settlement space. English gardens and airports cover a comparable area. Both are typically situated along arterial roads or thoroughfares at the urban fringe. In both cases, creating visual connections is a com-monly employed design principle. The placement of the runways, the tower, and the terminal enables visual connections between pilots and air traffic controllers. The arrangement of pathways, buildings, flower beds, bushes, and trees in the English garden conveys the visual impression of an idealized form of nature to visitors and observers. Economically speaking, the English garden was an important land estate of Georgian England, as the airport forms a significant economic motor in the city-region. And ecolog-ically, various plant and animal species are used in the manage-ment of airport landscapes (Dümpelmann, Waldheim 2016:35). Let's look closer at a concrete case.

City Airport Hamburg: Its Airside and Contradictions

The City Airport of Hamburg and its airside are exemplary for a kind of landscape that features numerous contradictions (Johann 2016, p. 141). The green spaces of the Hamburg airside include 355 hectares of grasslands and meadows along and between the land-ing strips (FHG 1999, p. 23). In sum, they cover more than twice as much area as Hamburg's 164-hectare Aussenalster (FHH 1990, p. 7) or Hamburg's 128-hectare Stadtpark (Kossak 1996, p. 266). Unlike city parks, however, the expansive green spaces of the Hamburg airside are located behind the airport perimeter fence, inaccessible to the city's residents; instead, they serve as a stopover along mi-gratory birds' migration paths and also offer ideal nesting sites in the city for these birds, posing potentially dangerous obstacles to airplanes, and vice versa. In order to avoid collisions, airport opera-tors hardly ever maintain the airside grass meadows (FHG 2014, p. 34). This lack of care of the green spaces keeps migratory birds from

building nests and periodically staying in these areas. The airside green spaces also contribute to a reduction of the urban heat island effect in Hamburg, while the airport and terminal coverage increases it (FHH 2012). Due to the airport's function, planning the areas surrounding the airport is subject to numerous restrictions aimed at protecting both the city and air travel (Johann 2016, p. 118). These restrictions impact the surrounding settlement space and lead to the creation of expansive and often heavily used green setback areas. However, they are hardly the result of any design process. In Hamburg, these green buffers feature bike trails, walkways, small gardens, a cafe, and recreational facilities. The urban residents, including bike riders, joggers, flaneurs, excursionists, dog owners, and plane spotters use these spaces for recreation and appreciate the view towards the airside, despite the noise created by airplanes (Johann 2016, p. 141). Hamburg's airside and its green perimeter are exemplary for the qualities and meanings of the landscape bordering airport infrastructure and its immanent contradictions. But what could be the advantage of applying the airport-as-landscape concept to other growing city-regions and airports?

Designing the Hybrid: Airside as Airpark In and For the City-Region

The interrelations between city and airport can be described as very tense. This is due to increasing urban development, increasing international air travel, and the expansion and transformation of airports in many European city regions (BBSR 2011; Johann 2016, p. 33). This gives rise to conflicts. Merely designing the interface between city and airport is insufficient to resolve these conflicts. But applying the concept of airport as landscape—that is, transforming the airside into an airpark—could strengthen and highlight the hidden ecological, economical, and even sociological characteristics of the airside, and show the complexity of the ambivalent interrelation of airports and city-regions. Designing the airside and its bordering green buffers into an airpark changes the public perception of airports and offers citizens specific recreational sites. The airport offers city residents a place of wonder that can foster the creation of a new identity, where the contradictions of modern society's mobility behavior can be seen and experienced. Its further development and design can help unleash potential for both the city and the airport.

For this purpose, an increased future cooperation between the disciplines of airport planning, urban planning, landscape planning, landscape architecture, and urban design and architecture is indispensable. Looking back, Koolhaas and Cosgrove have been important pioneers of their disciplines, if not really groundbreaking, as their dichotomist concepts of airports-as-city and airports-as-landscape display.

2.1.2

References

Bundesinstitut für Bau-, Stadt- und Raumforschung (BBSR) (2011). *Neue Perspektiven für Flughafen und Stadt. Informationen zur Raumentwicklung.* Heft 1. Bonn.

Cosgrove, D. (1999). "Airport/Landscape." J. Corner, ed. *Recovering Landscape: Essays in Contemporary Landscape Architecture.* New York.

Dümpelmann, S. and C. Waldheim (2016). *Airport Landscape: Urban Ecologies in the Aerial Age.* Cambridge, MA.

Flughafen Hamburg GmbH (FHG) (1999). Umwelterklärung. Accessed August 10, 2017. https://www.hamburg-airport.de/Umwelterklaerung_1999.pdf.

Flughafen Hamburg GmbH (FHG) (2014). Umwelterklärung 2014–2017. Accessed August 10, 2017. https://www.hamburgairport.de/media/Umwelterklaerung_2014-17_2014_11_03web.pdf.

FHH. Freie und Freie und Hansestadt Hamburg (1990). *Die Außenalster. Entwicklung, Biologie, Bepflanzung.* Hamburg.

FHH. Freie und Hansestadt Hamburg (2012). *Stadtklimatische Bestandsaufnahme und Bewertung für das Landschaftsprogramm Hamburg. Klimaanalyse und Klimawandelszenario 2015.* Accessed August 10, 2017. http://www.hamburg.de/hamburg-ist-gruen/3519286/stadtklima.

Güller Güller (Hrsg.). (2003). *From Airport to Airport City.* Barcelona.

Johann, R. (2016). *City-Airport Hamburg: Ein mit der Stadt gewachsener Flughafen? Entstehung, Kontroversen, Eigenschaften, Potenziale und Herausforderungen.* Groningen.

Koolhaas, Rem. (1995). "The Generic City." *S,M,L,XL.* New York, pp 1239–1264.

Kossak, E. (1996) *Hamburg: Die grüne Metropole.* Hamburg.

Mensen, H. (2013). *Planung, Anlagen und Betrieb von Flugplätzen* (2nd edition). Berlin-Heidelberg.

Waterside: Crossing the Border between Land and Water

Amelie Rost

From the realization of numerous floating buildings and projects in various metropolises around the world, as well as from recent bottom-up movements that not only create but also demand accessible space on water, a changed perception of water in the city can be determined and a curiosity to develop this space—also as "building land"—can be derived.

In a city-water relationship that has constantly changed over the course of history our perception of water in cities in the Western world is particularly influenced by the city-port relationship. In this relationship now the next phase of the five so-far-diagnosed phases by Hoyle in 1989 (Schubert 2010) seems to have been reached: after the conversion and development of former harbor districts freed up by structural changes in the port industry in the nineteen-sixties, the transformation is no longer just about the space at the water, but also about the space on water.

But what are the consequences when the border from land to water is crossed and the space on water is suddenly understood as urban transformation space and in this context as "building land"?   2.3.2 ▶

Segregation as a Result of the Current Use of Floating Architecture

The buildings on water that have been realized as yet, inter alia, those we have planned by our office, can be seen as a first approach to this new planning task. In a first reflection of these projects the following problems must be ascertained.

1. Spatial segregation

Taken from the idea of a houseboat, most projects are developed as hybrids between architecture and ship's architecture: on the one hand they are designed like land-based architecture (in de-sign-vocabulary, volumes, shapes, and floor plans); on the other hand they are designed with the self-referentiality of a ship's draft—purely at an object level. An integration in the urban context is missing. They are neither following a spatial nor a programmatic urban logic, but rather are just added to the urban fabric by mooring them along the waterfront. The already-existing spatial boundary between land and water is reinforced by the newly constructed barrier of the floating architecture, and thus opposes the desire to activate and open up the water as a publicly accessible space.

2. Social segregation
Many of the projects are only accessible to a limited group of users. In particular this applies to the use of housing. Gated communities are created on the water, which provide direct access to the water for the residents, but not for the public, resulting in social segregation between privileged residents and the general public.

Multiscale: Researching the Potentials of Floating Architecture
However, against the background of a changing city-water relationship, floating architecture is an instrument to develop urban (water-)spaces and holds—as an element of city planning—great potential for the future transformation of those spaces, which is not limited to the development of houseboat settlements or the use of floating architecture for flood areas. In order to exploit this potential, an approach and investigation of floating architecture with regard to its possible role for urban development is needed at both the urban and architectural scales.

1. Urban scale
In order to develop water areas with reference to their ecological, economic, and social functions in the city structure and to cana-lize the present investment interests in a reasonable way, urban planning models for inner-city water areas that define the urban planning aims and evaluate the future programming of those water areas in a broader context need to be worked out. The de-struction of valuable natural or landscaped areas and the privat-ization of important public spaces should be avoided; and the possibilities of new opportunities of networking or activating ur-ban areas by reprogramming the water should be exploited.

2. Architectural scale

Floating architecture—here an umbrella term that includes floating buildings and free spaces; amphibious houses; mobile, temporary, and permanently installed buildings—can play a key role in the future development of inner-city water areas. In order to take on this role and not remain a complementary add-on, floating architecture must not only be embedded in a contextual way, but also be understood and exploited in its properties and potentials (such as mobility or temporality).

In a permanent change of scales research is needed to explore how floating architecture and the particular characteristics of floating architecture can be used to achieve the previously defined urban planning aims.

2.1.3

Reference

Schubert, D. (2010). *Hafen- und Uferzonen im Wandel. Analysen und Planungen zur Revitalisierung der Waterfront in Hafenstädten.* Berlin.

2.2. Spatial Agency

- **1** Spatial Agency: From the University of the Neighbourhoods to Building A Proposition For Future Activities or How Urban Design Mobilizes the Performative Plan

- **2** The Spatial Turn to Processuality, Diversity, and Collaboration

- **3** Teaching and Learning to Act

Spatial Agency: From the University of the Neighbourhoods to Building A Proposition For Future Activities or How Urban Design Mobilizes the Performative Plan

Bernd Kniess/Anna Richter/Christopher Dell/ Dominique Peck

2.2.1

The Urban Design program at HafenCity University (HCU) in Hamburg is conceptually founded on an understanding of the city as not only produced in terms of its built structures, but also co-produced by the socially embedded practices of its actors and actants. These actors and actants—speaking with Bruno Latour (Latour 2005a), agency also refers to things and matters of concern that develop agencies—come together, are assembled, and interact in specific spatial settings that are conversely interwoven by diverse layers of power (political, economic, and material forces, decisions, practices, discourses, configurations, representations, etc.)

2.5.1 ►

and the transformations these cause. The interdisciplinary approach to and focus on practices and processes departs insofar from the planning disciplines urban planning and architecture, exploiting new areas of know-how and know-why within the realm of the social and cultural sciences, as we are no longer concerned with the production of buildings or physical structures alone but with their interrelationship with those who use these structures.

We realize that we are entangled with the existing, potential, and emerging assemblages, rather than being in an externalized or externalizing position from which it would be possible to explain in universal terms how the city works or how to plan it; indeed, prolonging Latour's statement—made in reference to the work of Rem Koolhaas—"on ne peut plus rien externaliser" (Latour 2005b), we would go so far as to question whether such an externalized position ever existed. From this point of view the city is no longer a bounded object; on the contrary, it has to be interpreted as a sociomaterial texture (cf. Farías 2011) of agental situations that is constantly in flux and never finished, always contested and rarely uniting. Methodologically, this epistemological shift from reading the city not as a closed but an open form enables us

▶ 2.7.1 to immerse ourselves in the present so as to study historical developments of this status quo and to draw out possible future trajectories.

While the notion that the urban and indeed space altogether is socially produced is slowly but steadily gaining ground, the conditions and modes of its constantly processed reproduction and the structural and spatial vectors of its agency are given less attention. The production of any material texture is furthermore strictly separated from its usage by the abstract figure of the end-user, the consumers of design and architecture. What counts in the design process are the client's needs, demands, and preferences reduced and abstracted to functions that have to be arranged in the right order and given good shape. The result, however, is often more than a skillful mix of function and form. Although we might know about the involvement of countless human and nonhuman actors in the processes of production and appropriation of things as well as the built environment, it seems that we

▶ 2.5.3 tend to oppress an awareness of their agencies, especially when faced with their contingent and thus difficult-to-manage character. What is at stake are modes of action and knowledge that enable a constructive exploitation of the hardly visible agencies, discrete, and nonrepresentational vectors that can be utilized as driving forces. Meanwhile, collaborative, participatory, and cooperative planning processes are tested and implemented, demanded and granted, although of course the nature of participation remains heavily contested and often tokenistic (Arnstein 1969; Paddison 2009; Richter 2010). While the role of the social has long been a matter of discussion mostly in the social sciences, it is recently receiving increasing attention in architecture and design (Richter et al. 2017). This causes a shift in the disciplinary perspective, for example, from "function" to "use" or from "needs" to "agency," as the notion of performance and alongside it indeterminacy and contingency of concerted action enter the discussion. Tonkiss (2017), however, observes that the social-production side of architecture and design is still often overlooked or deliberately disregarded. Tonkiss thus calls for "critical and practical efforts to socialize design" and argues that these "need to go beyond the consumption stage of design processes to take in the social relations of [space] production" (2017, p. 12). Thinking of Marx, what is needed is an analysis of the relations of production of space.

We assume that a building cannot be reduced to form or function any longer (if that was ever possible). And even if we think that objects—and thus buildings—have no agency, we have to admit that they can make things happen or prevent or hinder processes; they are doing something. As cultural scientist Hartmut Böhme has pointed out, things cannot appear in any other way than "as relating to our activities of a cognitive or practical nature" (2007, p. 14). Agencies are embedded in space, which in its materialization is no longer solely determined by its visibility but is at least equal to the amount of the invisible parts of its infrastructure and even "infrastructure space is doing something" (Easterling 2014, p. 14). In unpacking forms and functions and hacking infrastructural operating systems, the conditions of spatial productions can be analyzed and the markers of unfolding potentials or inherent agency can be observed and discovered. Easterling termed this disposition "the character or propensity of an organization that results from all its activity" (2014, p. 21). It is not only about the *what*—the materiality of space or the urban—but it is also, and foremost, about the relationality, i.e. *how* space and the urban are constantly reproduced in different constellations or assemblages. In order to detect and unpack spatial structures retrospectively with a view to prospectively reassemble and further develop them, a transgression is needed from object form to active form. In what follows, this

2.2.1

argument will serve to situate a central aspect of the research, teaching, and practice approach of the Urban Design program at HafenCity University within a broader perspective of the social production of the urban regarding its modes of realizing as well as its specific materialities, medialities, and temporalities.

The University of the Neighbourhoods, a long-term project that ran from 2008–2013 in collaboration with the International Building Exhibition Hamburg (IBA 2013), the cultural producer and provider Kampnagel, construction company Max Hoffmann GmbH, and HafenCity University Hamburg, provided an opportunity to turn the usual approach on its head. IBA 2013 made available to the project a plot with an old, derelict building. According to a conventional approach, any architecture or urban design undertaking faced with this situation would probably have torn down the existing building so as to practice the core disciplinary methods of planning and building—and it is no surprise that most entries of the previous students' competition had precisely made this proposition. Yet rather than tearing down the one-story building from the nineteen-fifties in order to build from scratch, only to then tear down again when the project ended whatever had been built in its stead, the project proceeded in an archaeological manner, laying bare the various intended and unintended transformations of the building over time, from its original function as a residential home for unmarried women to local health center for the district to derelict graffiti canvas of the so-called crack house. Testing and trying practices of un-building and stripping down enabled the team of staff and students to reappropriate the building with a view to uncover and bring back to life central functions and hidden potentials of the existing structure. Reducing the building to its core and overwriting it with new uses that had been deduced through emerging uses as well as negotiations served as a method to reflect on and engage with past, present, and future demands both regarding the building, the university, and the neighborhood. The project's name echoes this approach and the focus: University of the Neighbourhoods (UoN). This reversal of architectural and design procedures raised categorical questions about the building's functions and made it possible to open the form. Opening up the question of functions brought to the fore the usage of existing facilities during the process of appropriation and negotiation and served to once more categorically rethink the separation of functions. Boundaries and divisions were tackled both practically and theoretically, and by making the building physically and socially permeable through what we called "enabling-architecture," the project activated a range of functions, uses, and ideas relating to the house, the area, the neighborhood and community, the city of Hamburg, the international building exhibition, the university, and modes of dwelling. The experiment included designing new spaces within the stripped core so that the shell was furnished with new spaces that emerged from an analysis of its ongoing uses of holding seminars and workshops, cooking and eating in common, inviting neighbors, undertaking research in and around the UoN, and eventually moving into the building for auto-ethnographic research into dwelling-as-practice.

Having agreed to hand back the empty plot as the exhibition closed down in 2013, the University of the Neighbourhoods consequently followed its programmatic of reversing architecture by completely stripping bare, un-building, and tearing down the building. The radical reduction of an existing structure while using its potential and actual functions to the full provided the experimental setting in which central questions regarding dwelling, neighborhood, urban development, and inherited functional separation were addressed both in more traditional research projects and in actual uses in and of the building (Kniess et al. 2015).

The project Building A Proposition For Future Activities started in the year 2016 in the general context of the so-called refugee crisis in Germany and the local context of a proposed building site in Poppenbüttel on which the Hamburg-wide program Accommodation with Perspective Dwelling was about to be implemented. The civil society initiative Poppenbüttel Hilft e.V. from the direct neighborhood developed the idea to lobby for a community building to be self-built not *for* but *with* refugees in the new residential area and approached the research and teaching program Urban Design and Hamburg's district Wandsbek to get involved. Convinced by the idea, the Urban Design team was amazed when the initiative initially asked for a representation of the community building, a photorealistic rendering in architectural terms of the object of desire and with this a final product. Neglecting their own participatory approach, the intention with the image of a building was to convince other philanthropists to provide financial support for the project. Radically turning around the approach, the Urban Design team expanded its modes of showing. Now ranging from process drawings to the performative setting of a summer school on site, the production of representations always focused on the possible future users and users of the area. Several research projects undertaken by students looked into the refugee crisis, refugee accommodations, and accommodating structures, administration, and management; studied urban modes of dwelling-as-practice beyond the home; and investigated possibilities to problematize the legal structure of refugee accommodation. The notion of accommodation—as opposed to dwelling—is highly problematic as it denies any active designing of one's everyday life by reducing it to the container-space where one sleeps, eats, and stores his or her things. Housing (or dwelling), in contrast, "is a doing, it is dwelt or inhabited as much as it is built" (McFarlane 2011, 650; wohnbund e.V./HCU 2016).

2.2.1

Out of this emerged the central motif of the project: to enable refugees in and through architecture to become active in Hannah Arendt's action-sense (Arendt 1998). On the backdrop of refugees' legal situation of being accommodated, which prohibits dwelling-as-practice (cooking, eating, washing, among other central dwelling functions and practices), the Urban Design team sought to activate and mobilize Arendt's threefold notion of labor, production, and action in a way that allowed to simultaneously overcome the hierarchical order within which Arendt had devised her thinking on agency. Understanding agency, as introduced earlier, as an effect of action or effectiveness that emerges from within the "unforeseeable deviations" (Butler 2015, p. 32) of performative enactments, we transpose three of Arendt's criteria in relation to action into the mode of work (in the register of space production) and the mode of labor (in the register of dwelling). That is firstly the connotation of the Greek *archein*, the ability to begin (Arendt 1998, p. 177), which leads to an unorthodox relinking of *archein* to *architecton*; secondly the character of unexpectedness as "inherent in all beginnings" (Arendt 1998, p. 178); and thirdly the capacity to "act in concert" (Arendt 1998, p. 179). Mobilizing refugees' agencies in this sense meant to go beyond the idea that refugees could participate in the planning or building processes and to centrally engage with their everyday lives, their backgrounds, their interests, and their resources. While functional separation is being partially revised—for instance, through the introduction of a new site designation in the German Land Use Ordinance, the so-called urban areas—both urban developments and housing policy remain locked into the traditionally tight frame of unquestioned definitions. Current ways and modes of dwelling, however, no longer correspond with the floor plans and prices, let alone locations of what is currently being designed and built (cf. Glucksberg 2016). This crucially introduces the aspect of contingency into production and labor as a basic condition of spatial agency. We argue that stressing the contingency of space production and dwelling provides grounds for insisting on the open form and on representations that are adequate to show such open form, which leads us to the use of and research into diagrammatics (Dell 2016). In an even more radical sense, this line of argument consequently seeks to replace the teleological notion of the "production of space" with the open notion of the "improvisation of space."

▶ 2.6.1

The project Building A Proposition For Future Activities thus problematized the existing policy resulting from the application of paragraph 246 of the building code—an exception from planning law for the building permission of refugee accommodations without the legal basis of planning regulation. This exception makes the distinction between dwelling and being accommodated possible in the first place: accommodations do not provide for complementary functions such as spaces for work, leisure, or even common uses. To mobilize the multiple yet neglected or ignored agencies, the Urban Design team reassembled the practices, approaches, and issues rehearsed during the five-year UoN project: working with the existing status quo (a planned refugee accommodation *cum* social housing residential area), developing a motif (activating the multiple agencies of refugees), practice-research (coming into play as students, new neighbors rather than refugees, industrial school students, residents, interested public), developing individual motifs and roles as well as needs (who will use the community building for which functions, how will its program be developed, how do we translate existing and future activities into architecture, and how can the building be realized as self-build project?).

Departing from building law and the exception introduced above served as a means to problematize the nature of accommodation as non-dwelling and in doing so opened up the frame of reference altogether: no longer was Building A Proposition For Future Activities exclusively an architectural project (if ever it was), but instead considered the question: how do we live today and how can accommodated refugees mobilize their agencies?

The basic idea of self-build practices indeed turned out to be the main challenge. The planning and construction procedures themselves are governed by various rules and regulations. The procedures of a publicly financed and used community building, however—albeit small like this—reached an unprecedented scale. Every step of the procedure is defined and observed by countless actors. This causes doubts: how is self-build possible when liability security is directly linked to professional services provided by the commission of an institutional actor with legal status and maximum insurance coverage? How is self-build a possible route when all service phases of architectural and structural planning are commissioned, all building trades are contracted based on the tender documents, based on the execution planning, based on liability security? So, where does self-build actually start? On the construction site, in the project office, during the process of programming the building and who (especially the refugees addressed) is involved, where and when?

The open form and in consequence the open building process was the quintessential outcome of the problem referred to as refugee crisis (when in reality, it is more the refugees' crisis). The question around social production (of design, of architecture, of realizing accommodations rather than homes) thus turned into the active engagement with performative production. The constant request for closed-form products such as designs, plans, and renderings, and their unquestioned modes of (re-)production could only be addressed by getting involved and

2.2.1

becoming active in all three senses envisaged by Hannah Arendt—and by trans-gressing her hierarchical order of the human condition. Rather than representing a determined (and potentially very limited) future, the project worked with a *cadavre exquis* approach, starting in the very immediate present, mobilizing or letting go of specific vectors as participants stumbled across them, and performing the plan rather than the other way round. Twisting the metaphor, practice—not representa-tion—became the function of form.

Concluding Remarks

The two cases outlined here can only convey a rough sketch of how Urban Design at HCU understands spatial agencies. At first sight perhaps quite contrary, the two projects both proceed from the supposition that architects, planners, and urban studies scholars need to engage with the present, accept the urban as found, and unpack its having-becomeness in order to project forwards again.

References

Arendt, H. (1998). *The Human Condition.* Chicago.

Arnstein, S. (1969). "The Ladder of Citizen Participation." *Journal of the American Institute of Planners* 35.4: pp. 216–224.

Böhme, H. (2007). *Fetischismus und Kultur.* Hamburg.

Butler, J. (2015). *Notes toward a Performative Theory of Assembly.* Cambridge, MassA.

Dell, C. (2016). *Epistemologie der Stadt: Improvisatorische Praxis und gestalterische Diagrammatik im urbanen Kontext.* 1st ed. transcript. Bielefeld.

Easterling, K. (2014). *Extrastatecraft: The Power of Infrastructure Space.* London.

Farias, I. (2011) "Introduction. Decentring the Object of Urban Studies." I. Farias and T. Bender, eds. *Urban Assemblages: How Actor-Network Theory Changes Urban Studies.* London.

Glucksberg, L. (2016). "A View from the Top." *City.* 20.2: pp. 238–255.

Kniess, B., B. Becker, S. Gernert, B. Pohl, and A. Richter (2015). "University of the Neighbourhoods—Hotel as Method?" A. Fuad-Luke, A.-L. Hirscher, and K. Moebus, eds., *Agents of Alternatives—Re-Designing Our Realities.* Berlin.

Latour, B. (2005a). *Reassembling the Social: An Introduction to Actor-Network-Theory.* New York.

Latour, B. (2005b). "En tapotant légèrement sur l'architecture de Koolhaas avec un bâton d'aveugle..." *L'Architecture d'Aujourd'hui* 361.Nov./Dez: pp. 70–79.

McFarlane, C. (2011). "The City as Assemblage: Dwelling and Urban Space." *Environment and Planning D: Society and Space* 29.4: pp. 649–671.

Paddison, R. (2009). "Some Reflections on the Limitations to Public Participation in the Post-Political City." L'*Espace Politique* 8.2: pp. 1–17.

Richter, A. (2010). "Exploiting an 'Army of Friendly Faces': Volunteering and Social Policy Implications." *Journal of Policy Research in Tourism, Leisure and Events* 2: pp. 184–188. https://doi.org/10.1080/19407963.2010.482278.

Richter, A., H. Göbel, and M. Grubbauer (2017). "Designed to Improve? The Makings, Politics and Aesthetics of the 'Social' in Architecture and Design. Introduction to the Special Feature." *City* 21.6: forthcoming.

Tonkiss, F. (2017). "Socialising Design?" *City* 21.6: forthcoming.

wohnbund e.V./HafenCity Universität Hamburg eds. (2016). *wohnen ist tat-sache. Annäherungen an eine urbane Praxis.* Berlin.

2.2.1

The Spatial Turn to Processuality, Diversity, and Collaboration

Jan Lange

When we talk about the "spatial turn," the reference is usually to a metatheoretical paradigm that, at first glance, holds out the promise of a solid basis for interdisciplinary knowledge production. The concept, introduced by Edward Soja, at first parenthetically and only later labeled as heuristically significant, in being adopted has led to a widespread popularity of spatial thought patterns and inspired new questioning. Nevertheless, this does not imply a unification of disciplinary perspectives and categories. Thus, it seems to me that the future of the theoretical understanding of space also lies rather more in trans- than in interdisciplinary dialogue.

2.7.2 ▶

However, this is not the place for further speculations about the fragility of the common ground for an interdisciplinary turning point. It appears to me that the more exciting question is what challenges confront an urban design practice if it is serious about taking the spatial turn as an orientation a) to the social space, and b) to a broader societal participation. In this regard, my reflections are first and foremost anthropologically grounded. For research work with this specialized provenance, the focus is on analyzing space as an intrinsically dynamic orientation framework experienced as everyday culture.[1] To preach to the urban design disciplines from this lofty standpoint that it now behooves them to conceive of their own activity as social process and to pay more attention to local knowledge traditions and spatial references would be like carrying coals to Newcastle. In recent decades, ur-

2.1.1 ◀

[1] For a reinforced future collaboration with urban design disciplines, I find especially interesting in this repertoire studies in assemblage and actor network research because they concentrate on sociomaterial frameworks; that is, they expand the traditional claim of the social by the apportionment of things.

ban design instrumentalities and models have oriented themselves increasingly toward cooperation and participation, not least because of the demands by social movements for a voice, the letdown in governmental accountability, and the strengthening of economically oriented administrative leadership. At the same time, it strikes me that, at present, prevailing practice and organizational models do confront challenges, three of which I would like to briefly address here.

1. *Processuality:* Demands by civil society to make its voice heard continue to grow. Contemporary participation formats, as a rule, are calibrated for integrating the population's local everyday knowledge at the outset. As most projects progress, it then augments the urban planning expertise. This sort of practice, however, leads only in the rarest of cases to collective learning processes by civil society and does just as little to foster a future willingness to engage individually. It appears more appropriate to me, therefore, to invest energy in developing formats that open the urban design process so that spatial problem-solving tools are worked out collectively and action resources are handed over to civil society actors. Participation in that case is no longer an acceptance-creating instrumentality, but a   1.2.3 ◄
general deliberative quality of urban design projects.

2. *Diversity:* In pursuing the implementation of projects on the local level, urban design conceives of the residents affected by building work as a local action community. As the population becomes more diverse, however, the spatial references multiply. Consequently, those addressed in participative urban design are growing increasingly diffuse. In the future, efforts to make the multitude of positions comprehensible and concrete must therefore be intensified. Participative formats should increasingly function as discursive workshops in which civil society can confront its differing ideas and, moreover, plumb which self-conceptions it wants to champion vis-à-vis urban actors. The latter then must rise to the challenge of continuing to think about the problem of the lowest possible participation threshold in the social but also increasingly in the cultural dimension.

3. *Collaboration:* To the extent that urban design has a participative orientation, its knowledge practices per se can always be

2.2.2

understood also as research—the point is to integrate people's perceptions and wishes that cannot be anticipated. To satisfy this requirement, it is usual to reach into the social science toolbox. Insofar as the current operating procedure is implemented, it is predominantly reflexive knowledge in exclusive settings beyond social practice that is tapped in the process. The challenge of rising diversity, however, shows plainly that, besides the—seemingly worth considering—shift of participation into the public sphere, it must also seek to diversify survey methods. In this regard, collaboration with other knowledge systems seems to me worth a try. Especially the (rightfully) hyped artistic research points to contemporary avenues for making everyday cultural reflections tangible in all their idiosyncrasies.

▶ 2.5.2

Teaching and Learning to Act

Doina Petrescu

I am one of those who think that pedagogy and education do not necessarily take place in schools and in institutions, but also within the civic realm, in activist initiatives and political struggles, through economic undertakings, and ultimately in everyday life.

We are in a moment of crisis, in which, according to many, we move into a different era, beyond neoliberal capitalism.[1] What marks this era is the nature of the multifaceted crisis we face: it is a crisis of reproduction not only of production, as the very basis on which things and life are produced is under threat. In times of austerity politics and the loss of waged work globally, in times of unprecedented migration flows and resources wars, it is reproduction—namely, how we sustain ourselves and our world—that has become a "political battleground" (Petrescu and Trogal 2017). There is an imperative to change, to find new forms of organizing and means to sustain ourselves in the world. This demands new forms of collective politics, values, and actions, in which space and architecture must play a role. Here comes our role as architectural educators. All my teaching has tried to encourage students to look into how we can prepare for a sustained "reproductive" work both at a local and global scale. I have also been concerned with how to teach them to gain agency and be active as architects in changing the world from wherever is their position and location, in other words, teaching them to learn how to act.

One of the important instances of this approach to teaching was to involve my students in the Eco Nomadic School, an informal institution run over ten years in different rural and suburban contexts.[2] This consisted of a network of locally based projects from across Europe, the participants in which have been visiting each other to learn, teach, share, and discover the knowledge held in their communities. This network, initiated by atelier d'architecture autogérée, involved projects, practices, participants, and ordinary

1 See, for example, Paul Mason's *PostCapitalism* (2015) or Jeremy Rifkin's *The End of Work* (2000).

2 See more in Böhm et al. (2017).

people from six countries, nine regions, four cities, two towns, and six villages. The Sheffield School of Architecture's (SSoA) involvement was through a number of live projects, which I consider as a form of mutual learning and nonhierarchical, practice-based teaching that we have run for more than seventeen years as part of the masters programs.[3] At SSoA, we have developed a specific interest in the relationship between architectural practice and education, taking a critical view on the normative values in these fields and proposing alternatives. The Live Projects are one such pedagogical alternative that challenges supposedly "safe" academic environments within which we, as academics, and the students operate. Live Projects push students out into the world, instead of letting them remain passively contained within the educational institution, so that they become agents acting both within and between the fields of research, practice, education, and civic life. During a period of six weeks, students get immersed in the complexities of a real-life situation and real client; they are exposed to the social, political, economical, and ecological conditions of the outside. Eco Nomadic School offered one of these instances in which students not only worked on crossing disciplinary boundaries but were also involved in transversal collaborations that facilitate a critical redefinition of given parameters and conditions.[4] They became part of "communities of practices" and informal learning networks that developed through practice—not specifically project teams, but informal groupings drawn together by common challenges, opportunities, or passions (Wenger 1998). Students met gardeners, wood builders, people interested in household economies, but also artists, activists, cultural workers, designers, feminists, curators supporting with their knowledge a peer-to-peer learning process. This nomadic school without fixed location and affiliation, allowed a diversity of knowledge and know-how to circulate without hierarchy between participants in diverse formats: conversations, product making and workshops of all sorts, field trips, mini-conferences, storytelling. In these conditions, learning becomes learning *from* and *with* others through pedagogies based on "ethics, democracy and civic courage" (Freire 1970). This pedagogy sits underneath the small visible part of education hosted in specialized capitalist institutions within the huge iceberg of the knowledge production. It sits in direct relation with the grassroots level, and the knowledge connected to everyday life and communal living.

3 For more on live projects in Sheffield see http://www.liveprojects.org/.

4 Eco Nomadic School-related Live Projects:
• Community Economies, Italy (2016): http://www.liveprojects.org/2016/community-economies/
• Civic University, UK (2016): https://civicuniversity.wordpress.com/
• Growing (in) Todmorden, UK (2011) http://www.liveprojects.org/2011/growing-in-todmorden/
• Ecoroof, France (2009) http://www.liveprojects.org/2010/ecoroof-paris/
• Cultural Agencies, Turkey (2009) http://www.rhyzom.net/workshops/live-project-cultural-agencies-istanbul-2009/
• Remote Control-Reimagining cultural accommodation in rural border regions, Northern Ireland (2009) http://www.rhyzom.net/workshops/live-project-remote-control-reimagining-cultural-accommodation-in-rural-border-regions-northern-irel/

This is pedagogy in times of responsibility and care, times of reinvention and change, times when architects' skills, knowledge, and affective power are the most valuable and when teaching and learning to act should indeed be on every architectural school's agenda.

References

Petrescu, D. and K. Trogal, eds. (2017). *The Social Reproduction of Architecture*. London.
Böhm K., T. James, and D. Petrescu, eds. (2017). *Learn to Act*. (Paris: aaa/peprav)
    http://www.rhyzom.net/nomadicschool.
    /manual-for-local-inter-generational-resilience-and-innovation-april-2016/.
Wenger, E. (1998). *Communities of Practice: Learning, Meaning, and Identity*. Cambridge, UK.
Freire, P. (1970). *Pedagogy of the Oppressed*. London.

2.2.3

2.3. Transformation

- 1 Navigating Transformation
- 2 (Urban) Transformation Design

Navigating Transformation

Klaus Overmeyer

More than ever before, urban and regional planning is now being confronted with the consequences of worldwide upheavals. The increase in complexity and multifaceted interactions in the economy and in society are posing new challenges to the planning disciplines. Current practice in architecture and urban construction is still focusing on the quality of design and the final planning of spaces. The future will see enhanced methods of process design, which include the actors and forces driving the production of space in the drafting of the city.

The shift from formal spatial-oriented planning to an actor- and process-oriented planning culture has now become firmly established in Germany in the field of superordinate regional and urban planning concepts. At the Habitat Conference in Quito, Germany presented a contribution showing how the sustainability goals in the adopted New Urban Agenda are being implemented in German planning practices (BBSR 2016). Case studies taken from municipal planning practices clearly showed that all strategies for empowering the parties concerned involve promoting bottom-up activities or increasing the flexibility of decision-making structures. Enhanced participation in today's urban development is often tied to sharing ever-scarcer resources. Designing and using space in the public interest is gaining in significance.

At the same time, however, the examples also show that actor- and process-oriented approaches are more difficult to implement if the organizational task is more definitive. As long as changes are related to larger spaces, such as a neighborhood or a region, remain abstract, affect only a few people directly, and stretch out over long periods of time; it is easier to include the public at large in planning processes. However, as soon as a specific development area or plot is at issue, a more heated discussion often arises between those actors who want to fashion building legislation, invest, and implement final plans quickly; and those who want to have a say and keep options open.

The urge to control processes from the top down and restrict participation to the legally required minimum increases if the scope of the task is more specific. In order to reduce complexity and be able to calculate and carry out projects reliably, an attempt is made—even in urban building projects with a development period lasting many years—to stipulate a final picture as early as possible and to reduce the group of actors involved to those who finance, approve, plan, and implement the project. Of course, no large project nowadays can do without participation procedures. As a rule, however, these are aimed at informing the public and obtaining suggestions for the experts doing the actual planning. It is less a matter of discovering together the talent a place may have to offer, of developing values, goals, and tasks through conversation, or of integrating the project ideas of local groups into the planning. Because a final picture is to be communicated and further fixed by means of the necessary planning procedures as quickly as possible, no alternatives, temporary solutions, or prototypes are provided for, let alone the formation of user-led organizational structures. Every effort is made to keep unforeseeable factors from intruding on the planning and perhaps causing it to fail.

The right balance of state control, free-market dynamism, and citizens' initiatives must be sounded out anew for every project. This causes many planning processes to keep coming up against the same hurdles, and one not insignificant effect of this is to put the professional image of architects and planners to the test.

Establish a Clear Idea of Goals and Tasks
The goal of conventional building tasks is clear. Builders or development agencies formulate a space allocation plan that becomes the basis of the draft for the (landscape) architecture or urban planning. As experience with projects in complex urban contexts affecting large numbers of people or requiring large time frames has shown, solely defining the uses and areas is no longer a sufficient basis for planning if you want to create a vibrant spot suited to people's future issues and needs. For example, in the cases of the Parkstadt Süd in Cologne or the procedure at the Spielbudenplatz for the subsequent construction of the Esso-houses in Hamburg, the values, qualities, and goals of the tasks were decided cooperatively. At the Spielbudenplatz, this was achieved by means of

◀ 1.4.1 a preliminary participation procedure in which PlanBude, a transdisciplinary team designing and implementing the participation process, worked together with the local population to create the St. Pauli Code (PlanBude 2017). This code is a catalog of values for the future neighborhood to which the drafts of design and utilization must measure up.

In the urban planning process for the Parkstadt Süd, the formulation of goals and planning contracts were embedded right in the starting phase of the co-operative procedure. In the first three months of the process, planning offices and the urban community together worked up their own scope of tasks, guided by specific questions: What qualities and values will distinguish the future accommodations and open spaces? Who are the future users and what needs will they have? What basic conditions are given? What are the particular aptitudes of the area? What open questions are there at the site? And what are the rules for the process? (City of Cologne 2017)

The scope of tasks was compiled with the aid of interactive formats, such as a Parkstadt Safari with ad-hoc mapping, an increasingly detailed picture documenting the identified potentials and inspection orders, and public forums on focal points of the upcoming development. The spatial analysis of the five planning offices involved was also incorporated into the scope of tasks and became a shared foundation to be used for further revision.

The advantage of a joint definition of goals is obvious: in the process, differing interests in view of the future of a space become visible and focused; the possibilities a place could offer are increased by making use of the knowledge of many people; and negotiating the target corridor creates trust and a common basis for further steps. This gives rise to a kind of latitude that has been acquired jointly and can be used to take the measure of planning ideas before they are further developed.

The method of participatory development of the scope of tasks also makes potentially conflicting goals apparent early on; for instance, when the interests of the city as a whole to densify neighborhoods come up against the local population's not-in-my-backyard, or NIMBY, attitudes. What is important is for administrators, policymakers, or the responsible initiator of the planning to clearly define and articulate beforehand what is negotiable and what is not.

Process is Organization Development

Whatever the direction, processes lead to change. So far, the question of how planning processes influence the organizational form of the actors involved has received little attention. It is obvious that very differently organized groups will clash in these procedures—a usually hierarchically structured administration, political parties, companies, associations, planning offices, informal coalitions, and individual activists. Planning processes often have the effect of triggering the organizational development of those involved. Administrations set up inter-agency project groups; policymakers forge alliances; and individual initiatives are reformed by the process or ally themselves with others into an umbrella organization.

The right organizational form becomes a relevant factor whenever the aim is to give weight to a position in the process, to speak with one voice, to make decisions, or to assume responsibility for the results.

2.3.1

1.3.2 ◀

When processes falter or even fail, this is often due to the organization of the actors. Strongly hierarchically structured organizations often have well-practiced implementation procedures. They can hamper dynamic planning processes, however, if responsibilities are passed back and forth and, in the end. nobody feels responsible; or when solitary decisions are made at the top level but do not find a consensus in the organization. At the same time, elaborate planning processes signify an enormous effort for initiatives comprised of volunteers working on an honorary basis. Often, the energy needed to create efficient organizations out of informal relationships to strengthen a particular stance in public discourse is lacking, along with time-consuming discussions of the individual position and participation in other events. Processes would be overtaxed if the formation of organizations were part of their task. This is the responsibility of those involved. A deep understanding of how the actors in planning processes are organized is helpful in several respects:

- In the preliminary phase of process design: a successful process depends on a good organizational culture; therefore, the roles, responsibilities, and decision-making channels should already be stipulated during the preparatory stage. Planning processes offer many administrations an opportunity to try out new forms of collaboration on a specific project.
- During the process: no process goes off without complications. It is worthwhile to look at past process phases in the course of regular revisions and—where possible—to reflect on the organizational form of the actors and groups involved. As a rule, this is a critical point because few are willing to shine a light on their own organizational form but it can help to dispel blockages in the process.
- In further development: viable organizations are a key condition for planning processes pursuing user-led development goals that intend for responsibility for subprojects to be assumed later by those involved as operators of commercial parks and cultural and open space sites, as park initiatives, construction groups, or sponsors of social services. In large part, the organizations that will later utilize the site are already in place. Depending on their design, however, processes can also be a seedbed from which new organizations can arise and take form to later assume the responsibility for implementing the planning.

Test and Let Fail

Most planning processes take a long time by their very nature. The actual participatory phase is relatively short by comparison. Hence discontent often arises among public participants concerning the fact that very concrete future possibilities of a location are discussed while the actual implementation will not take place until years later. Communicating the long-time horizons of development processes is one aspect. Another problem is the detachment of further participation from the actual urban development process. Planning still continues even after the result of a planning procedure has been established. The transition from picture to construction, which as a rule is the responsibility of official authorities, planning specialists, and financiers, proceeds in secret for long periods and only becomes visible when the cranes start turning. The people and institutions that put their ideas into the conception phase are sure to be notified of the status of planning as it continues, but theys are no longer co-authors of the process, and only regain significance at the end, as possible consumers of what has been built.

This leaves out the opportunity to adjust the control mechanisms during the process, to allow for mistakes and learn from them, to experiment with places and utilizations, or to develop prototypes before final decisions are made. So far, there are few planning processes that include a program allowing for step-by-step urban development and are thus open to the possibility of practical participation. A key to a process-oriented, user-led development is the attitude and orientation of the underlying planning.

Treibhaus Landschaftsarchitektur and teleinternetcafe came up with a pioneering concept in this context for the Kreativquartier 1.2.2 ◄ (Creative Quarter) in Munich (City of Munich 2017). As part of the twenty-hectare development area on Dachauer Straße, the planners' prize-winning 2012 design suggested a five-hectare Kreativlabor (Creative Laboratory) in which a dense neighborhood with commerce, new living quarters, social facilities, retail trade, and creative uses was to successively arise from the already existing interim utilizations and buildings. While the formal planning, with its development and master plans for the entire Creative Quarter is already far along, there is as yet—five years after the laboratory won the competition—no convincing idea of how development can purposefully proceed in the conflict between self-organized interim utilization and the vision of urban development.

In 2014, representatives of the administration, local users, and external experts developed a joint model (not yet published) for a two-year test phase. With the aid of curated formats on the grounds, questions related to the development of the laboratory are to be resolved within the set time period. What utilizations are suited to the public spaces of the laboratory and how can better connections in the neighborhood be structured? How can temporary utilizations and new, permanent programs best profit from one another, and what rules would this require? What user groups are interested in developing subprojects in the laboratory? What partners and funds are necessary for this? How could an umbrella organization for the laboratory be designed, and how can the public authorities break even on the laboratory?

Test phases like those conceived in the Munich case can be an adequate means of gaining actors as co-producers of development projects and making participation concrete. In the Creative Laboratory, the test phase has so far been implemented as a kind of informal muddling through, not as consistent milestones of an augmented planning process. There are various reasons for this: there was no common understanding among the actors concerning what the test phase was to accomplish and what it should be good for; policymakers did not adopt any resolution on implementing the test phase as a milestone in the planning process; and the responsible political departments are working on their tasks by the book, but not trying to implement a joint idea—the municipal department is allocating, renting, and clearing out areas; the planning department is creating planning law; and the culture department is ensuring that there is room for as many artists as possible. The municipality has to do justice to the entire populace and gets into trouble when individual initiatives are given preference. The local user groups are fragmented and have diverse priorities. Not all realize that the development of the laboratory needs joint goals, organizational forms, and actions.

The Munich example shows that there are hardly any empirical studies of how to enrich time-tested planning procedures with the knowledge gained from practical trials of places and then to allow the results to be incorporated.

It also becomes clear that the outcome of a competition can only be a first step on the way to actor- and process-oriented development. Process design turns out to be a separate field of competence through which it is necessary to get beyond formal planning procedures and reach the goal of furthering participatory processes and joint decisions between administration, builders, policymakers, users, and architects.

Learn to Design Processes

In its building culture report 2014–2015, the Bundesstiftung Baukultur (Federal Building Culture Foundation) recommended introducing a Service Phase Zero, or planning the planning (Bundesstiftung Baukultur 2017). This is driven by the realization that the usual architect's services no longer represent all the tasks of complex planning processes, especially with regards to participation, process design, dialogic formats, real estate policy, and contract allocation practice. But is it enough to add another service phase to those already found in the official Fee Structure for Architects and Engineers, or to offer architects in training additional seminars in process design? Can we hold it against future architects if they design spaces with passion but without taking into consideration local milieus, changes in housing

◄ 1.4.4

market policy, or co-producers appearing on the scene? Many construction tasks will be discharged in coming years in the same familiar way: with time-tested procedures, well-chosen drafts, and a convincing implementation. There will, however, be a growing need for designers who do not shy away from the complexity of the world to come and who intelligently combine the art of designing space with that of designing processes. The ways and methods leading there are still new. Let's make use of them!

References

Bundesinstitut für Bau-, Stadt- und Raumforschung (BBSR), ed. (2016). *New Urban Agenda Konkret—Fallbeispiele aus deutscher Sicht*. Concept and realization: Philipp Misselwitz, Klaus Overmeyer, and Cordelia Polinna. Bonn.

"Konzept." *PlanBude*. Accessed August 6, 2017. http://planbude.de/category/konzept/.

"Beteiligung der Öffentlichkeit." *Stadt Köln*. Accessed August 6, 2017. http://www.stadt-koeln.de/politik-und-verwaltung/stadtentwicklung/parkstadt-sued/beteiligung-der-oeffentlichkeit.

"Kreativquartier." *Stadt München*. Accessed August 6, 2017. https://www.muenchen.de/rathaus/Stadtverwaltung/Referat-fuer-Stadtplanung-und-Bauordnung/Projekte/Dachauerstrasse-Werkstattgespraech.html.

"Kurzfassung Baukulturbericht 2014/15." *Bundesstiftung Baukultur*. Accessed August 6, 2017. https://www.bundesstiftung-baukultur.de/sites/default/files/medien/967/downloads/baukulturbericht_handlungsempfehlungen.pdf.

2.3.1

(Urban) Transformation Design

Saskia Hebert

Everything is constantly changing; nothing stays the same. Even our built environment transforms continually since space is embedded in time—and not only in the linear time we imagine leading from a distant past to an unknown future, but also, and above all, in the cyclical time of day and night, summer and winter, workdays and holidays.

Change is not necessarily negative. It is a part of life, and of the historical and cultural development of space and societies. When ongoing transformations are perceived as critical or even threatening, this is usually due to two things: their speed and their direction. Hence the extremely dynamic acceleration processes of modern times, which demand ongoing efforts to adjust to them (Toffler 1970, Rosa 2005), can be seen as an imposition, just like changes that lead us to expect a turn for the worse.

While processes such as digitalization, urbanization, and migration are taking place today with a palpable dynamism—which in some cases is also causing disruptive, that is, abrupt and fundamental, changes in the way individuals perceive their world—other, slower transformations stay covered in the background. Hence, the realization that climate change is a consequence of the industrialization and extractivism (Klein 2014) of the past two hundred years is for most people still an abstract scientific finding rather than something they can feel to be true, even though the weather is "going haywire" more and more often. The anthropogenic changes here on "Spaceship Earth" (Buckminster Fuller 2010) are happening so slowly that individual frames of reference have easily been able to adapt ("shifting baselines," Welzer and Sommer 2014).

Therefore, one of the most basic, existential questions facing the design disciplines of our time is whether social change in the sense of a more sustainable, future-proof way of living (Hauff 1987) can be designed—that is, whether a transformation by design is possible—or whether we are doomed to suffer transformation by disaster. Design here does not, of course, mean fighting earlier mistakes that were committed by design disciplines marked by a naive faith in technology, shortsightedness, and insufficient complexity, with yet more design of the same kind (Fezer 2016). There is no need for aesthetically embellished plans for saving the world, for even smarter yet still unnecessary products, for geoengineering or strategies that allow the externalization societies in the global North to polish up their environmental life cycle assessment at the expense of the other hemisphere (FHNW 2017, Sassen 2014). If design wants to be both sustainable and effective, it will have to stop thinking in terms of product and start thinking in terms of process, seek allies, and show some backbone—regardless of whether you call it eco, social, sustainable, transformation, minimal, activist, or critical design (Burckhardt 2012, Papanek 1985, Jonas et. al. 2016, Banz 2016, Arch+ 2016). The discipline's methodological toolbox contains some interesting tools in this regard, of which only a small range can be mentioned here: conceptual or speculative design, for instance (Dunne and Raby 2013), develops scenarios of possible futures that make utopian or dystopian suggestions available for wider public debate, including a necessary discussion of goals and values of change.

Design, or simply *Entwerfen* in German, can not only project the future into the present, but also generate in the here and now concrete simulations of leaps in time that let us actually experience a changed reality. Iterative, performative, and collaborative processes, with sketches, renderings, films, and narratives, as well as models and 1:1 prototypes, can create aesthetic situations that can be perceived with all senses (Böhme 2001) and in which we no longer "face the future" (Flusser 2007), but can experience it—in the here and now. To be clear, this does not have much to do with plans and predictions ("The best way to predict the future is to design it," said Buckminster Fuller), but rather with a process-oriented, transformative (design) research (Schneidewind and Singer-Brodowski 2014) and an open debate on how to "convert existing situations into preferable ones," the definition of design given by Herbert A. Simon (2008).

2.3.2

This sort of discourse faces many challenges for it must integrate a variety of standards and different actors. In the sense of a necessary "great transformation" (WBGU 2011, Polanyi 2015), design always has to think globally, yet at the same time it must deliver precise analyses and specific propositions for the *Eigenart*[1] and the respective transformational potential of local places (WBGU 2016). It has to deal with abstract topics such as freedom or global and intergenerational justice, but also with their very specific manifestations in urban communities, common goods (Helfrich 2012, Dellenbaugh et al. 2015), and new habits. And of course, it is a general question how we as designers can help to keep the spaces that we build open (Sennett 2006, Hebert 2016). For the future.

1 A German word meaning "character."

References

Arch+, ed. (2016). Arch+ 222: *Project Bauhaus 1: Kann Design Gestaltung verändern?*

Banz, C., ed. (2016). *Social Design: Gestalten für die Transformation der Gesellschaft.* Bielefeld.

Böhme, G. (2001). *Aisthetik: Vorlesungen über Ästhetik als allgemeine Wahrnehmungslehre.* Munich.

Buckminster Fuller, R. (2010). *Bedienungsanleitung für das Raumschiff Erde und andere Schriften.* Hamburg.

Burckhardt, L. (2012). *Design ist unsichtbar: Entwurf, Gesellschaft & Pädagogik.* Berlin.

Dellenbaugh, M., M. Kip, and M. Bieniok et al., eds. (2015). *Urban Commons: Moving beyond State and Market.* Berlin.

Dunne, A. and F. Raby (2013). *Speculative Everything: Design, Fiction, and Social Dreaming.* Cambridge, MA.

Fezer, J. (2016). "Parteiisches Design und die Probleme anderer." Lecture in the conference Un/certain Futures. HBK Braunschweig.

FHNW Academy of Art and Design Basel (2017). Call for Papers. "Beyond Change." des Swiss Design Network.

Flusser, V. (2007). *Von der Freiheit des Migranten.* Hamburg.

Hauff, V., ed. (1987). *Unsere gemeinsame Zukunft—Der Brundtland-Bericht der Weltkommission für Umwelt und Entwicklung.* Greven.

Helfrich, S., Heinrich-Böll-Stiftung, ed. (2012). *Commons—Für eine neue Politik jenseits von Markt und Staat.* Bielefeld.

Hebert, S. (2016). "Schwerpunkt Stadt—ein Reisebericht." D. Giesecke, S. Hebert, and H. Welzer, eds. *FUTURZWEI Zukunftsalmanach 2016/17.* Frankfurt am Main.

Jonas, W., S. Zerwas, and K. von Anshelm, ed. (2016). *Transformation Design—Perspectives on a New Design Attitude.* Basel.

Klein, N. (2014). *Entscheidung. Kapitalismus vs. Klima.* Frankfurt am Main.

Papanek, V. (1985). *Design for the Real World: Human Ecology and Social Change.* London.

Polanyi, K. (2015). *The Great Transformation: politische und ökonomische Ursprünge von Gesellschaften und Wirtschaftssystemen.* Berlin.

Rosa, H. (2005). *Beschleunigung: die Veränderung der Zeitstrukturen in der Moderne.* Frankfurt am Main.

Sassen, S. (2014). *Ausgrenzungen: Brutalität und Komplexität in der globalen Wirtschaft.* Frankfurt am Main.

Schneidewind, U. and M. Singer-Brodowski (2014). *Transformative Wissenschaft: Klimawandel im deutschen Wissenschafts- und Hochschulsystem.* Marburg.

Sennett, R. (2006). "Open City." ed. London School of Economics and Alfred Herrhausen Stiftung.

Simon, H. A. (2008). *The Sciences of the Artificial.* Cambridge, MA.

Toffler, A. (1970). *Der Zukunftsschock.* Scherz.

Wissenschaftlicher Beirat Globale Umweltveränderungen (WBGU), ed. (2016). *Der Umzug der Menschheit—Die transformative Kraft der Städte.* Berlin.

Wissenschaftlicher Beirat Globale Umweltveränderungen (WBGU), ed. (2011). *Welt im Wandel: Gesellschaftsvertrag für eine Große Transformation.* Berlin.

Welzer, H. and B. Sommer (2014). *Transformationsdesign: Wege in eine zukunftsfähige Moderne.* Munich.

2.3.2

2.4. Temporalities

- •1 Temporal(ities): A New Perspective into the Design of Time, Rhythm, and Atmosphere in Urban Places
- •2 URBAN_NIGHT_TIME_SPACES
- •3 Temporalities: Temporal Turn?

Temporal(ities): A New Perspective into the Design of Time, Rhythm, and Atmosphere in Urban Places

Filipa Wunderlich

Manifesto—Thoughts on cities / notes to the urban designer:
Cities are not movement; they are flow
Cities are not static matter; they are choreographies, improvised plays,
*   eventful narratives, and bundles of sensorial and affective meaning*
Cities are not activity or practice; cities are experiences
Cities are not organization and logistics, complex operations involving people, facilities
*   and supplies; they are processes, managed and unmanaged, formal*
*   and informal, planned and unplanned*
Cities are not noise; they are soundscapes
Cityscapes are not only visual; they are sound, touch, odors, and scents
Cities are not grey, they are full of color
Cities are not new; they are palimpsests—reused and altered matter in evolution,
*   bearing the traces and scars of eventful pasts*
Cities are not history; they are memories
Cities are not facts; they are ethnographies, individual quality experiences set in
*   motion, which are sensorial, emotional, and meaningful*
Cities are not screens; they are theater plays, performances
*   in which we the audience gets involved*

2.4.1

Cities are not a collection of stills or sequential representations;
    they are fluid and rhythmic
Cities may be influenced by industry and technology, but they are
    most importantly crafted

Cities are both territories and atmospheres!
Cities are not temporary, but temporal!

1. Introduction

Urban migration into cities and metropolises is generating a need for rapid and intense development, often of significant height and scale. Especially in megacities such as London, New York, Hong Kong, Tokyo, and others, urban growth results in a rapidly changing and intensifying morphology, and goes along with often negative impacts on the social fabric and the quality of everyday patterns of life.

Technological advancements have resulted in an acceleration of urban life. The Internet and communication via email and social media is prompting a retreat into the workspace, the domestic space, and the virtual space. Wireless connectivity, portable mobile devices, geospatial positioning and information systems, the sharing economy, augmented reality apps, games and the like offer new forms of engagement with the city fabric, but also have an impact on the way people behave in the city. People tend to depend less on real urban features, and become less conscious of the present time and space and the present-moment sensorial experiences. The focus is shifting away from the senses (the haptic, the sounds, the smells, and even the visual) towards screens and earphones, altering the experiential realm in the city. City spaces experience more accelerated collective behaviors along with experiences of agitation and stress, fast movement punctuated by disengaged practices in the space of the city (for example, people sitting, waiting at bus stops, walking, and playing while staring at screens). Technological advancements are further playing a role towards the acceleration of time and behavior and the overall disengagement from everyday social life in the city, weakening participation in places and processes of social production.

Social density (or crowdedness) alongside spatial density and architectural complexity, the overall acceleration and intensification of everyday life, and experiences of alienation and isolation are factors that contribute towards the greater proportion of mental health problems that can be found in contemporary large cities (Adli 2017).

Urban design research into the fundamental new challenges in cities that derive from densification, technological advancements, and impacts on mental health, however, is still in its infancy. The built environment disciplines, in particular the urban design practice, have so far devoted little attention to the design of civic and social space and in support of physical and mental well-being in urban environments. Many questions remain unanswered, such as how urban design can explicitly respond to social conflict and difference in urban space, and how it can deliver spaces that are healing and have an overall positive impact on mental health in the city.

These challenges cannot be addressed through old-fashioned urban design thinking derived from a modernist understanding of space and time where the aesthetics of design are primarily focused on the visual, the static, and the material condition of cities. What is required instead is a much more holistic and experimental urban design approach that focuses on people and the experiential realm of the city. This needs to consider the interplay of many aspects, such as time, the senses, affect and emotion, and the processes through which they are experienced. Aspects of performance and the choreography of places, thus, become fundamental elements to design with and for in the space of the city.

This approach will resonate well with the crucial theoretical advances from within the social sciences in the past two decades, which brought about two important paradigm shifts, or turns, into the discussion of the urban condition. The first of these important shifts in understanding the urban is the so-called spatial turn, which offers a more holistic understanding of place. It introduces a new dimension, that of spacetime, in which the production of physical space is inseparable from social spaces and processes (Lefebvre 2004; Massey 2005; Thrift 2003, 2008). More recently, another paradigm shift is developing, the so-called affective turn, in which, the embodied experience is center stage and the focus is on performativity, the senses, affect, and emotion as the principal means by which to understand the human condition versus the production and experience of the built environment (Deleuze and Guatarri 1989; Massumi 2015; Greg and Seighworth 2010).

Deriving from these new theoretical currents of thought on urban spacetime, other interdisciplinary approaches to the nature, production, and design of the built environment are gaining momentum. This is the case of the sensorial urbanism group of thinkers, which include studies on soundscapes, smellscapes, the role of touch, and tactile landscapes (Zardini 2005; 2016); performative urbanism, which looks at the intention and constellations of events as the means of production of urban places (Wolfrum, 2015); atmosphere or ambience, which focuses on a combination of features, from the senses to emotions, to generate new forms of reading and comprehending the city from a sensorial and affective point of view (Le Laboratoire AAU–CRESSON and CRENAU,

2.4.1

Grenoble and Nantes; Centre for Sensory Studies, Concordia University, Montreal); and also the composite approach on the value and role of place-temporality and rhythm in the design of the city (Wunderlich, 2013, 2014), which is looked here at in more detail below.

These innovative approaches to the nature and production of the urban environment are only slowly permeating into the built environment debate, in particular, into the research and teaching of urban design. In this context, a paradigm shift is needed in regards to the way urban designers understand, analyze, and design for people in the city. If the urban design discipline likes to evolve and develop meaningful ways of responding to contemporary urban challenges as mentioned above, it will need to open up to advancements in the social sciences that teach us to look at urban space not as fixed but ephemeral, not as visual but sensorial, not as representation but nonrepresentational, intentional, and performative. It should shift the focus from the physical to the social space, add the dimensions of spatiality and temporality, and embrace the senses, performativity, and affect.

This is the wider context within which this paper on temporality should be read and the ground dimensions for a new field of urban design research and practice: temporal urban design.

2. Temporal Urban Design

Cities are ephemeral, and, contrary to what one may be drawn to think (with the hangover of modernist thought and education), its buildings, streets, squares, and parks, and altogether its material and visual forms are only the stage sets for the city's everyday life rhythms and its overall temporal performances. It is argued here that the latter is what defines the actual urban design of places.

The main focus of this type of urban design is on what happens (in urban space), how is it performed and how it feels. It is a kind of urban design that is sensorial (experiential), as it is involves all the senses. It is performative, as it continuously creates new urban realities, new meanings, and, as such, it is also affective, meaning it induces emotions, including states of flow that foster well-being in urban space (Csikszentmihalyi 1988; Wunderlich, 2013). Most importantly, this kind of urban design is temporal. It is experienced and perceived through time (that is, being in a performative state rather than frozen in time) and is defined by time's sculpting elements—the rhythms that are inherent to places' performances and choreographies.

A place's specific sets of performances and choreographies shape unique place-temporalities. Place-temporalities are continuums of orchestrated rhythms that as a whole define and induce vivid senses of time in one particular space. The multiplicity of rhythms can be sensed and tangibly engaged with in the space. Place-temporalities juxtapose in their entirety, constitute the city.

The aesthetics of temporal urban design is one of social and playful praxis, temporal production, and improvisation, analogous to the aesthetics of other experiential and performative art forms, such as music or dance. In fact, urban place-temporality is a temporal art form (Dewey, 1934; Dufrenne, 1973) with performative character that influences people's experiences and impacts their emotional and affective well-being.

The connecting element between a place's sense of time, sensoriality, affect, and performativity is rhythm, and it is that which ultimately induces the place's mood and atmosphere. Rhythm is also the principal design element of this new form of temporal urban design.

3. The Components of Temporal Urban Design: An Alternative Aesthetics and the Focus on Place-Temporality and Rhythm

As briefly introduced above, two central aspects of temporal urban design are place-temporalities and place-rhythms. Both have a dual characteristic: they are equally 1) a sense, and 2) a process, and thus can be sensed and observed.

Place-Temporality—A Distinct Sense of Time

Place-temporality is the equivalent on time of what character is on place. Place-temporality is the existential and phenomenological sense of time in a place. It is the embodied time that is sensorially and affectively perceived in a place. Some cities and places have particular senses of time of their own; for example, they can be perceived as slow or as fast. Intrinsically linked to this unique sense of time are other meaningful qualities and senses of atmosphere in places. such as, in the case of slow places, being calm, ordered, easy to understand, engaging, and harmonious, or, in the case of fast places, stressful, busy, complex and agitated. Place-temporality is a temporally distinctive qualitative condition of a place. More than a mere emotion, it is a meaningful (both sensorial and affective) appreciation of time. It induces a state of flow, a state of immersion in which the pace of our own practices accelerates or slows down collectively as we immerse ourselves in the rhythmic practices of everyday life. It offers a sense of temporal identity to urban places.

Besides being a sense, place-temporality is also a process, and as such it can be studied and mapped. It expresses and represents itself in urban space through at least four typical sensorial attributes that are intrinsically related: 1) a vivid and distorted sense of time; 2) a sense of flow; 3) a distinct soundscape; and 4) rhythmicity. It is through the means of rhythm that the sense of time, flow, and soundscape express themselves in urban space. The vivid sense of time and flow have been mentioned earlier. Yet, soundscape also plays a major role in the perception of place-temporality. Place-temporality soundscapes are acoustic colorations where foreground and background can be heard distinctively; these sounds offer information on their physical characteristics and express aspects of their social and cultural identity. However, and ultimately, the most important and core attribute of place-temporality is rhythmicity.

2.4.1

intensity:
n. events

proximity and distance between accents

tension

release

release   tension

Rhythmicity—The Expression and Representation of Urban Place-Rhythms

Place-temporality is expressed, materialized, and structured through multiple temporally resonant urban place-rhythms. Place-rhythms constitute rhythmic (recurrent and synchronized) temporal events that are expressed both spatially and temporally. They can be traced by the type of event and their recurrence and articulation over time, including duration patterns, frequency, and intensity, or in other words, their accentuation patterns (how many and when they coincide in time) (see figure 1).

In my doctoral thesis I studied the sense of time and rhythm in the urban environment. This explored both the spatial and temporal expression of urban rhythms and established direct parallels to musical rhythms and their aesthetics (Wunderlich 2010a; 2013). In this research I demonstrated that, although they are principally temporal, urban place rhythms can be identified, graphically interpreted, and illustrated. More than one year's ethnographic fieldwork, which included various site-specific practices such as video recordings, time-lapse photography, site-specific writing, and the production of time-based maps of movement and social rhythmic events, was carried out at Fitzroy Square in London. A multiplicity of place-rhythms were identified at the square. This included everyday social routines, patterns of movement and other sensory practices, circadian and seasonal cycles of nature, and visual and haptic patterns of physical space.

In respect of their spatial expression, place-rhythms can be grouped into three primary categories: social, natural, and physical rhythms (Zerubavel 1981; Lefebvre 2004). My research breaks each group further down into subgroups: social into societal, cultural, and functional; natural into daily and seasonal; and physical into dynamic and static rhythms. Place-rhythms are place-specific and unique in the way they vertically relate to one another, or in other words, how they superimpose temporally.

The temporal expression of urban place-rhythms can be captured in the form of spectral rhythmic diagrams (see figure 2), which show the overall temporal articulation and accentuation of particular place-rhythms. The diagrams visualize the duration, frequency, intensity, and accentuation of rhythms. The juxtaposition of spectral rhythmic diagrams generates a place score (see figure 3) that illustrates how place-rhythms resonate in time to form unique place-temporalities, just like urban symphonies of events.

Figure 1: Walking place-rhythms: two hours of rhythmanalysis (spectral rhythmic diagram and its analysis), the rest hour, 10 a.m.–12 noon, on a summer day at Fitzroy Square, London, © Filipa Wunderlich

2.4.1

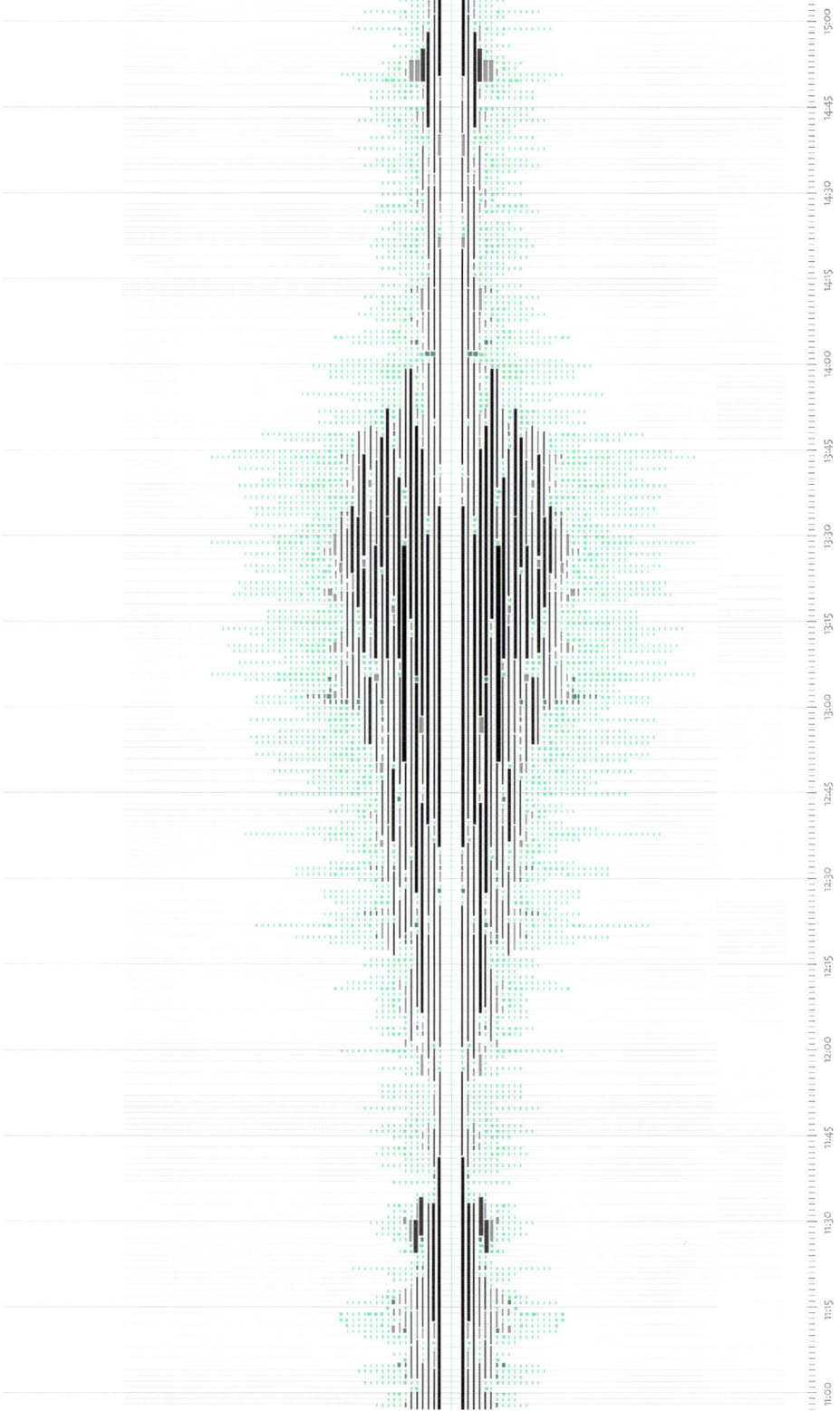

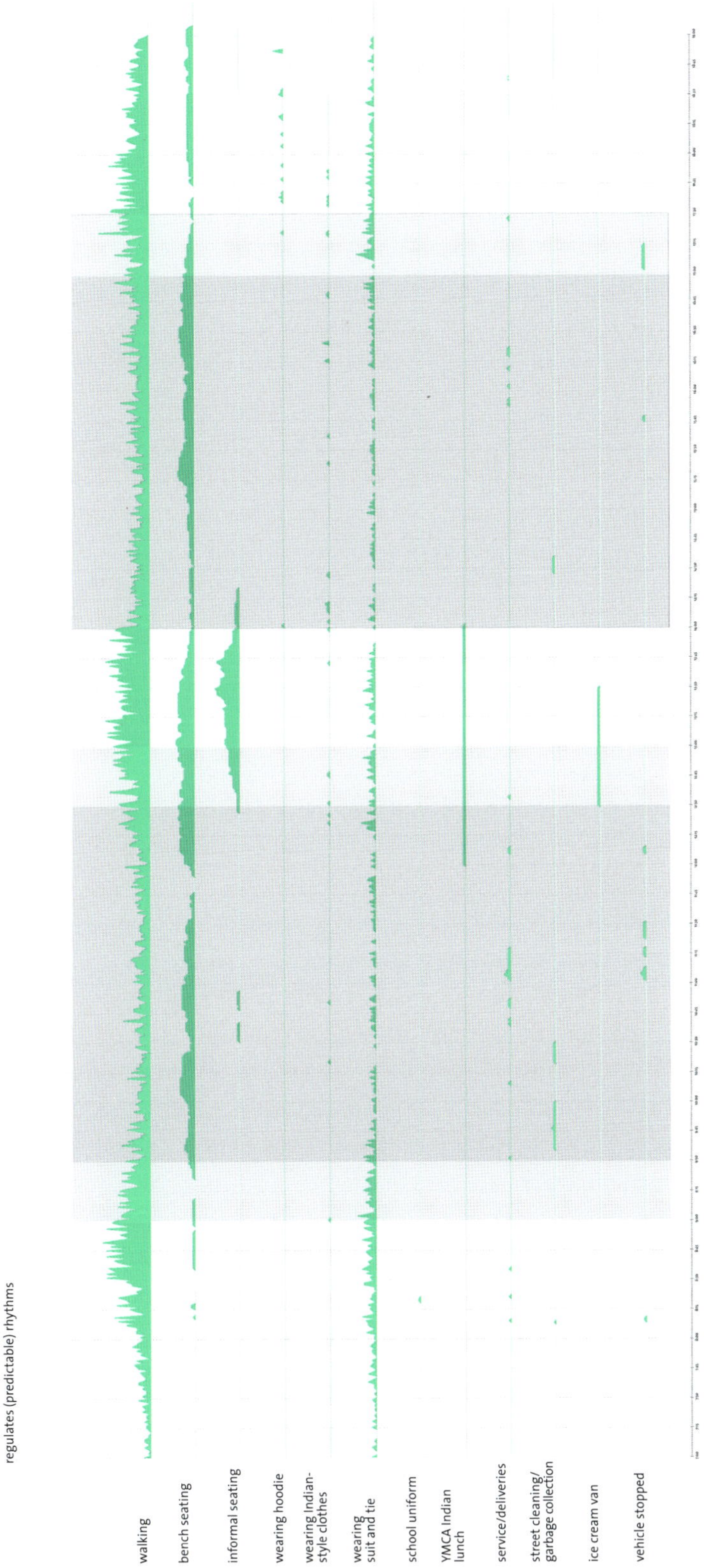

Figure 2: Spectral rhythmic diagram: superimposition of social everyday life place-rhythms, four-hour sample, 11 a.m.–3 p.m., from a typical summer's day at Fitzroy Square, London, © Filipa Wunderlich

Figure 3: The juxtaposition of spectral rhythmic diagrams of regulated (predictable) social everyday life place-rhythms generates a place-score, 12-hour sample, 7 a.m.–7 p.m., from a typical summer's day at Fitzroy Square, London, © Filipa Wunderlich

2.4.1

regulates (predictable) rhythms

walking
bench seating
informal seating
wearing hoodie
wearing Indian-style clothes
wearing suit and tie
school uniform
YMCA Indian lunch
service/deliveries
street cleaning/garbage collection
ice cream van
vehicle stopped

A New Temporal Aesthetic—The Sense of Temporal Beauty

The exploration of place-rhythms falls squarely into a new field of study—the aesthetics of temporality. This discusses the sense of temporal beauty in respect to a places' rhythmic performance. Two principal dimensions of temporal aesthetics can be identified. One is the theatrical dimension (in earlier work referred to as place-temporal performance) (Wunderlich 2013). This focuses on performance and performative character, looking at the choreographies of place-rhythms, mapping their rhythmic structures, how they articulate over time and interrelate, and the meanings and critiques of place that may be induced by it.

For example, at Fitzroy Square, at the end of the weekday, fast and regular walking rhythms of crowds of office workers passing the square on their way home dominate the place's temporal experience. This is superimposed by the slow and distinct cultural regular rhythm of mainly Asian youth from one of the nearby housing estates gathering around one of the benches, sitting and standing, with their hoodies, and sharing unique body gestures and codes. The recurrent and regular juxtaposition of these rhythms give a distinct scenic temporal quality to this place, one that is meaningful and engaging, as it creates awareness of the cultural differences, tensions, and inequalities in the neighborhood.

The other is the dimension of affect (in earlier work also referred to as place-tonality) (Wunderlich 2013), which focuses on the sensorial and affective aspects of place-rhythms. This looks at how one senses place-rhythms and our emotional response to them. It looks at the extent to which they induce senses of flow, and with them, the sense of balance, equilibrium, resonance, and embodied pleasure, and conjure an overall optimal place-temporal experience.

An example for this in Fitzroy Square are the sunny summer lunchtimes, when the dominant and influential natural rhythms of the large plane trees in the central garden provide a patchwork of shade and light, and juxtapose for the short intense lunchtime period (when the gardens are open to the general public) with the slow social rhythms of people walking and sitting, alone and in groups under the trees, accompanied by soundscapes of loud chatting and laughing, and accentuated occasionally by the unique sounds of birds; all together, inducing senses of flow as place-rhythms combine into an harmonious sensorial whole, and induce a sense of well-being.

This aesthetic exploration opens up an important new field of study with significant relevance for urban design, as it establishes a tangible relation and structure of a theoretical framework that links the temporal aspects of place and the sensual response and meaning associated with it. It means that temporal attributes matter, can be studied, and can (and should) be discussed when approaching the experiential quality of urban environments and well-being.

4. The Next Steps—Situating the Practice(s) of Temporal Urban Design

Thinking of how to practice temporal urban design, one crucial question is whether one can actually and explicitly design for the sense of flow, induce sensorial engagement, enhance and facilitate specific social processes through time, and promote or alter existential senses of time, temporality, and rhythm in the city overall. This has not typically been the domain of interest and practice of the architect, planner, or urban designer so far.

To do so urban designers will need to open up their horizon of practice, embrace an interdisciplinary outlook, and embark in methodological discovery and innovation processes (Wunderlich 2014). Here, there is much to be learned from the performative arts, where atmosphere, mood, and senses of time, rhythm, and overall temporalities have always been the main focus.

Designing for rhythmicity in the city and, in particular, urban place-rhythms, can assist us in managing social density, with the aim to disperse or concentrate, dissipate or intensify, and accentuate social place-rhythms in the city spaces. The focus of design should not only be the accommodation of movement, spatial practices, or events, but also the shaping of their intensity and temporal articulation—how these movements, practices, and events resonate and express themselves both spatially and temporally, in other words, to attend to performance patterns and temporal aesthetics in urban space and time.

Designing for the sense of time and the aesthetics of place-temporality overall, by concentrating on rhythm and rhythmicity in urban space, means designing for mental well-being in urban space. Urban place-rhythms have the potential to induce states of flow, and thus can offer states of fulfillment, pleasure, and gratification, and by that, induce optimal experiences in urban space. In this context, temporal urban design's aim is to deliver places with unique senses of flow, time, and overall eurhythmia, expressed and represented through resonant performances of natural, social, and physical rhythms.

5. Conclusion

Temporal urban design is fundamentally an interdisciplinary field of research and practice. The practice of temporal urban design is defined by two main domains of inquiry. The first is the in-situ research of place-temporality and place-rhythms, which analyzes aspects and furthers an understanding of their spatial and temporal expression in urban space, and which represents and interprets a place's rhythmicity and temporality with the aim to inspire and inform design propositions. The second domain is that of the temporal urban design response processes and products. Situating the practices and products of temporal urban design into the interdisciplinary field is paramount. Temporal urban design practice can be inspired and supported by other emerging fields of practice, such as temporary urbanism, sensorial urbanism, and participatory urbanism, as it aims to shape a new field of practice with its own unique principles and scope of action, that of urban place rhythmicity, sense of time,

2.4.1

and overall temporality. Here, quantitative participatory urbanism methods of data collection in particular can complement an area of study that would otherwise remain mostly broadly qualitative.

Temporal urban design is a new field of research and practice that is collaborative and participatory as much as a creative and experimental approach to the design of temporality and rhythms in urban places. Interventions may be temporary or long-term, steered and directed by the understanding of places as temporal frames, where its sense of time, sense of flow and rhythmicity is experienced in a performative manner, and can be mapped through a unique continuum of rhythms and as such, temporally orchestrated and designed for.

The question remaining is: what then would this mean for the urban design profession? Fundamentally, temporal urban design asks for a review, or a paradigm shift, of the urban design disciplinary focus and approach to the aesthetics of urban places, within which methodological innovation in both research and practice is imperative. The focus shall be shifted into the domain of time and the processes of production of place, its expression, and representation. In this context, temporal urban design adopts place-temporality and urban rhythms as the principal elements of urban design aesthetics, embracing the sense of time, its sensoriality, performativity, and affect as paramount in the process of designing for more fulfilling, gratifying, and ultimately healing urban environments, in other words, designing for and supporting mental well-being in the contemporary city.

Given the ambiguity and porosity of the field of urban design, temporal urban design, as an inherently interdisciplinary approach to the design of the city, alternatively has the potential to break free from the dominance of either architecture or planning disciplines, and instead establish itself as an independent area of urban studies of research and practice, one which is situated at the crossroads between the performative arts and the built environment disciplines.

References

Adli, M. (2017). *Stress and the City: Warum Städte uns krank machen. Und warum sie trotzdem gut für uns sind.* Munich.

Csikszentmihalyi, M. and I. S. Csikszentmihalyi, ed. (1988). *Optimal Experience: Psychological Studies of Flow in Consciousness.* Cambridge, UK.

Deleuze, G. (1989). *Cinema 2: The Time-Image.* Minneapolis, MN.

Dewey, J. (1934). *Art as Experience.* London.

Dufrenne, M. (1973). *The Phenomenology of Aesthetic Experience.* Evanston, IL.

Gregg, M. and G. J. Seigworth, ed. (2011) *The Affect Theory Reader.* Durham, NC.

Lefebvre, H. (2004). *Rhythmanalysis: Space, Time and Everyday Life.* London.

Massey, D. (2005). *For Space.* London.

Massumi, B. (2015). *The Politics of Affect.* Cambridge, UK.

Thrift, N. (2003). "Performance and ..." *Environment and Planning A: Economy and Space* 35.11: pp. 2019–2024.

Thrift, N. (2008). *Non-representational Theory: Space, Politics, Affect.* London.

Wetherell, M. (2012). *Affect and Emotion: A New Social Science Understanding.* London

Wolfrum, S. and N. Frhr. v. Brandis (2015). *Performative Urbanism: Generating and Designing Urban Space.* Berlin.

Wunderlich, F. M. (2010a). "Place-Temporality and Urban Place Rhythms in Urban Analysis and Design." Doctoral thesis, 2010, UCL, University of London.

Wunderlich, F. M. (2010b). "The Aesthetics of Place-Temporality in Everyday Urban Space: The Case of Fitzroy Square." T. Edensor, ed. *In A Geography of Rhythms.* London.

Wunderlich, F. M. (2013). "Place-Temporality and Urban Place-Rhythms in Urban Analysis and Design: An Aesthetic Akin to Music." *Journal of Urban Design* 18.3: pp.383–408.

Wunderlich, F. M. (2014). "Place-Temporality and Rhythmicity: A New Aesthetics and Methodological Foundation for Urban Design Theory and Practice." M. Carmona, ed. *Explorations in Urban Design.* London.

Zardini, M., ed. (2005). *Sense of the City: An Alternate Approach to Urbanism.* Montreal.

Zardini, M. (2016). "Towards a Sensorial Urbanism." A. Schwanhäusser, ed. *Sensing the City: A Companion to Urban Anthropology,* Basel.

Zerubavel, E. (1981). *Hidden Rhythms: Schedules and Calendars in Social Life.* Chicago.

2.4.1

URBAN_NIGHT_ TIME_SPACES

Christine Preiser/Jakob F. Schmid

Interviewer: Today I am talking to two researchers working on the urban night and more specifically on urban nightlife. Jakob Schmid and Christine Preiser—welcome to the studio.

JS/CP: Thank you!

Interviewer: Jakob, you are an urban planner; Christine, you are a sociologist … before we go more into the details of your specific projects, let's start with the things they have in common: what connects your research?

CP: First of all, of course, it is the interest in the urban night, the city between 10 p.m. and 6 a.m., which is still not taken into account or even neglected in urban planning and sociology in Germany.

JS: We are both fascinated by urban nightscapes, a term that combines the notion of night and landscape, and has been established to describe the texture of the urban night that can be quite different from that of the city at daytime. We share a relational understanding of place and space as it is promoted by de Certeau (1980) or Löw (2001). So we are interested in the places, the physical entities, that form these nightscapes—the nightclubs, the bars, the paths between, their relation to other places of the city. But also the nightlife or the nighttime economy that is formed as a space by and of people, practices, social dimensions, and sometimes conflicting rules.

CP: It is quite common to describe urban nightlife as "leisure time," "time-out," "carnival," or "play," and we both understand the urban night as a "heterotopian" (Foucault 1984) territory. This

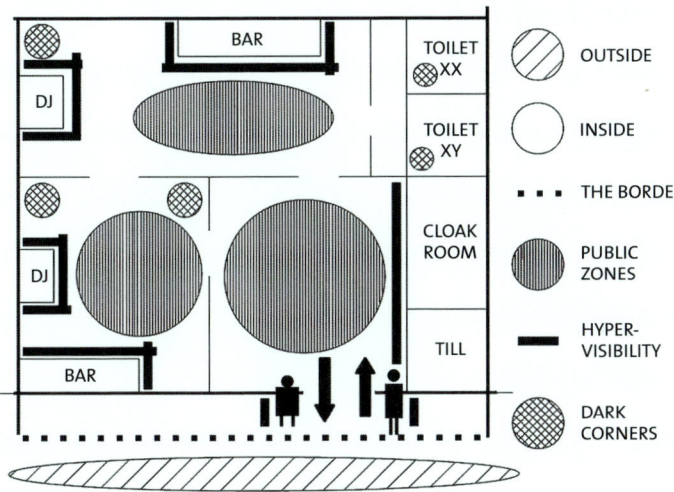

always implicates—like the definition of the night itself—the notion of temporality. Heterotopian territories and their specific participants, logics, and modes of access only exist for limited times. They are always interconnected with territories from which they differ, such as the urban daytime.

Interviewer: How does this translate into your research?

JS: As an urban planner I look at the city as a whole. I used nightlife-related entries in a popular online directory to analyze the spatial distribution of nightlife premises in thirteen German cities. This included nightclubs, but also cinemas and theaters among others. We translated the data into maps that help us to understand the spatial distribution of nightlife activities in each city. The maps show that every city has its unique nocturnal fabric, but there are also similarities. Each nightscape has its hotspot(s) and its peripheries. Like elsewhere in European cities, the hotspots of nightlife are rather close to central business districts but not to the high streets. Those areas provide important conditions for nightlife venues such as less expensive commercial space and a more noise-friendly environment. If we read nightlife as an indicator of gentrification processes, those maps also speak of changes to come in the city at daytime.

CP: I am working with ethnographic research methods so my approach is a quite different one and more on the micro-level of the

Figure 2: Map of the spatial distribution of nightlife premises in Berlin, © Jakob F. Schmid and Patrick Stotz / stadtnachtacht – Map tiles: Stamen Design CC BY 3.0. – Base Map: CC BY SA

urban night. I conducted open participant observations in three nightclubs in two German cities to gain an understanding of nightclubs as specific territories. Bouncers are not only the border guards and gatekeepers of these territories. They also have a major influence on the rules that apply inside the nightclub and how the inside is connected to the outside. What is allowed inside, but is forbidden outside and vice versa? Where is it (not) allowed inside? To what extent will the inside be shielded from the outside, especially from authorities such as the police? My research shows that bouncers make several territorial distinctions. They distinguish basically and strictly between the outside and the inside and tolerate zones of enhanced secrecy inside—for certain nighttime practices. This applies for all three nightclubs, but it depends a lot on the respective bouncers as to how strict they are and to what extent they let people "play" and have a "time-out." All this is connected to a specific time, because eventually the party will be over, the doors will close again and the guests will have to wait till the next weekend or night.

Interviewer: This sounds challenging to combine in an interdisciplinary approach?

JS: It is sometimes, but the combination is very promising, also when it comes to knowledge transfer outside of science. If we bring the different perspectives together, we gain a profound knowledge of the spatiotemporal structure of the nocturnal territory and are able to zoom in to understand how nightlife is created and experienced through practices ...

CP: ... so that the night will eventually be properly taken into account by urban planners. Who will know that not everything can be planned in a field of play?

Interviewer: Thank you!

2.4.2

References

Certeau, M. (1980). *L'invention du quotidien. Arts de faire*. Paris.
Foucault, M. (1984). "Of Other Spaces: Utopias and Heterotopias." *Architecture, Movement, Continuité* 5: pp. 46–49.
Löw, M. (2001). *Raumsoziologie*. Frankfurt am Main.

Temporalities: Temporal Turn?

Dietrich Henckel

The need for a wider and systematic recognition of urban tempo-ralities in urban studies and planning practice is, in my view, un-questionable even though the diffusion of research in different disciplines is growing and the body of literature increasing. Even in many planning documents or statements by urban planners the importance of temporal issues and the demand for explicit temporal planning is mentioned, yet with rather little impact so far.

Urban temporalities are not at all a new question, but have been limited in scope within specific disciplines with a rather nar-row spectrum of topics and are often dealt with only implicitly and not explicitly. This is also true for planning departments, es-pecially those which have, in one way or another, established schedules for services (for example, public transport, urban light-ing, and schools, to name a few). But mostly it has been a mere technical effort with little regard to the impact on citizens' behav-ior (and vice versa) and on the interrelations between the differ-ent departments, disciplines, temporal scales, rhythms, and cycles.

Many disciplines have at least parts that deal with temporali-ties. That urban history would is obvious; but economics also con-siders the question of time preferences for investments; time ge-ography explicitly puts the focus on the interrelation between space and time; and time sociology is another example, though it was not originally oriented to urban issues.

The growing interest in urban temporalities has some sources, including:

- Due to changes in the temporal structure in society (ac-celeration, extension, flexibilization), temporalities that have been taken for granted for long periods of time are losing relevance, and new temporal conflicts (problems of synchronization and desynchronization, perceived scarcity of time, temporal stress) are rising.

- Due to changing temporal scales (the relations between past, present, and future) and spatial scales (internationalization and globalization) the temporal fitting over these different scales gets much more complex. 1.1.2 ◄
- The diffusion of information technology and digitalization that produces data with time prints in never-known fields with unprecedented quantities and qualities ("big data") allows—along with new analytical tools—for temporal analyses of behavior of people, of technical systems, and their interrelations. The use of these technologies (however problematic with respect to privacy issues) massively enhances the possibility to understand the (temporal) behavior of cities, urban systems, and other spatial configurations, and in the end also to improve explicit temporal planning.

Therefore, I am convinced that urban temporalities are a growing field of research in urban studies. In my view this accrues for many disciplines, but it also calls for a much more inter- and transdisciplinary perspective, which is often claimed in science but not so often realized.

The need for a more systematic integration of temporal issues in planning practice is also easier claimed than implemented. One problem is the intangibility of time, which makes it difficult to introduce in mostly material planning procedures. Another problem is the undefined responsibility and the lack of political power and institutionalization (visible in the minimal impact of the Italian urban time planning, which has also a legal basis).

I am skeptical whether the growing interest in and a closer focus on temporalities, the need for a growing explicit scientific endeavor in urban studies, and the claim for interdisciplinarity and explicit integration into urban planning should be called a temporal turn. My skepticism relates to the seemingly growing number of "turns" and the fact that for some authors the spatial turn is described as a replacement of the temporal fixation. If temporal issues get more recognition and the inseparable interrelations between time and space are taken into account, there is no need for a "turn."

2.4.3

2.5. Co-production

• **1** The Co-production of the City: Learning from
 Advocacy Architecture in Brazil

• **2** Sociological Glances on the "Social Turn" in
 Architecture and Design

• **3** The *Other* Engagement: A Critique of the "Co-"

The Co-production of the City: Learning from Advocacy Architecture in Brazil

Ana Paula Koury

Introduction

Urban gigantism is a feature of urbanization in the largest countries in Latin America. Besides Mexico, the Brazil is the largest case study of urban society in the continent. The urbanization process in Brazil was embedded in the social, political, and economic issues and understanding it is indeed a knotty problem. However the tricky task could provide us worthy clues for the future of urban society in the world, considering global urbanization is one of poverty and precariousness and frequently faces worse situations than Brazil has experienced in its past.

This article aims to trigger a debate on the role of architecture and planning in urban democracy under poverty. The vibrant thoughts and innovative solutions including urban and social techniques that arose in Brazil since the nineteen-sixties could inspire experiments in urban design worldwide. On the other hand critically analyzing Brazil's recent past can also be important to refresh the history of urban planning agenda inside the country.

The urban population in Brazil reached 45 percent (32 million inhabitants) of the whole in the nineteen-sixties, surpassing the rural population in 1966. Urban rates continued to rise quickly until the end of the twentieth century. According the *Sinopse do Censo Demográfico de 2010* (Synopsis of the 2010 Demographic Census) in 2010 the urban population reached 84.5 percent, totaling 191 million inhabitants (IBGE 2007; IBGE 2010). The concentration of poverty in metropolitan areas happened two decades after the demographic transition. In 1985 poverty in Brazil reached 41 percent of population (53 million people), 55 percent of them were living in cities and 18 percent in metropolitan zones (Santagada 1990, pp. 121–43). The numbers outlined the great challenges of the urban process in Brazil.

2.5.1

Advocacy Architecture and Urban Planning

The largest cities were growing through informal settlements in their outskirts. The Santos school of architecture was founded in 1968 and influenced the studies of informality in Brazil. The academic studies stressed the urban reality of underdevelopment through practical approaches. The students were encouraged to visit the slums and informal settlements and to address the urban reality.

The attitude toward Brazilian underdevelopment was part of the criticism directed at Brasília, the federal capital built from 1956 to 1961. Brasília was an icon of Brazilian modernity and was severely criticized by two architects from the young generation, Sérgio Ferro (1938) and Rodrigo Lefèvre (1938–1984), who were faculty members in the Santos school leading an important report on informality during their activities there. The report showed the majority of the slums in the shanty-towns were owned by workers and were built by the community. The results were interpreted by Francisco de Oliveira (1933) in 1972, who pointed out that the ownership of the slums reduced the worker's cost of living, leading to their own wages being depressed. On the other hand the informality had been central to guaranteeing the overexploitation of workers, in which Brazil's selective modernization and inequalities were rooted. Oliveira's economic analysis was a benchmark of the role of informal settlements in Brazilian economy.

A Plan for a Migrants Neighborhood: A Radical Democracy in São Paulo City

Migrants arriving in droves in São Paulo metropolis from the poorest regions of the country fed the growth of informal settlements in the peripheral areas. Between 1970 and 1980 the migrants reached 3.6 million people, and they frequently didn't find jobs or even shelters.

Lefèvre presented a neighborhood migrants plan in his PhD thesis in 1981. The thesis was entitled *Projeto de um acampamento de obras: uma utopia* (Proposal for a Building Work Camp: A Utopia) and envisioned a social management plan to deal with the migrants. According Lefèvre's proposal the migrants would be divided in groups of two thousand people, which would then be distributed in transitional shelters provided by the state in the places they would be settled. In the transitional shelters there would be an interdisciplinary team to receive the group of migrants. The architects in the team would lead a collective proposal for a new building to accommodate the building site and the school of construction, both part of the work/learn proposal. The group would start the process of constructing their own neighborhood in the city, deciding their priorities and how to organize themselves (Lefèvre 1981, p. 253).

The group producing their own place to live—their home and neighborhood together—would also develop a sense of community; and through the building-site school, they would acquire the knowledge and qualifications to be employed in the civil construction sector. Thus the building-site school would play a key role in the assimilation of migrants into the urban fabric through improving the sense of belonging in the new urban neighborhood and qualifying its dwellers to have formal jobs and finally to be assimilated in the urban economy. Lefèvre presented the proposal as a transitional solution for the issues of the growth of migrants and poverty in São Paulo metropolitan zone in the nineteen-eighties (Lefèvre 1981, p. 3, 263).

The proposal of **self-built and self-managed** communities 2.2.1 ◄ would also work politically. The migrants would determine their own lives and communities, allowing them to claim their place in the political arena in the future. The idea was to increase awareness of their own needs and to stimulate their ability to be protagonists in achieving their goals, initially through the building-site school proposal, and subsequently through political engagement. Lefèvre was a reader of Paulo Freire, an important Brazilian pedagogue who developed a methodology to literacy for adults in the early nineteen-sixties. Freire's methodology was based on "problem-situations" to induce adults in achieving Brazilian formal language skills and concurrently achieving political rights, because illiterates were forbidden to vote. Lefèvre had quoted Freire several times in his thesis to explain the ideas of utopia and popular protagonism he mentioned in the text. According to Lefèvre the migrants' settlements were the "problem-situation" defined by Freire as a key element to start the pedagogic process of political engagement to achieve the right of the city. The assistance team who will initially receive the migrants would only provide the elements requested by the group to help them to address their own situation.

Lefèvre was an architect of single houses, but also had led huge teams at a construction company where he had designed hospitals, airports, and public buildings in Brazil, Africa, and Portugal. Despite all his contributions in architectural design it was the social utopia presented in his doctoral thesis that became his legacy for future generations. He linked his technical knowledge of design and the Brazilian social utopia of popular protagonism, pointing out a new way to produce the Brazilian city under poverty and informality. The technical assistance combined with Freire's pedagogy would transform the migrants and peripheral dwellers into the worthy producers of the São Paulo metropolis under a new pattern of city growth and new conception of the modernization process toward a radical democracy in Brazil under poverty. Although Lefèvre's proposal has never been implemented, it influenced architects since the nineteen-eighties, who turned to assist the popular and organized dwellers movement in

2.5.1

the period which urban poverty had grown mainly in the metropolitan zones.

The organized urban movements became one of the most significant political powers in the transition to democracy in 1985. They had an important role in the approval of the urban law in Brazil, which was introduced by the 1988 constitution and defined in 2001 by the federal law called Estatuto da Cidade (City Statute). The federal law was a success for both the organized urban movements and the generation of architects that supported them. It guaranteed—in terms of the law—the right to the city in Brazil.

The Pitfalls of the Participatory Process in the Democratic Period
The City Statute law in Brazil requires all the cities with over twenty thousand inhabitants to develop its master plan through a participatory process. The master plan defines urban development according to social interests to guarantee the welfare of the city's citizens. Once approved, the master plan becomes law, allowing the city government to force the urban landowners to follow the guidelines defined by it.

The planning authorities develop master plans through direct public consultancy, whose results are debated in public. However, despite the good intentions of the planning authorities the promise of social and individual prosperity cannot work easily in contemporary cities. The recognition of the legitimacy of conflicts between different urban groups—and their different visions for future for the cities—would be the first step to consolidating urban planning beyond the participatory planning process based on direct public consultancy and would be a valid communicative action for change that really improves democratic experiments in urban management (Mouffe 1992, pp. 1–14).

Fostering Advocacy in the City Management Experiments
To improve the critical approaches in the urban management experiments that were going on in São Paulo metropolis within the frame of the master plan revision in 2014, both the city government and the universities convened a number of workshops. The Itaim Paulista workshop Estudos Urbanos SP: Novas Linhas de Mobilidade (Urban Studies SP: New Routes of Mobility) led by the DAAD/CAPES cooperation between the HafenCity University (HCU) and Instituto de Arquitetura e Urbanismo (IAU) of University of São Paulo from March 18 to March 26, 2014 was part of these initiatives.[1]

1 The workshop was led by professor Renato Anelli (IAU USP) and Martin Kohler (Hafencity Universität, Hamburg). It was part of the co-operation that begun in 2009 as part of the German contribution to the 8th São Paulo International Biennale of Architecture.

Itaim Paulista was the eastern-most neighborhood in São Paulo city. The area is sized 21.7 square kilometers, in which there are 300,000 inhabitants; that makes it one of the densest and most populated administrative regions of São Paulo city, with 17,195 inhabitants per square kilometer. Although Itaim Paulista is located next to the Tietê River's environmental protection area and is crossed by six creeks, it has one of the lowest rates of vegetation per inhabitant, which increases the effects of air pollution and forms heat islands in the eastern part of the city.

The HCU-IAU workshop focused on the João Neri bus corridor, 2.7.3 ▶ which would improve the Itaim Paulista mobility system through its connection to the city center and the surrounding cities in the metropolitan zone. The results were shown through a proposal for a new approach in peripheral urban development based on a green bus corridor. Beyond the urban design proposal the studies made by the workshop group had identified conflicts between the mobility planning system and the environmental protection areas along the creeks; and conflicts triggered by the evictions needed to improve the mobility system, which would affect damaging the local economy. The debate fostered by the team pointed out the limits of the participatory planning policy within the framework of the São Paulo master plan revision (Anelli and Leitão 2014).

In 2015 São Judas University held the II São Paulo Meeting: Planning by Conflicts to study the challenges of Itaim Paulista local government. The studies included interviews with local government and engaged citizens; documentation of the creeks; a historical study of the place; and the monitoring of the regional plan approved in 2016. The studies involved architecture and urbanism students, some of whom lived in the Itaim Paulista neighborhood. The results focused on producing technical support for the engaged community to participate in the janitorial activities and to produce urban furniture. The ongoing project is opening new understandings on the place of civil society in the local government in São Paulo city neighborhoods and also identifying the difficulties in applying the planning system approved in the last term of Fernando Haddad, major of São Paulo from 2013 to 2016, who fostered the participatory process in the planning system. The difficulties in promoting the integrative planning system inside of the administrative levels of municipal bureaucracy and in mobilizing the key civil society players in the peripheral neighborhoods to foster the debate on urban development is appearing in

2.5.1

this case study as the main obstacles within the planning system to improve the urban democracy experiment in Brazil. On the other hand the civil engagement at all levels of the production of the city is a huge phenomenon also noted in this on-going empirical study.

References

Anelli, R. and A. Leitão (2014). *A. Corredores Ambientais Urbanos: desafios para o desenvolvimento do Plano Diretor Estratégico de São Paulo, articulando as escalas metropolitana, regional e local.* São Paulo, III Enanparq (Anais).

Instituto Brasileiro de Geografia e Estadística (IBGE) (2007). *Censo demográfico 1940–2000. Estatísticas do século XX.* Rio de Janeiro.

Freire, P. (1980). *Conscientização. Teoria e Prática da Libertação.* São Paulo.

Lefèvre, R. (1981). "Um acampamento de obra: uma utopia." PhD dissertation, Faculty of Architecture and Urbanism, University of São Paulo .

Mouffe, C., ed. (1992). *Dimensions of Radical Democracy: Pluralism, Citizenship and Community.* London.

Oliveira, F. de (1972). "A Economia Brasileira: crítica à razão dualista." *Estudos Cebrap.* São Paulo. pp. 4–82.

Santagada, S. (1990). "A situação social no Brasil nos anos 80." *Indicadores Econômicos* 17.4: pp. 121–143.

Instituto Brasileiro de Geografia e Estadística (IBGE) (2010). "Sinopse do Censo Demográfico de 2010." Accessed June 8, 2017. http://www.censo2010.ibge.gov.br/sinopse/index.php?dados=11&uf=00.

Sociological Glances on the "Social Turn" in Architecture and Design

Hanna Göbel/Monika Grubbauer/Anna Richter

The so-called social turn—the rejection of expert knowledge in favor of non-experts' participation, self-organization, and improvisation techniques—in architecture and design practices and debates has not only opened up potentialities in a number of disciplinary fields and projects, but also attracted critical attention by sociologists concerned with a perceived invasion into their very matter of concern. The social presents a strong yet often-unquestioned category in a number of architecture- and design-related discussions and practices, suggesting participatory, just, and inclusive procedures and some kind of positive impact on local communities. The precise meaning and the normative dimension of the social in such discourses and practices are far from clear, though. Sometimes used interchangeably as qualifier and quality, the social figures also as a placeholder for entities as diverse as civil society, community, initiatives, gatherings, as well as the wider public. Our concern with the alleged social turn is the sometimes inadvertent, sometimes intended confusion of the social as descriptor and the social as normative judgment, that is, lived relations between people, things, places, ideas versus distinctions from traditional architecture and urban design projects (see the recent Special Feature in *City* 21.6). This results in three critical glances on the recent debates' constellations of the social:

1. The social in social sciences traditionally served as a means for critical inquiry relating to class and class conflict, addressing

2.5.2

political questions about participation and inequality, for instance, in social housing. Having gained a more embodied, material, and practice-based connotation in social science debates, and particularly in architecture and design contexts, the social no longer primarily refers to capitalist and power relations, but has come to be associated with and used as a shorthand reference to community involvement, bottom-up approaches, and DIY practices. This often produces a range of new and productive interdisciplinary collaborations and projects but reflects little on the political economy of investigated practices.

2. Another issue is the often small and local scale on which social architecture and design projects (temporarily) take place. Paradoxically, although concerned quite explicitly with social benefits, the affirmative self-reference to small scale also offers convenient ways of not having to engage with the broader political, cultural, and economic context beyond a specific project in substantial ways. Furthermore talking about social projects rhetorically allows displacing the anti-social conditions in all their complexity (privatization, developer-led planning), ascribing the latter to forces seemingly beyond reach (for example, "market forces," gentrification) and delegating its examination to other disciplines and realms in a rather naïve way.

3. The social turn also offers a welcome and timely opportunity to reflect on the "socializing" of architecture and design, as there is clearly a need for making building practices more accessible for community building and useful for members of society who are not part of the investor-client posse. The involvement of local communities is not only a question of agency but also depends on expanding tools and methods 2.2.1 ◄ of operation. The toolkit of architects and designers now includes a range of diverse methods such as interviews and story-telling, game-playing, mapping techniques, collaborative workshops, guides and manuals, public events, and the use of social media. Practitioners are beginning to engage with communities in participatory processes as part of "tactical learning" experiences (McFarlane 2011) of marginalized groups as well as dialogic forms of urban democracy. These implementations— if they don't fall into the affirmative trap of self-celebratory projection—can possibly serve to

question the top-down and unsustainable paradigms of current urbanism.

We argue that rather than focusing on the social turn in architecture and design, scholars, activists, architects, planners, and designers need to critically engage with the existing anti-social urbanism and its constellations due to which such so-called social projects and the accompanying discourses are emerging.

References

McFarlane, C. (2011). "The City as a Machine for Learning." *Transactions of the Institute of British Geographers* 36.3: pp.360–376. doi: 10.1111/j.1475-5661.2011.00430.x.

Richter, A., H. Göbel and M. Grubbauer (2017). "Introduction to the Special Feature: Designed to Improve? The Makings, Buildings and Aesthetics of 'Social' Architecture and Design." *City* 21.6: pp. 769–778.

The *Other* Engagement: A Critique of the "Co-"

Tatjana Schneider

I have just come back from a conference (Architecture Connects 2017) that sought to explore "architectural education and research that collaborates with people, organizations, and other disciplines in real world contexts for their mutual benefit." What we saw were presentations of projects that involved people in games and consultation events. We were shown photographs and films showing spatial interventions that came out of the collaboration with one or more community interest groups, had discussions on the methodologies of engagement, and listened to people arguing for the need to think about appropriate educational models in the context of twenty-first-century challenges and crises. Again and again, we heard people emphasize the need for co-production between different actors in order to get successful projects; different presenters mentioned the need to work with communities rather than for them; and many others spoke about the necessity of situated working, situated learning, and situated doing. The underlying message of many contributions was about the need for an architecture that recognizes the desires and wishes of its users. Hence, many of the projects we saw focused not on the final product but on processes that didn't have clear briefs as a starting point. Instead, concepts for a space developed over long(er) periods of time through collaboration and negotiation with a whole range of actors.

These discussions are nothing new—not even in the field of architecture and urban design. Indeed, they have been debated intensely since the nineteen-fifties at the very least. Think, for example, about N. John Habraken and his seminal contribution in the field of housing through the inclusion of users in the production and reproduction of their spaces. Or, Oskar and Zofia Hansen who talked—from an intensely architectural point of view—about the need for the development of user participation and flexibility in buildings beyond the purely technological. Of course, many other approaches could be added that were contesting either a top-down production of space that did not give room to the everyday needs of its inhabitants, or a tabula rasa approach that favored large-scale infrastructures and personal car-based mobility over localized and situated forms of planning. Here, Jane Jacobs could also be named as someone whose work on the need for sociospatial diversity, mixed-use, and an activation of the streets at different times of the day fueled some of the most fervent and prominent battles against displacement of existing communities through planning in the nineteen-sixties. And, in other fields, too, theorists, writers, and critical thinkers have devoted much of their work to a critique of a static, nonsituated, and product-focused understanding of architecture. The much-referred-to late French writer Henri Lefebvre comes to mind here, too, who, again and again, raged against the architect's abstraction of space and, instead, emphasized the role of the user in making and remaking space through a continuous process of production.

At this point one might ask why it might be necessary to bring up these historical references again? Are those not outdated at the very least? Arguably, a lot of examples from around the globe show that architecture, urban design, and planning have moved on. The 2016 Architecture Biennial in Venice might be a case in point here, where practices that emphasize incremental planning, people-centered approaches, and projects that foregrounded ethical and ecologically driven agendas took center stage. Consider this together with the conference I attended and supplement it with other experiences, publications, and projects that each and every one of us knows and could add to the long list of this other engagement with the mechanisms of producing space: the sum of all this might be seen as an indicator that, undeniably and definitely, space is increasingly produced by focusing on the citizen-led, bottom-up, and democratizing processes and practices of production.

And yet, there is much about this that troubles me intensely. It seems, too, that I'm not alone with that feeling of unease; more recently, it is has been gathering momentum in the field of critical urban studies too. But let me be a little bit more specific here and classify my discomfort. Claims about the transformational potential of this way of working are not scrutinized sufficiently—neither in education, practice, or the media. We find statements about the political and social dimensions of a project that, when looked at more closely, might be a one-off, one-day, urban-furniture intervention. Overstatement of the success of projects, whether hyper-local or network-based, has almost become the norm. The proliferation of festivals and events around the topics of everything "co-" is no longer questioned. And, on top of that, there is widespread historical amnesia. Yes, the production of space and the challenges that surround it are different today, the actors are different, and technologies have shifted; however, a historical awareness might certainly point to some of the pitfalls or limitations of some interventions.

Take this short text here as a plea to embrace critique and maybe even pessimism as a tool of operation. Losing those tools seems absurd, even downright dangerous. Process-based and other forms of learning that are linked in the field of theory to debates around empowerment and democratization are not served by attempts to iron out or neglect discussions on power—which include, for all involved, a much more rigorous engagement with ownership of as well as access to land and resources. When much discussion centers on processes (understood as the counterpart to product) as a key aspect to reach "a better world," this is an appeal for more criticality around those very processes and the context they are embedded in. In order to confront a-historicity, quick and nonjustifiable claims, interventions that are organized simply for the sake of doing, as well as retreats into happy project bubbles that only serve the agendas of neoliberalization, we—as citizens— need not only to listen to but also produce more friction. We need to make things more difficult and complex rather than more simple; we need to question statements and assumptions rather than taking them at face value. This is not easy at all—especially in a context where urgent questions might also need urgent answers. To meet immediate housing needs, for example, with a response that suggests land-tax reform is just as problematic. And yet, it is those bigger interdependent contexts of politics and ecologies as well as finance and cultures that are important for any type and way of engaging. Ignoring those frameworks and their way of operation will lead to the production of Band-Aids that cover social or spatial "wounds," but never understand the symptoms of why an issue might be there in the first instance. Finding ways that bring together those questions of structure and systems with societal questions is therefore necessary. Doing it "co-" might be one way. But, fundamentally and more importantly, ambitions and their consequences need to be articulated. If this "co-" shall become something that can directly and essentially address global crises, producing friction—continuing to question why, for whom, and with whom things and spaces are produced—it is key to move beyond the current state of indifference towards everything and anything "co-."

2.6. Improvisation

- 1 Option Improvisation: Why It Is Critical to Conceptualize Improvisation in Architecture and Urban Design

- 2 Art and Urban Development: Is It Dangerous for Nonartists to Look at Art Practice When Considering How to Act as Urban Designers?

Option Improvisation: Why It Is Critical to Conceptualize Improvisation in Architecture and Urban Design

Christopher Dell

This article tackles the conceptualization of improvisation in the context of urban design. It suggests improvisation as a programmatic notion that offers the possibility to think of the city differently. It argues that the key aspect that renders the concept of improvisation useful in architecture and urban design is its option to approach contingency in urban situations constructively. I will outline what it takes to access this option, beginning with an understanding of the city as contingent and improvisational relations of actors, actions, things, and sites. The integration of the concept of improvisation in architecture and urban design seeks to overcome an understanding of the city occupied with the production of the city, which, I argue, falls short in architecture's and urban design's modes of being propositional about the future. A logical progression of such an approach lies in the notion of representation. Representations of improvisation cannot be understood as isolated denoting signs, but representations themselves

1.3.2 ◀

2.6.1

constitute a practice of improvisational writings and readings of the city. Its topology depicts the structure of the relationality between actors, actions, things, and sites in specific urban situations. Given the fact that one might be surprised to see improvisation connected with planning disciplines, this text should not only be seen as the supposition of a paradox but it can also itself be seen as an exemplification of improvisation. Not only by form but also by content, the motifs of this article take their departure from improvisation as compositional strategy in music. This strategy can be generally defined as the constant rearranging and reconfiguring of motific structures in relation to a form-making process during a musical performance. This process is conditioned, determined by, and transformed under the specific material, social, and spatial conditions of each performance, thereby serially adding structural constellations in the making.

Inspired by the characteristic of improvisation to let its form develop out of structural motifs, this article unfolds its argumentation by developing four motifs. The first motif sheds light on the

◄ 2.2.2   fact that the spatial turn—proposing new ways of theorizing the space—has expanded the focus of the work and theories of architects, urban designers, and planners by the practices that constitute the city. The motif thereby calls attention to the importance of the definition of these practices. Urban practices also have been on the lead in social sciences, which have coined the umbrella

◄ 2.3.1   term "the production of space" in the effort to define making of the city. Evolving from the contrast of the notion of production with the notion of improvisation, the second motif argues that in this discourse the use of the notion of production falls short in describing the contingency and nonlinearity of urban practices. Given the task of tackling disorder and contingency, the third motif evolves around the question of how improvisation positions itself to order or constitutes an "other" of order. Once an improvisation is over and no longer acting directly upon reality, a gap occurs—the improvisation loses its place exactly where representation begins. The fourth motif, which follows from these thoughts, leads to the epistemological question: can one represent improvisation? With this motif I introduce diagrammatics as the representational mode of improvisation. Vice versa, improvisation is the action model that is needed to understand diagrammatics. What is more, improvisation puts diagrammatics in use while it organizes itself in a diagrammatic way.

Motif 1: From Object to Process

"The unthinking acceptance within urban studies that time and space act simply as objective, unvariant, external containers for the urban scene is now collapsing ... In this perspective, social ordering occurs through complex efforts of both humans and non-humans to engage other actors through performative actions that are fundamentally heterogeneous and impossible to generalise" (Amin and Graham 1997, pp. 411–429).

With these words the English geographers Ash Amin and Stephen Graham describe how the disciplines of planning, architecture, and urban design have gone through a radical change in recent years. This change has taken place in respect to the interpretation of the city as a spatial entity. Foremost inspired by what has been labeled as "spatial turn" in the social sciences, there is evidence of a clear shift from reading the city as an object to city as a process. Understood in these terms a definition of space takes rise in which space is regarded as a social product.

To understand space as coming about through social action not only challenges traditional notions of space—conventionally it was either seen as material that is contained in a form or as a priori condition of form coming into being—but it also puts forward new ways of designing, of planning practice and methods. Drawing attention away from a tabula rasa planning to research on and in support of the constitutive effects of urban action, analysis searches to reveal yet undiscovered links or relationships in given urban situations. Foregrounding action in the design furthermore proposes to read the making of the city through forms of structured mediation that do not only lead to the generation of built objects but also to new constellations of acting humans, things, and discourses on sites.

Understanding space in this way implies that the urban can no longer be generalized as a fixed or closed form. Far from being systems with their own internal coherence, contemporary cities have to be regarded as open forms. One might argue that rather than having to do with urban space as a neutral entity, it is indicated that architecture and urban design today are presented with space as a contingent and pluralistic epistemological field. Not only does this shift thematize the loss of objectivity and neutrality of space, but it also addresses its relational becoming. As indicated, this becoming should be understood as a relational constellation between humans and nonhumans—that means things, discourses, sites—which not only constitutes but also brings forth urban space by performative actions.

To say that these actions are performative signifies that the actions are not linear but nonlinear, that is to say, contingent. Why is that so? It is the confrontation of humans and things that constitutes the main driver of contingency here. To assert that things act should not be read as a mysterious humanization of objects. Quite the contrary, what is indicated here is that things do something in the sense that they interfere with, affect, constrain, or enable human action. Indeed, this doing is neither linear nor rational but the causation and formation of contingent constellations.

2.6.1

At the same time, research into the dimension of the city as a contingent product raises fundamental questions about the representations that are used when one thinks, talks, negotiates about, or shows aspects of the urban. As for any issue such as the city to become epistemological as well as political, there is a need to translate and transpose the issue to a scientific or political engagement by representation.

Motif 2: From Production to Improvisation

However, there are plenty of puzzling aspects missing in the discourse on the urban. For instance there is a remarkable absence of critical research on modes of action and their structural constitution. In addition to that I will argue that critical reflections on performativity and its contingent and indeterminate character are very rare among urbanists. When tracking the progression and varying orientations of the critique of traditional approaches, it is crucial to understand the drawn conclusions about what has been termed and widely acknowledged as the "production of space" by rethinking the notion of action itself.

Consequently, the second motif evolves around the argument that thinking the urban through the lens of improvisation calls for opening up and reconsidering the conception of the making of space and its unspoken ideologies while taking into account the understanding of space as social product. This is not an offer for an all-encompassing methodology and strays rather far from a manual for how to act. The potential here might be for a renewed conceptualization of action in relation to the city as being its resource. What is offered here might be an approach to do research by both critically intervening in and representing spatial relations. So, I argue, stimulating the renegotiation of spatial contexts appears within reach again. Improvisation invites the researchers to rethink the way space is relationally produced, to reveal latent or potential elements, structures, relationships, and material and social conditions through the active positioning of oneself in an affirmative criticality. Yet, improvisation of space cannot be understood outside its relational connotation—not positive in terms of a better planning—but in terms of articulating constructive action in contingency in alliances, projects, and institutions. The complex ramifications of improvisation as technology, when exposed, questions simplifying binary oppositions by putting forward the relational practice in the field of diverging and conflicting interests and forces that constitute the city. Improvisation aims at redistributing and reconfiguring these forces on a working plane.

Without going too deep in the argumentation, one can sum up that the theorization of production puts forward a strong characterization of production as teleological. This argumentation involves the positing of a goal, and therefore a goal-positing consciousness—what is called a plan in architecture and urban design—to production, a goal that can be imagined in the realm of the intelligible and then acted out in a result-oriented fashion in the realm of the sensible.

Tackling this argumentation sheds light on the discrepancy between the notion of production and the above-explained shift in theorizing space. While its teleological meaning carries implications of a tabula rasa concept, the term production lacks criticality towards the articulation of space as borders and notions of territory in particular in relation to the spatial unfolding of action as its nonteleological aspects, which means that one should reject the notion of production of space as inadequate to describe the contemporary city.

Motif 3: From Order to the Other of Order

The third motif argument considers that the epistemological status of improvisation is that of a paradox. First of all, it bears a conflict between order and disorder, thus improvisation cannot and doesn't want to wholly pacify the doingness aspects of the urban because it is the source of its movement. This paradox is described best by Lefebvre, to whom "the urban reality today looks more like chaos and disorder—albeit that one conceals a hidden order—than an object. Rather than being an object that can be examined through contemplation, the reality of the urban phenomenon would be a virtual object" (Lefebvre 2003, pp. 57–58). To say this points to the fact that improvisation of space at the same time disrupts and conceals a hidden order. The "blending" of order and disorder described here is never a merging. For the disruptive force of improvisation to be preserved, it must somehow remain external to the order that it would disrupt. Yet improvisation as pure "externality" would preclude the necessary "meeting of the heterogeneous" that enacts the urban. I argue that improvisation must be "other" to order, but not purely "other." This otherness leads to the condition that all representations of improvisation are driven by nonrepresentational layers.

In that sense improvisation does not only pose a problem of understanding the city in the traditional meaning; it also changes the relation of the practice of thinking and the city. What improvisation confronts in the epistemology of the city above all and in a unique way is the generative function and capacity of symbolic form. To read, to think, to understand ultimately means to change. It is never only reflective on a passive referent but also recursive in interaction with the referent. Put simply, one can account for the fact that all it takes to change the city is reading a single urban situation as improvisation and creating a new symbolic form for it that contains representational and nonrepresentational layers while being structurally framed. One can say that only in symbolic forms—words, thoughts, images, imaginaries—does the city present itself to our thinking; but any making of symbolic forms enacts a differentiation of the relationship between thinking and the city. Read in this perspective, the principle of the symbolic form turns out to be not arbitrariness but contingency. By improvisation, the symbolic form transforms within a continually changing structural framework that is formally open and functionally underdetermined. Its framework is full of potentialities while being constituted by its structural ties to thinking and the city. This brings to mind that improvisation

2.6.1

and structure are not opposites. Always operating beyond representation, structure delivers the grammar of a situation. Its transformative potential is brought to light by improvisation: improvisation is the mode of action that uses structure as material for iterative and recursive reshuffling, rearranging, and reconfiguring of the elements of a given spatial situation. Concerning its temporality, there is something retroactive about structure. Far from providing a predetermined cause, it rather constitutes a temporal entity in which improvisation constructs what retroactively is discovered as determination.

Motif 4: From Diagram to Diagrammatic Play
Evidently, it has become standard repertoire in the urban discourse to assert a logic to space-producing actions. But one cannot speak of such a logic without representing and considering urban practices and their representations as a way of conceptual understanding. Yet a critical discussion of the modes of the representation of action is still lacking. Instead, I locate my resources for thinking about the representation of action on the observation of the architectural and urban design practice. One can indicate a change in representation procedures that somehow anticipates the improvisational turn—without ever mentioning this notion—and that is articulated foremost by a rise of diagrammatic reorganization of representation. (Dell 2016a)

This diagrammatic field can be specified in three categories. The first category refers to the diagram as a sign-type of icons. Principally icons are signs that denote their referent by some sort of similarity. The characteristic aspect of the diagram, however, is that it bases its iconic function on not a formally representational but a nonrepresentational structural mode of similarity. That means its representation is not directed to the fixed form of the referent but relates to its internal structure "in terms of interrelated parts, facilitating reasoning possibilities" (Stjernfeldt 2007, p. ix). What reappears here in the semiotic register is the above-indicated shift in improvisation from arbitrariness to contingency. The diagram's iconic function is founded on the contingent structural similarity between signified, signifier, and the sign's referent. Consequently, far from ending at the function of mere decoding, the diagram enables and provokes reasoning processes as well as raises epistemological questions on how one composes knowledge with, through, and by signs and sign-making.

The diagrammatic mode in which current urban research organizes its representations as heterogeneous, relational, and hybrid constellations of photographs, figure-ground plans, drawings, scribblings, texts, diagrams, collages, and renderings constitutes the second category of diagrammatics. Its denotations of urban situations makes use of the sign strategy of the diagram—the structural reference as displaying the topology and relationality of the parts it depicts—but transposing it from the sign to the organization of an arrangement of signs. This transposition brings the composition of the representational space as a relational arrangement of representations into focus—traditionally the diagrammatic visual organization on a page of a book or journal, on a sequence of pages, in a composition of a whole book or journal, on display in an exhibition, or the composition of an arrangement of displays in an exhibition. This is why one can say that the second category problematizes the composition of the spaces of representation as relational and in their relationality.

The question of the relationality of the spaces of diagrammatic representations leads to the third category, indicating what Krämer has described as "Diagrammspielen" (Krämer 2013, pp. 162–174). Drawing on the spatial analysis of diagrams, Krämer points out that all reasoning with and about diagrams—in which, in a complex manner, iconic and linguistic, sense and sensible, the explicit and the implicit interrelate—depends on a mode of a historically informed way of working with diagrams. This mode can be best comprehended as an improvisatory playing with and relating of the disperse and heterogeneous orderings of diagrammatic structure, which in itself contains and demands specific capacities and knowledge. In other words, to work with diagrams, to experience and experiment with their epistemological structures and their reconfiguring capacities means to improvise with signs (Dell 2016b).

Epilogue: Towards the Improvisational Organization of a Propositional Body of Work

A growing number of researchers use diagrammatic formats that combine heterogeneous materials and methods apparently due to the improvisational dimension of the research, the participation of different actors and agents in interplay and interaction taking on a new relevance for the engagement with the investigation in urban situations. (See exemplary article "Spatial Agency" in 2.2.1 ◄ this volume.) This development highlights changes in design practices over recent years, moving from designing objects to designing research processes and their representations in the context of action orientation and improvisation. Thus the urban research manifests itself as an orchestral arrangement of transdisciplinary actors in spatiotemporal relations, which, as such, is structurally organized in a time-based mode. While the time aspect grows insignificantly, along with the due analysis of time as a factor in research action and as an opportunity to bring aspects of relational action into focus, space nevertheless remains the primary reference category in the urban discourse.

2.6.1

Based on the above-listed arguments I wanted to denote why it is important to study improvisation in architecture and urban design. Improvisation—understood here as a technological, sociomaterial urban practice—sets the conditions for the permanent reoccurrence of the city as an event. Based on this concept my article sheds light on the fact that on a conceptual level an alteration in understanding the city is indicated, shifting from the production of space to the improvisation of space. Nonetheless, the research practice thematized here is far from negating *the plan*. But rather than beginning with a result-oriented plan, it puts the emphasis on *planning in the making*. The orientation toward process and open form gains its specific character in relation to a broader understanding of action and the production of space and to the temporal and discursive framing of processes and their mediation. Above all improvisation means a type of action that analyzes, works with, and creates relationships between actors and agents. Not least, the debate opens perspectives on questions concerning the social characteristics of urban space. At issue are possibilities for using the improvisational perspective as a means of rethinking and reimagining the city, subjecting it to revision in a process of constant rearranging, redefining, and redesign.

Taking the above into consideration, my text differentiates between two modes of improvisation: first is the repair mode, and second is the technical mode. The first mode is the one that is traditionally used to indicate when a planned action went wrong. The second mode I call improvisation technology. The word "technology" here refers to its etymological background, interpreting "techne" as art of doing and knowing how and "logos" as form of knowledge. The technological mode deals with how the improvisation is historically classified as a procedure in the current situation as a practice of urban life, in other words, how it is historically conditioned. It very significantly draws focus to those techniques of organization that combine, connect, mix, and fuse. Thus it is not only the medialities and materialities that intertwine and enter into relational interplay with and among each other, but also structure and action, times and spaces. The context of such crossings reveals an explicit improvisational field of action that constructively undermines or opens up the rigid borders of the structure-versus-agency dichotomy, where so-called spontaneous actions stand against structural norms. Instead, improvisation technology aims at a formal approach that works nonnormatively with norms and diagrammatically with structures. This is the starting point for the various paths and forms of investigation presented here. They don't try to represent a homogenous whole or describe a full circle but wander different lines, in which the reoccurring and the different converge in a historical trace of thinking and working at a specific variant of a theory of space.

References

Amin, A. and S. Graham (1997). "The Ordinary City." *Transactions of the Institute of British Geographers* 22.4: pp. 411–429.

Dell, C. (2016a). *Stadt als offene Partitur.* Zürich.

Dell, C. (2016b). *Die Epistemologie der Stadt.* Bielefeld.

Lefebvre, H. (2003). *The Urban Revolution.* Minneapolis.

Stjernfeldt, F. (2007). *Diagrammatology.* Dordrecht.

Krämer, S. (2013). "Diagrammatisch." *Rheinsprung. Zeitschrift für Bildkritik* 11/2013: pp. 162–174. http://rheinsprung11.unibas.ch/archiv/ausgabe-05/glossar/diagrammatisch.htm.

2.6.1

Art and Urban Development: Is It Dangerous for Nonartists to Look at Art Practice When Considering How to Act as Urban Designers?

Liza Fior

Art has been given a place in urban development and design in the last thirty years, as in the campaign for 1 percent of capital budgets for development to be spent on art. But its place is generally just that, a minority share in any discussion: 1 percent of time, 1 percent of listening, 1 percent of cubic meters. Conversely curators and funding agencies can inflate this contribution through mythologizing and instrumentalizing the contribution the art project makes.

The tedium of listening to the practitioner as compared to the theoretician in a conference setting can be the practitioner's very show-and-tell approach—"and then we did this and then we did that." The relationship between urban design and art is not something that consciously shapes our practice, yet it looks like it does.

For this contribution, I will discuss muf's work and the way that artists' ways of doing things play out in muf's practice, looking at projects that are not art commissions, but instead are projects on which artists have worked.

Naming

Renaming as a method, as in the as-found space, where the initial design move is simply the stating of the properties of the existing as a way of describing its value.

Examples include the derelict railway line renamed as park in Making Space in Dalston (2008); the street renamed as public space in Street Interrupted (2012), where the transformation was signified by a mature tree being placed in the middle of the street; and, most recently, the positioning of an illuminated nose in front of an informal cultural center (Jordbro Kulturhuset, Sweden) due for demolition and replacement by a "real" cultural center. The nose, fixed to a broken light column, states, "*This* is the cultural center in front of your nose," while also acting as a street lamp.

Enactment

Playing things out through inhabitation is performative, open-ended, exploratory. In muf's artist-led projects the potency of the performance-based work is clear; experiences, unlike objects, cannot be taken from you.

Examples can be found in projects such as Art Camp, where groups of children working over the course of a week in parallel with artists explored buildings and sites just before they were demolished or developed. The children and artists were the last inhabitants, and in their occupation describe the value of open-ended space, something that is a rare commodity in London in 2017.

Studio Practice

Performative, open-ended trials in the same place where a built thing will later be made—it could be said that this makes a site and public realm into a studio.

An example is Ruskin Square, a corporate project where muf is designing the spaces between buildings in an attempt to enrich them with possibilities of multiple use, such as spaces for hundreds of people to gather or one person to escape their colleagues,

2.6.2

or planting that will go a little wild. When we were first commissioned in advance of construction commencing, we enacted the possibilities of the spaces-to-be for a brief period (two years) by negotiating access into the building site, introducing a protected route through a wild garden and to a series of spaces including an open air room and cricket nets. This was a means to up the ante for the developer, the client, and the local authority, demonstrating the value of social spaces by acclimatizing these stakeholders to real people hanging out behind the hoarding line, within a wild biodiverse setting.

Authorship

1.6.1 ◄

Craft is a form of authorship. The most common contract for both public and commercial projects is design-build where the contractor takes responsibility for building a scheme in a way which is not entirely faithful to the design drawings. This contractual process can lead to a flattening, an approximation of intention. But if part of a scheme is authored as an art project, it can bring a necessary unevenness of care and precision to this approximation. (It can also just amplify the mismatch between the two.)

Examples where intentional unevenness has worked mixing contractors and craftsmen include projects such as Barking Town Square and Altab Ali Park.

Durational Work

Durational work, where time itself is the medium or subject, could 1.2.2 ◄ be said to be obvious in its application to urban design. But seldom is time itself foregrounded, nor how long it takes to plan, to draw, to negotiate, and to build.

Feminist Art Practice

The **personal** is political—and the work you make can be shaped by this fact. Awareness of where you sit in terms of power relations is further refined if you apply an intersectional reading of your role, considering gender but alongside this, race or class or education. This awareness can enrich your understanding of what might be lacking or added in your reading of place, and also enrich the proposals you make.

Relational Aesthetics

Critic Lucy Lippard used the phrase "serial monogamy" to describe the perils of an artist with a participative practice entering situations, making relationships, and then leaving. The question of what your role is, what you owe, what you leave, and in what ways your work is a co-production is one that is worth asking. It is true that spending time at a site brings a greater accuracy to a project through understanding a place through those who live there, but it's not enough: retaining a relationship post- occupancy brings its own accountability.

1.1.4 ◀

Site-Specificity
Surely it is a no-brainer that urban practice should be site-specific. Those who are au fait with the discipline of master planning know that there is a tendency to apply ideal and standardized systems and geometries onto a place.

muf's methodology of
> "value what's there
> nurture the possible
> define what's missing"

is not anti-ambition, but proposes a pause for breath, thereby imposing a discipline of understanding context before making a response.

On Being Appropriated by the Market
It can ruin lunch to walk the streets of east London, seeing your language of celebration of the fabric and culture of a place being used for its commodification, whether on the sales hoardings or in material language of the architecture itself. It can give the urban designer and architect the experience which the artist knows so well: architects, authors of critical practice, and urban designers— you are implicated, too.

2.6.2

2.7. Multidisciplinarity

- **1** **Multidisciplinary and Generalist Education: Architects Mastering the Brazilian Cities' Growth**

- **2** **Transdisciplinarity: The Basis for the Increase of Urban Knowledge?**

- **3** **"They Came Togather"**
  A Screenplay of an Urban Workshop Encounter

Multidisciplinary and Generalist Education: Architects Mastering the Brazilian Cities' Growth

Renato Anelli

This paper presents a brief history of the relationship between generalist professional duties of the urban planning architect in Brazil and the corresponding qualification structure, with effects on his/her role on the urbanization process.

The Brazilian legislation defines as activity restricted to urban planning architects: "Coordination of multidisciplinary planning team regarding the city plan or layout, master plan, urban requalification plan, urban sector plan, local intervention plan, social interest housing plan, plan for land regularization and preparation of neighborhood impact assessment."[1]

The extension of the duties of urban planning architects, which include from interior architecture to urban and regional planning, corresponds to the conception of the generalist qualification that regulates the architecture and urban planning courses. The correspondence between education and profession dates back to the creation of the Federal Council of Engineering, Architecture, and Agronomy (CREA) in 1933, in the context of the organization of a modern state in Brazil after the Revolution of

1 Council of Architects and Urban Planners (CAU), Resolution No. 51, of 12/7/2013.

2.7.1

1930. At that time, there was an interest in differentiating professional engineers and architects graduated from polytechnic colleges or academies of fine arts from those working in construction, that is, master-builders and contractors. The purpose of the duties set forth in the regulation of professions of engineers, architects, and land surveyors was to introduce the mandatory diploma for the professional activity and did not clarify the specific duties of architects and engineer-architects. In addition to the building project and construction, the legislation also mentioned the performance of urban planning, landscaping, and "great architectural decoration."[2]

The simultaneity with the development of Brazilian modern architecture impregnated the professional and educational with the principles of this movement, particularly the creation of a project system capable of expanding from the scale of the utilitarian object to city planning, going through building projects, urban segments, and landscaping. The principles established and disseminated by the International Modern Architecture Congresses for the European scenario in the interwar period found their own meaning in the fast twentieth-century Brazilian urbanization. Since 1945, the main courses of architecture were integrated as schools in the new high education system of universities.[3] Concurrently, the Brazilian Institute of Architects (IAB) was being consolidated as the main professional organization of architects, spreading out to other capital cities.

From Brasilia to the Metropolitan Complexity Challenge

The Brasília plan competition in 1956–57 depicted the colonizing challenge of planning a capital city in the middle of the hinterlands of the country. The majority of architects handled the program to build a city for five hundred thousand inhabitants. Proposals unveiled the state-of-art of urban planning in Brazil, showing different conceptions comprising scales of a building to that of a city. The architects played a major role in leading teams, in general composed of other architects, engineers of diversified expertise, agronomists, and, to a lesser extent, sociologists, economists, and experts in education and public health.

Lúcio Costa's plan was characterized by the simplicity of its presentation: a typed technical description illustrated by fifteen sketches and a general plan in a 1:25,000 scale. It was chosen in view of what it represented: its symbolic meaning completing the modernist Brazilian project started in the nineteen-twenties.

2 Federal Decree No. 23.569, of 11/12/1933, Article 30.

3 The National School of Fine Arts was incorporated into the University of Brazil in 1945, and the School of Architecture of the city of Belo Horizonte was incorporated into the Federal University of Minas Gerais in 1949. In 1947, the Schools of Architecture and Urban Planning of the University of São Paulo and of the Mackenzie Presbyterian University were created in São Paulo.

However, it should not be omitted that it was incumbent upon the Urbanization Company of the New Capital (NOVACAP), a publicly held company organized in 1956, to develop the plan, further to managing the construction of the city and its infrastructure, and being in charge of managing its utilities. The brief nature of the initial plan was sufficient to define concepts and general schemes, subsequently developed by a complex structure, sufficiently effective to be transformed into the second-most important metropolitan center of Brazil in this century (IBGE 2007).

After the inauguration of Brasília in 1960, the problems in large cities worsened and the country exceeded the limit of 50 percent of the population living in urban areas, pursuant to the 1970 census. In 1963, the IAB proposed new approaches to the problem of cities at the Housing and Urban Reform Seminar, including proposals that urban planning should be linked to regional planning to reduce migration flows to large cities; financing instruments should be created for social services, housing, and urban infrastructure; incentives to new industrialization in building construction would be crucial for mass production; and new strategies that required a new professional profile. This agenda had already been introduced in the main universities of the country, which pressed for new reforms in the education and professional statutes so as to acknowledge that the industrial design, decoration, landscaping, and planning were included in the architect's professional duties. As to professional regulation, architects started a movement of independence in relation to engineers through the failed bill of 1958. This initiative was only successful in 2010, when the Council of Architects and Urban Planners was created (Oliveira 2012, p. 321).

Between the years of 1959 and 1962, the College of Architecture and Urban Planners of the University of São Paulo (FAU USP) went through a reform that introduced the departmental structure in which the teaching of planning, buildings, industrial design, and visual communication was organized in sequences of disciplines within the design department (Contier 2015, pp. 134–143). Together with these disciplines that expanded the scope of architecture, in addition to maintaining disciplines of technological nature, school curricula started to receive contributions from human and social sciences. With the departmentalization institutionalized by the University Reform of 1968, new options for specializing in specificities that unbalanced the generalist unit were then offered. Knowledge and methods from other sciences

2.7.1

enriched the qualification of architects, but introduced new approaches of the large modern architecture and urban planning systems.

By this time, a new law included the planning activity, still on a quite generic basis, between the professional assignments of the architect, engineer, and agronomist engineers, still keeping the overlapping of skills:

"Planning or project, in general, or regions, zones, cities, works, structures, transportation, exploitation of natural resources and development of industrial production and agriculture and cattle raising."[4]

4 Law 5194, of December 24, 1966, Article 7, Item c.

The complexity arising from the growth of cities and the increased social recognition of the architect's activity changed the practice deeply. If until then architects such as Lúcio Costa could devise alone the plan for a whole city in a few lines, over the nineteen-sixties the preparation of integrated development master plans and urban infrastructure network plans mobilized Brazilian and foreign consulting companies, grouping together complex multidisciplinary teams. Apparently, this is when the expression used in the current professional legislation appears, which considers an exclusive assignment of the urban planning architect the "coordination of a multidisciplinary planning team." This refers to a large exchange of experiences among professionals from different areas, and the urban planning grew as a practice and knowledge, even considering that the application of plans has been quite limited and the lack of control over urban grown has remained (Anelli 2012).

▶ 2.8.1

◀ 2.1.1

Certain professionals stood out for the diversified activities, of generalist nature, of their architecture and urban planning companies, such as Jorge Wilheim (1928–2014) and Joaquim Guedes (1932–2008). Both established large offices that exploited the range of professional assignments of the urban planning architect in Brazil.

Jorge Wilheim Consultores Associates (1953) dedicated, since the beginning, to large-scale architectural projects, of which the most recognized one was his proposal for the city of Curitiba in 1965, later developed by Jaime Lerner's team. From the nineteen-eighties, he combined his private activities with the public position of head of planning departments of the city and state of São Paulo.

Joaquim Guedes (graduated FAU USP, 1949) started his career developing architectonic projects and working for the Society of

Graphic and Mecanographic Analyses Applied to Social Complexes (SAGMACS) organized by Louis-Joseph Lebret, an important introducer of European urban planning methods in Brazil. In 1957 he organized his first company, Technical Assistance Services for Municipalities, where he prepared his proposal for Brasília competition. Later on, in 1965, he organized the company Joaquim Guedes and Associates, which would employ a large group of architects in the preparation of master plans and projects of cities of mining companies, such as Caraíba (1976) and Barcarena (1980).

The generalist education enables leadership of these teams of salaried employees, who specialized in a sector within the company.

Bottom-Up Planning and Social Movements Advocacy

However, this large company model did not survive the end of the military regime. On the one hand, the economic crisis reduced the state's demand for projects. On the other hand, the criticism that the centralized and specialized model of developing plans and projects were technocratic progressed, supporting the idea that the bottom-up models would be the most suitable to the return of democracy. As already mentioned by certain authors, what had been supplementary—planning and participation—was now used excluding as opposed categories (Innes and Booher 2004; Koury and Lara 2016).

1.3.2 ◂

The model of a large consulting company grouping together expert professionals and coordinators of multidisciplinary teams went into decay due to its high cost and lack of demand. The economic crisis with a long recession reduced the capacity of public investments, and the adoption of these minimum state policies in the nineteen-nineties relinquished the urban planning practices as they had been built so far.

In these years, the model that thrived was the self-employed professional, who adjust themselves to the opportunities available, frequently bordering on informality and precariousness of agreements. Accordingly, the generalist education was efficient, but in a sense opposite to the previous one, since it allowed for the flexibility required to meet uncertain demands that oscillated according to the development of the economic crisis and political guidance of the government authorities.

1.4.4 ◂

And an uncontrolled expansion of new architecture and urbanism courses[5] had perverse effects on the professional practice, since all of them have legal authority to qualify their graduates as urban planning architects regardless of any subsequent control to

5 The number of architecture and urban planning courses increased to 466 in 2015.

2.7.1

the obtainment of a certificate. The reduction in the compensation level and institutionalization of precarious professional relations was widespread, reducing the technical capacity of the complete professional field. Despite the culturally recognized practice of important names, the majority of professionals worked in a highly competitive, discontinuous, and underpaid market.

In these years, new ways of professional organization arose, of a collective nature, among which are the nongovernmental organizations of technical advisory for social movements organized in collective efforts. Inspiration came from the revolution of 1974 in Portugal. Under the direction of Nuno Portas, the the Local Ambulatory Support Services (SAAL) brought together architects such as Alvaro Siza Vieira and Gonçalo Byrne for the production of housing projects in direct cooperation with social movements for housing. In São Paulo, between 1989 and 1992, under the direction of Erminia Maricato and Nabil Bonduki, the municipal Superintendence of Social Housing organized and financed the movements for housing in associations to exercise the project self-management, construction, and organization of housing complexes. Architects were hired by these associations in two ways: firms of consolidated professionals developed the projects and groups of young architects advised in construction, both with no direct interference of government authorities. Over the nineteen-nineties, this practice became common, even considering the oscillation of politics in the management of cities and states.

The regulation of urban legislation proposed by the Constituent Assembly of 1988 was made effective only thirteen years later, in 2001, as the City Statute (Law No. 10.257). From then on, government authorities required again urban planning services in large scale. However, the dismantling of government planning and project bodies through a implementation of minimum state policies had emptied the capacity of city councils to develop master plans or even to monitor their preparation.

Motivated by the resumption of economic growth between 2003 and 2013, several public institutions hired again professionals for urban planning and management, but they had to seek expert services out of their staff. The focus of these plans was the social participation, and, therefore, they were supported by consultants organized in nongovernmental organizations or university research centers.

Generalist Education and Flexibility

The census conducted by the Council of Architects and Urban Planners in 2012 provided a more accurate profile of areas of work of urban planning architects in Brazil[6] (CAU BR 2012). In spite of the generalist education, the major area of work is in design (architecture and urban design—conception: 34.73 percent), followed by construction (architecture and urban design—execution: 15.88 percent) and interior architecture (14.92 percent). Work in public service accounts for 5.29 percent of responses, urban and regional planning for 3.99 percent, and landscape architecture for 3.36 percent.

Considering that the research was conducted when the City Statute's incentive for development of master plans and government management of urban development was in place, work in this area was very low, ranging between 4 percent and 5 percent.

We can conclude that the generalist qualification and professional duties do not correspond to a balanced distribution of fields of work of Brazilian architects and urban planning. The Brazilian case makes us think about the limits of legal specifications in teaching and in teaching and assigning professional skills professional skills in view of the reality of the field of work of the urban planning architect. In fact, the coverage of the generalist qualification provides a great capacity of adapting to the oscillations of demands, either public or private. However, the conflict between the higher complexity of each area and the superficiality of this education is far from being overcome.

Continuous education has apparently been the path followed by graduated professionals. The most common ways of searching for specialization are courses, seminars, and fairs (82 percent), according to the same CAU census. In the two years prior to the census, 25.49 percent of the urban planning architects took any kind of graduate course, but only 6.86 percent got a master's degree and 1.21 percent were in in PhD programs.[7] The current graduate system was established in the University Reform of 1968, whose purposes were more focused on research and expansion of higher education through the qualification of faculty than providing continued education of specialization and refresher courses.

In 2013, the CAU reaffirmed its alignment with Resolution No. 51 on the generalist model, following UNESCO/UIA, which recommends:

"The basic goal of education is to develop the architect as a generalist. This is particularly true for those who are working in a

6 It should be noted that this data refers to the urban architects registered with the Council of Architects and Urban Planners, which, at the time of the research, totaled 83,754 professionals.

7 It is important to state that, in Brazil, an urban planning architect may graduate only after a five-year course, and master's degree is a scientific and academic type of course, taken after obtaining the diploma and professional qualifications.

2.7.1

◄ 2.2.1 developing context, where the architects could accept the role of an "enabler" rather than that of a "provider," and where the profession can meet new challenges."

The emphasis on the developing contexts acknowledges the difference in the international scenario, in accordance with the countries' economic and social conditions. We expect that this paper has introduced foreign readers in the role of urban planning architects, of generalist education, in the Brazilian urbanization process. This historical progression may have implications beyond the limits of Brazilian national particularities, providing input for an international debate that builds new perspectives for the professional teaching and practice of architecture and urbanism.

References

Associação Brasileira de Ensino de Arquitetura e Urbanismo (ABEA). (2015). "Cursos de Arquitetura e Urbanismo no Brasil." December. http://www.abea.org.br/?page_id=11.

Anelli, R. (2012). "Urban Planning, Urban Design and Architectural Design in São Paulo during the Military Regime." 15th International Planning History Society Conference. São Paulo. http://www.fau.usp.br/iphs/lib/IPHS%202012%20ANELLI%20Renato_eng.pdf.

Conselho de Arquitetura e Urbanismo (CAU BR) (2012). "Censo dos Arquitetos e Urbanistas do Brasil." http://www.caubr.gov.br/censo/resource/site/pdf/nacional/Folder-censo-CAU.pdf.

Contier, F. de A. (2015). "O edifício da Faculdade de Arquitetura e Urbanismo na Cidade Universitária: Projeto e Construção da Escola de Vilanova Artigas." PhD dissertation: Institute of Architecture and Urbanism, University of São Paulo. São Carlos.

Innes, J. E. and D. E. Booher (2004). "Reframing Public Participation: Strategies for the 21st Century." *Planning Theory & Practice* 5:4: pp. 419–436.

International Union of Architects/UIA (2011). *Charter UNESCO/UIA for Architectural Education*. http://www.uia-architectes.org/sites/default/files/charte-en.pdf

Institute Brasileiro de Geografia e Estatística (IBGE) (2007). *Regiões de influência das cidades*. http://www.ibge.gov.br/home/geociencias/geografia/regic.shtm.

Koury, A. P. and F. L. Lara (Org.) (2016). *Planejamento versus Participação: um falso dilema*. São Paulo and Austin.

Oliveira, A. F. de (2012). "A regulamentação do exercício profissional da arquitetura no Brasil." PhD dissertation in Architecture and Urbanism: Universidade Federal da Paraíba, João Pessoa. Salvador.

Transdisciplinarity: The Basis for the Increase of Urban Knowledge?

Kirsten David

The call for new professions that cross existing disciplinary borders has to be understood as a consequence of the growing complexity of urban problems (Grubbauer 2017). Our existing knowledge system—the result of our education and research systems—seems to be no longer able to deal with the (latest) developments of urban space and urban living, that is, the urban environment.

Can transdisciplinarity help to educate the required professions or to extend the knowledge of existing professions?

Transdisciplinarity itself is seen in different ways. On the one hand, transdisciplinarity is described as real interdisciplinarity, as (partial) liberation of science from its historical increasingly parceled-out being (Mittelstrass 1997). Annulling disciplinary particularities, transdisciplinarity reestablishes the initial unit of science. This is necessary because problems do not (always) originate within disciplinary borders. Accordingly they need cross-border identification and solution processes (Mittelstrass 1998). On the other hand, transdisciplinarity is seen as a cooperation between science and practice passing the borders of the science system (Defila et al. 2006). Hanschitz, Schmidt, and Schwarz (2009) tie both positions together and define transdisciplinarity as a problem-oriented approach to research. It resolves disciplinary boundaries in favor of participative generated solutions (Hanschitz et al. 2009). That is to say, the authors postulate the cooperation between science disciplines and practitioners or industry partners who are equally relevant for the solution of a problem.

On one point the authors of the different positions agree: conditions for transboundary cooperation are openness and respect while discussing critically the epistemological premises of one's own and the other's involved disciplines and/or science-external partners. The basic attitudes need to be curiosity and the real will to understand each other; Mittelstrass puts it in a nutshell, saying that the liberation of science out of disciplinary borders must begin in one's own head as lateral thinking, asking questions which nobody asked before and learning what isn't known in one's own discipline yet (Mittelstrass 1989).

If we now look at two of the *old* urban professions, we find that transdisciplinarity is nothing new. In the field of urban planning, transdisciplinarity—understood as an association of the artistic with scientific methods—already roots deeply in the qualitative metropolitan research as a result of the complexity of the urban environment (Streule 2014). And architecture has always been connected closely with craft and building construction practice. As a research discipline architecture is still young and needs to define its own epistemological approaches. Meanwhile the specific architectural knowledge culture and knowledge production are described as transdisciplinary (Flach and Kurath 2016). In consideration of the multilayered architectural knowledge and the practical orientation of architecture, transdisciplinarity in this case has to be understood in the sense of Hanschitz et al (2009).

Even if these two old urban professions interpret and use transdisciplinarity differently, the necessary base that transdisciplinarity—however defined—asks for is inherent in both of them: the ability to work and think laterally. This specific way of thinking—lateral, cross-linked, system-oriented or, as Vester sums up and suggests, biocybernetic thinking[1]—must be seen as a basic skill or method for the understanding of complex problems or phenomena (Vester 2001). And since transdisciplinarity aims to analyze border-crossing, complex problems, biocybernetic thinking is a basic method for transdisciplinary work.

Based on this context the original question has to be answered as follows: transdisciplinarity is not an aid to educate new urban professions or extend existing knowledge; it is the condition! And even though transdisciplinarity in the field of the urban environment still needs to be concretized and formulated in detail, the basic condition for a transdisciplinary increase of

1 Vester demands on planning and acting system-compatible by realizing and controlling the system-immanent meshed processes. His idea is based on biological cybernetics, the science of control and regulation processes in organisms and ecosystems (Vester 2001).

knowledge already is given. By becoming aware of our basic transdisciplinary skills in complex thinking, and using them in a more considered way, we—the old urban professions—are able to define the gaps in our urban knowledge system and to develop appropriate specifications of new urban professions. Furthermore we are able to pass this basic skill on to those professions.

But to organize and keep this process constructive, it requires a special trust base: the aim of new urban professions uniting our disciplinary knowledge stokes fear among the old urban professions of becoming less important. At the same time the process depends on the affected old professions. They have to be ready to examine critically their knowledge, epistemology, and methods and maybe even deconstruct them to create a new interwoven and more complex knowledge.

If we want to assume responsibility and solve our increasingly complex urban problems, we have to take on this challenge.

References

Defila, R., A. Di Giulio and M. Scheuermann (2006). *Forschungsverbundmanagement. Handbuch für die Gestaltung inter- und transdisziplinärer Projekte.* Zürich.

Flach, A. and M. Kurath (2016). "Architektur als Forschungsdisziplin. Ausbildung zwischen Akademisierung und Praxisorientierung." *Archithese* 2.2016: pp. 73–80.

Grubbauer, M. (2017). "Urban Research Today: Modes of Dialogue and Disengagement between Theory and Practice." W. Pelka and F. Kasting, eds. *Perspectives in Metropolitan Research (3): Science and the City. Hamburg's Path to a Built Environment Education.* Berlin.

Hanschitz, R.C., E. Schmidt and G. Schwarz (2009). "Transdisziplinarität." E.E. Krainz, ed. *Transdisziplinarität in Forschung und Praxis. Chancen und Risiken partizipativer Prozesse.* Opladen.

Mittelstrass, J. (1989). "Wohin geht die Wissenschaft? Über Disziplinarität, Transdisziplinarität und das Wissen in einer Leibniz-Welt." *Konstanzer Blätter für Hochschulfragen* 26: pp. 97–115.

Mittelstrass, J. (1997). *Der Flug der Eule. Von der Vernunft der Wissenschaft und der Aufgabe der Philosophie.* Frankfurt am Main.

Mittelstrass, J. (1998). *Die Häuser des Wissens. Wissenschaftstheoretische Studien.* Frankfurt am Main.

Streule, M. (2014). "Trend zur Transdisziplinarität—Kritische Einordnung einer ambivalenten Praxis qualitativer Stadtforschung." *Forum Qualitative Social Research (FQS)* 15.1, Art. 17, http://www.qualitative-research.net/index.php/fqs/article/view/1995/3614.

Vester, F. (2001): *Die Kunst vernetzt zu denken. Ideen und Werkzeuge für einen neuen Umgang mit Komplexität.* Stuttgart.

2.7.2

"They Came Togather" A Screenplay of an Urban Workshop Encounter

Timothy Pape/Martin Kohler

First Appearance—"They Came"
(The curtains rise but the stage is dark. Three spotlights illuminate different actors—left, middle, right of the stage. Anonymous and abstract, just like ghosts from distant galaxies, they judge their city: three statements, three spirits, no conversation.)

(MOBILITY) "I came to see how far I get by bus. With the new Bus Rapid Transit system it will be further and faster."

(PLAN) "I came to see the shacks and houses along the river. I am employed to provide a better territory based on travel time and not exactly on the distance."

(RESIDENT) "I am here. This is my shop and this is where our people meet. If the Bus Rapid Transit comes, it will bring new people. But it might also destroy my shop." *(Silence)*
"And then, where will we meet? Where will we work?"

(The lights fade and the curtains close.)

Second Appearance—On the Creek in Itaim Paulista

(A spotlight is directed on the center of the stage: Zona Leste, the northeast zone of São Paulo, where the workshop takes place. Industrialization has swept an irregular pattern of houses and streets without basic sanitation and accessibility over the former territory of indigenous people and Atlantic rain forest. Left alone by the state the new inhabitants arriving from all over Brazil and the world constructed settlements in valleys along creeks and rivers named São Mateus, Mooca, Vila Zelina, Penha, Tatuape, Vila Pru-dente, Ipiranga, or Itaim Paulista. In the flood plains between the rivers Tietê, Tamanduateí, and Aricanduva large agglomerations emerged, the periferias. Spaces of marginalization and great pover-ty. Over the years some pockets of wealth punctured this landscape and a new middle class arrived from the center. While making the social divide ever more visible in a highly diverse setting, the perife-rias remain marginalized, overcrowded, and with a lack of basic public services. This is the home of 4.2 million people.)

(RESIDENT ONE, unhappy) "**Too many people!**" *(Pauses.)* "**And the creek?**" *(He pulls a wry face.)* "**They only use it for throwing trash, normal trash, but also wood and foam from the industries.**"

(Now he laughs sarcastically and points at the trash along the creek while slowly walking a couple of steps towards it. It is ten o'clock in the morning, March 20, 2014, right at the crossing of Marechal Tito Avenue and Lajeado creek, close to the rail tracks that lead to down-town. RESIDENT ONE continues.)

"**Fifteen years ago I used to fish in the creek. It was deep, forming pools for swimming here and there. But the area was different too. A more rural neighborhood with** *chácaras*" *(the Brazilian word for "ranches").*

(RESIDENT ONE is sixty-four years old. For fifty-five years now he lives in Itaim Paulista. Twenty-five years ago he founded his own engine repair office next to the creek.)

"**Today life is more difficult here.**"

(Meanwhile a couple of people passed by and wandered through the trash on the river. A boy sharped his knife on the lamppost and picked something up on the riverside. RESIDENT ONE)

2.7.3

"People are searching for treasures in the trash, but nobody cares about the river. Once in a while somebody from the district hall comes and removes the trash." *(Pauses.)* "Or the rain does it and brings other and more. We have frequent floods here."

(He pulls out his cell phone. A video shows a turbulent and raging torrent of water, carrying away bottles, half trees, tires, plastic bags, and all sorts of absurd things. It's difficult to see. It's too fast. And the sun is reflecting on the cell phone.)

"This was two weeks ago. The water level was this high." *(RESIDENT ONE points at dirty traces on the his garage wall—more than two meters above the water level.)* "It completely covered the tubes over there." *(He now points at the immense round tubes that channel the water under the crossing train tracks.)*

(RESIDENT TWO, the boy with the knife, intervenes.) "It carries away everything. Even houses."

(Again RESIDENT ONE) "Yes, but you see them only in pieces."

(And yet another resident.) "Yes, sometimes even pieces of dead bodies, human bodies."

(The floods seem to be a passionate and blustery discussed issue.)

(RESIDENT ONE) "I thought of getting in contact with Greenpeace, but I gave up."

(A pause of silence gives the sentence a dramatic aura. Then a voice from offstage emerges.) "The aim of the São Paulo Strategic Master Plan is to create bus corridors to induce the creation of housing and jobs in areas easy to access by public transportation. In reality though, a lot of these planned mobility axes coincide with the creeks—parallel and occasionally intersecting—with the problem that most of them are subject to regular flooding and at the same time are occupied by informal settlements."

(While the voice from offstage is philosophizing, the spotlight moves to a group of actors on the right side of the stage who have

performed in the shadow until now, trying to shed some light on the details of the structural and morphological surroundings.)

(URBAN DESIGNER) "The area is characterized by the linear path of the Lajeado stream through the valley, without changing geo-morphological situations or transposing basins. However, with its enlargement, the area spans the railway line and reaches the banks of the Tietê River."

(WATER ENGINEER) "The Lajeado basin is a watershed of roughly 9.2 square kilometers connected to the river system of the Tietê. The topography is characterized by steep hillsides and creeks running from south to north."

(GEOGRAPHER) "Itaim Paulista has a population of 185,184 inhabitants with a density of 200 persons per hectare. The average rent is 550 Reais."

"Average…," *(the PLANNING THEORIST intervenes,)* "is but just another perspective. Woe betide anyone who forgets that it is only due to the various ways in which we view our urban things, and thus position ourselves as knowing judges, that we tend to create conflicting truths."

(While the spotlight on the right is fading, a cold and white light pours the whole stage from the left leaving no shadows. Only close to the source of the light are there still faces ruling the scene while all other actors are reduced to bleached and anonymous outlines.)

(The face of ACCESSIBILITY starts to explain.) "In order to make the planned public transport network of average capacity possible in the next fifteen years, the City of São Paulo defined structuring axes for the urban transformation in the so-called Strategic Master Plan."

"Many of these axes coincide with watercourses, and again many of them are subject to flooding and occupied by informal housing." *(It echoes from the anonymous outlines.)*

(Meanwhile HISTORY faces the scene.) "Such conditions are due to policies implemented from the nineteen-seventies, which called for plumbing works channeling the rivers together with

Figure 1 (p.282–283): Situations, © Workshop Estudos Urbanos SP, 2013

2.7.3

the construction of avenues on or adjacent to the water-courses."

(GOVERNANCE summarizes.) "Well, I guess all should start with one plan for the whole city. Derived from extensive participation it defines Macro-Areas, Special Zones of Interest, and Local Area Plans to adapt the general rule to specific conditions."

"But there is no definition of what a Local Area Plan is." *(It echoes again.)*

(And more and more visible an OPPOSITION is forming.) "The specific conditions are known by the people working and living in these areas. They are not documented and not respected. And they oppose the Strategic Master Plan!"

(The LAW concludes.) "Yet which is law." *(And the curtains close.)*

Third Appearance—"On the Tray of Discussion"
(The curtains rise again. In a black surrounding, different groups of actors are illuminated. They hold sketches and parts of the urban creek appearance in their hands—as we always take something with us from a visit, from an encounter.)

(The moderation welcomes all actors.) "We are between the second and third phases of our workshop now, a moment where we should reflect and adjust the workshop structure together and move the focus from present to future."

(Every workshop has an initial structure. A composition, timetable, meetings, and a proposal of how to approach an urban question together, in adding up experiences, coordinating resources, and creating a dynamic of congestion and conflation. In this case the proposal was to work in four phases: Opening, Gathering, Devising, and Presenting. But a workshop is not about timetables; it is all about timing. It is not about division of tasks; it is all about co-operating difference. There is even nothing wrong with hierarchies, if variety is given. The dynamic development of interrelations, variations, and differences is the great strength but also a great challenge that needs to be moderated. MODERATORS are part of the team, and act in process of collaboration: improvising on cues from

the groups, channeling movements, formulating proposals, and curating the process structure—a shared resource that has to be continuously adjusted. This involves asking simple questions:)

"If we cross out the word 'scenario' and write 'Maria' instead. What would that be?" *(Suddenly, a heated dead-end debate on scenario methods stopped.)*

(A German URBAN PLANNER, pertly) **"It's about future."**

(A Brazilian ARCHITECT counters.) **"It's about a scene or situation."**

(The STUDENT adds.) **"Maybe just an image."**

(According to the ENVIRONMENTAL ENGINEER) **"It is part of our methodology here. It's a method!"**

(While in the discussion until now "scenario" was lost in its abstract letters all alone on a dark green chalkboard, this variety of good company perspectives on it moderated the further discussion between.)

"Daniela Tapia Martinez, Mariana Rösel de Lourenço, Lisa Deister, Ana Tereza Gironi da Costa, Gabriela Oliveira Santos, Soyani Tardiolli de Figueiredo, Guilherme Eduardo Destro, Michael Koch, Rayne Subtil Leite, Carol Heldt, Fúlvio Teixeira de Barros Pereira, Alexandre Leitão Santos, Dajana Schroeder, Milena de Lima e Silva, Marlon Rubio Longo, Anne Caroline Malvestio, Timothy Pape, Renata Utsunomiya, Tiago Rodrigues, Vitor Calcenoni, Karine Piedade Pedrosa, Nelson Hamilton Garcia, Fransueldo Pereira da Silva, Leandro Vincente de Andrade, Eduardo Tavares de Carvalho, Mariana Jezilda de Mederiros Fontana, Harmi Takya, Martin Kohler, Patrícia Marra Sepe, Tais Tsukumo, Anderson Inancio Lopes, Hélia S.B. Pereira, Wiesbrock, Renato Anelli, Marcelo Montano, Luciana Schenk, Thiago Guimaraes."

(A composition of different names, backgrounds, cultures, nationalities, educations, professions, experiences, approaches, conceptions, convictions, and actualities. Professors, students, practitioners, and researchers. From São Paulo, Hamburg, Stuttgart, São Carlos, and Santiago. An encounter between differences that are working together for a compact period of time in one place and on the same

2.7.3

topic. This variety is the substrate of a workshop in urban research.)
(An ACTOR laughs.) **"And it leads to long discussions."**

"Well, already after four hours we found an agreement. We accept the inevitableness of the realization of bus corridors but challenge it by developing scenarios. Like a shared framework to understand different driving forces as base for an integrated planning approach."

(Workshop moderation is about framing a discussion, not producing one.)

(ACTOR ONE) **"But I don't understand why we should accept the bus corridor? It's just a bad plan."**

(ACTOR TWO) **"But it is a plan that exists. And not accepting the bus corridors won't be changing the future."**

(ACTOR ONE) **"Yes, but we have better solutions than this! A tram, for example, that needs little space and causes little pollution."**

(A third ACTOR intervenes.) **"How about collecting these more radical ideas as well? We can create a fourth group to collect utopian ideas. They probably won't get built, but they might influence people's minds."**

(ACTOR TWO) **"And what is realistic anyways? We have to come up with proposals."**

(URBAN DESIGNER) **"An integration of creeks, bus corridors, living, and working."**

(TRAFFIC PLANER) **"Let's call it a mobility corridor."**

(SOCIOLOGIST) **"Or a social corridor."**

(WATER ENGINEER) **"Or what about a green corridor with buffer zones for the floods."**

(The discussion and design of scenarios continues deep into the night. The lights fade and the curtains close.)

Forth Appearance—"Togather"

(The curtains rise and all actors and surroundings of the former appearances merge while they are all illuminated by single spotlights. The voice of a RESIDENT from the appearance on the creek breaks the silence.)

"Do you see this tree?" *(She points at a small tree at the creek.)* "If the flood is not taking it, they come with machines to cut the vegetation along the river. We'll see, how long this one will last."

(RESIDENT TWO) "And if you go to district hall to complain, they will not care. They do nothing for us."

(MOBILITY ENGINEER) "Well. Hasn't it been a great improvement when the city finally tarred the streets in the area?"

(WATER ENGINEER) "Yes!" *(Smiling ironically with a suffering face.)* "Cars and water flow fast. And when it rains, all the sealed streets amount to great inflows for the creeks—floods become flash floods."

(RESIDENT ONE is still showing his videos of the flood on the cell phone.) "In the last flood my truck was dragged away along with the current. It was parked in front of my office and the water reached such a level that it was dragged into the creek and disappeared in the tubes from the railway. I found it on the other side. With a dead horse, sofas, and closets. A battlefield of tragic traces." *(He points at a picture on his cell phone.)*

"But we tarred all streets to do something good for the community!"

"And we built the train!"

"And we will build the corridors!"

(The curtains close silently.)

"And who builds São Paulo?"

Fifth Appearance—Editorial Note

(The curtains remain closed. In front of the curtain two of the actors are illuminated by spotlights. A VOICE from offstage says sotto voce.)

"This is a play of fiction, but it is based on a workshop that took place in São Paulo in March 2014. The authors were part of the workshop, but the credits belong to all participants. In the interest of protecting the privacy of individuals, some names and identifying details have been changed."

(ACTOR ONE) "Urban theory and urban practice are a repetitive confrontation of different interests and conceptions, which often lead to unbridgeable controversies and oppositions. The potential of the dynamic composition of urban research workshops could be understood as always providing a third, hence an additional, perspective mediating the oppositions. This opens up new views, opportunities of access, and reflective debate. And it paves the way for follow-up research."

(ACTOR TWO) "In fact this is not about solutions, but about asking better questions. And this might be the most valid contribution of workshops: generating questions and doubts among all actors who are throwing their established convictions and cultural certainties into an open dialogue that is mediated by their differences."

[Acknowledgements: The workshop was funded by the Federal Foreign Office of Germany as part of the German year in Brazil 2013–2014. It was supported by the German House for Economy and Innovation (DWIH), São Paulo. It was made possible by the personal and intellectual resources of Universidade de São Paulo, HafenCity University Hamburg, University of Stuttgart, and by the committed participation of the Prefeitura de São Paulo and the local authorities of Itaim Paulista. The screenplay draws exclusively on material produced in the workshop.]

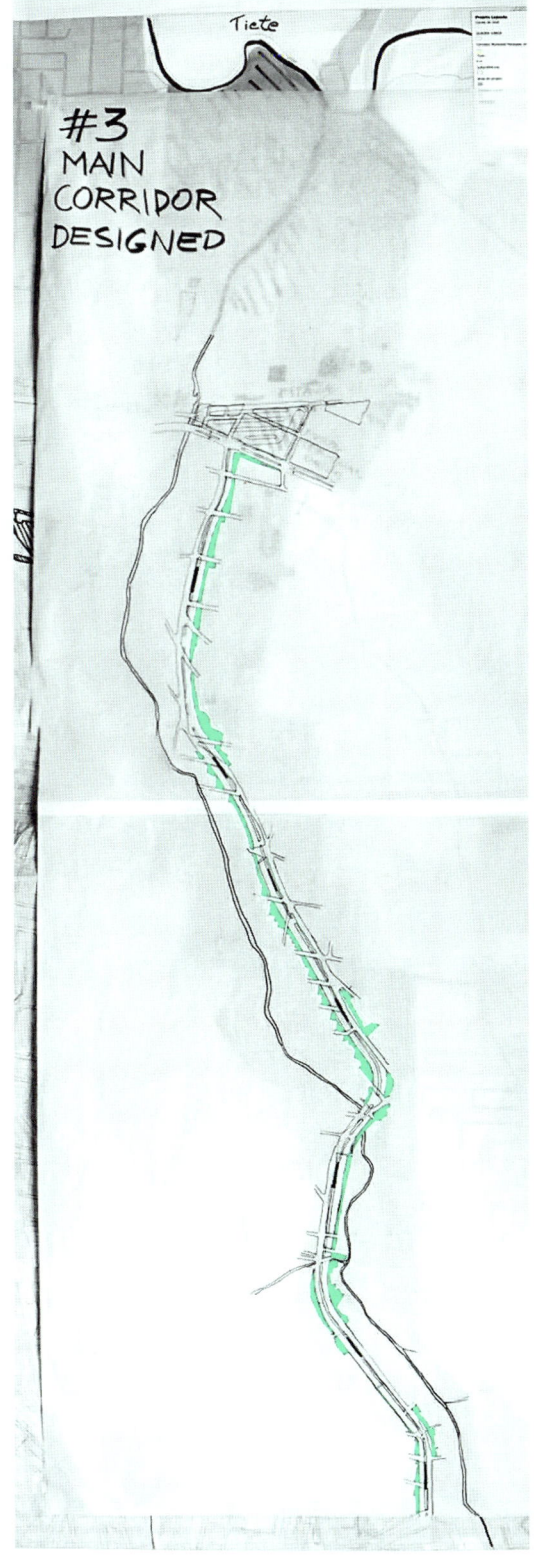

Figure 2: Main corridor, © Workshop Estudos Urbanos SP, 2013

2.7.3

2.8. Exchange

- 1 Producing Spaces of Exchange at the Periphery of Disciplines

- 2 Urban Practices: Vocabularies for a Creative Science and a Reflective Design

Producing Spaces of Exchange at the Periphery of Disciplines

Kathrin Wildner

Exchange and interaction are central categories in ethnographic research on social systems. Exchange is seen as a basic condition of human trade and a prerequisite for the survival of social groups. Objects, services, ideas, or marriageable members are often exchanged, allowing one social group to open to others, and thereby avoiding falling into a state of sheltered homogeneity and stasis. In the process, such interaction touches on mutuality and extends to a principle of reciprocity. A central foundation that makes interaction and exchange possible is the group's acknowledgement of its own identity—a differentiation between "self" and "other."

This paper does not discuss ethnic groups or subcultures, but academic disciplines. Concretely, it throws new light on the ways in which urban planners work as they begin to open out to other disciplines, as well as to actors in civil society. Although various external ideas on (the production of) the city can play a key role in the exchanges between urban planning experts, debates tend to get tangled up on details: the extension of education programs and traditional job descriptions, or the redefinition of professional payment structures via boards and chambers, those wardens of academic disciplines.

In this contribution, exchange should be understood as a mode of communication. In its broadest meaning, this includes the exchange of empathy, experience, understanding, and knowledge. The central questions and challenges of this paper

Translation by Sonja Hornung/
Richard Pettifer

2.8.1

center on where and how the traversal of boundaries between disciplines can take place. When and how is exchange possible? What types of situations and spaces exist that allow permeability between the boundaries separating disciplines? And if we are to understand this process as a transition—or as a transfer—how might such situations be set up or produced?

The lens through which I examine the question of an inter- or transdisciplinary exchange is the symposium Disziplinäre Grenzgänge (Crossing Disciplinary Boundaries), which was organized by urban planners from the HafenCity University in Hamburg in July 2016 and also provided the occasion for forming this collection of texts.

Participatory Observation and Active Listening

As an urban ethnographer attending the symposium, I was assigned with providing some concluding reflections on the task, methodology, and process of the event in the context of its declared aims. I was invited to take part as an active listener, but also to observe, so that I could reflect on the symposium at its end with my own commentary. As an ethnographer, I am well acquainted with the unresolvable problem of participatory observation. Neither completely a part of the situation, nor with the adequate distance required for gaining an overview, a continual confrontation with one's own subjectivity is necessary. Through this reflexive understanding of participatory observation, I collected and structured my impressions on the event, its programming, and coordination in order to compress this all into a form that would support a debate extending beyond the event itself.

Among the broad range of possible questions to be investigated with regard to cross-disciplinary boundaries, I decided to concentrate on the production of those spaces that facilitate exchange between disciplines. Additionally, I will focus on the notion of space across several scales and scopes. Firstly, the title of the symposium equates space with a border zone in the sense of a metaphoric space between disciplines: a zone where overlaps and exchanges are possible. At the same time, this raises questions relating to the periphery, and the relationship between the center and the periphery. A further spatial level addressed in the symposium is that of our shared object of research, the city as a space of possibility, as a place for testing things out and for experimental arrangements. Ultimately—and this is the main focus of my text—the space of the symposium itself, the staging of its setting, constitutes a further layer to be analyzed as a site of exchange.

The Boundary: Between-Space

A plethora of questions could be the boundary between disciplines: Where do the borders of disciplines lie? How do they appear—as fields, perspectives, competencies, or something else? Does the boundary have something to do with crisis—the crisis of disciplines? What happens at the edges of disciplines, and what constitutes the center?

At the symposium, the center was quite clearly defined as urban planning. Every participant, no matter what discipline they hailed from, were invited to cast their gaze from the edges, to reflect on their own relationship to urban planning, and to set new inter- and transdisciplinary processes into motion. Through this, the symposium assigned particular significance to precisely this between-space: along the border, on the edges.

Periphery—in this context transferred to the between-spaces at the edges of disciplines—is described as a semiautonomous space, full of surprising new constellations, as different forms and contexts meet one another. In a discursive sense, metaphors and possibilities form a space with its own rules and formats. What meaning do such between-spaces have for the people moving within them? Those people who move in the space between or along borders, or who regularly trespass across borders, are called *Grenzgänger*innen*: frontier workers, cross-border commuters, or boundary-crossers.

Like the participatory observer, the boundary-crosser moves between two positions or spaces, and is able to adopt multiple perspectives at once. However, the professional boundary-crosser attributes clear functions to each place, shuttling back and forth between them. She passes across boundaries regularly in order to go to the other side for school, study, or work.

In this sense, interdisciplinary boundary-crossers step outside of their customary specialist and social context, moving through unknown terrain. Their alienated position allows them to cast a distanced gaze towards the space on the other side of the border, and, with the same gaze, to look back towards the familiar place they have just left behind. This, however, still leaves questions open regarding the ways in which boundaries are traversed. Can the divisions between disciplines simply be duly crossed by means of certificates and diplomas? Will you be invited to the other side? How permeable is the border? Are there already holes in the fence or do they first have to be contrived?

The City: Space of Possibilities

The common ground shared by all participating in the symposium was the city. Despite disciplinary differences relating to concepts, approaches, and the ways in which fields of research are staked out, the examination of the city, the questions relating to what cities might be or become, could be described as a shared field. Interestingly enough, in the process of discussing urban space, the exchange frequently focused not on concrete places, but on discursive questions: the construction of concepts, theoretical perspectives, and academic disciplines with their own rules and formats, even though, as we shall see, the staging of urban places was to form a central moment in the symposium.

In this paper I understand cities to be transnational hubs and cosmopolitan centers, but above all, to be fields of conflict, and spaces for possibility in societal negotiations. The simultaneity of various lifestyles and negotiation processes

2.8.1

materialize on the physical level of urban space, sedimented in architecture, infrastructure, traces, signs, and symbols. City is not only an urban assemblage, but also a dense and complex space in which power relations and social structures are both reproduced and constantly renegotiated through cultural practice. Questions regarding the constitution of the city, its material conditions and social implications, its stakeholders, discourses, images, and imaginations play a central role in both the production and the planning of urban space (Wildner 2015, pp. 168-185). Cities are spaces of everyday practices, laboratories of knowledge, and spaces for research, as well as sites of planning. Thus, urban spaces are not just objects of research, but also concrete sites of investigation, intervention, and exceptional fields of experimentation.

The Symposium: Staging Spaces

In this case, the entire symposium Crossing Disciplinary Boundaries—and the process of speaking about interdisciplinary access to the field of urban planning—was itself an experiment. As aspects of methodology form central prerequisites for the production of knowledge and thereby of understanding, let's draw attention to the experiment's design and spaces.

Of particular relevance is the fact that the symposium did not take place in the representative spaces of the HafenCity University (HCU), but rather across carefully chosen urban sites. A central space was a hall in Oberhafenquartier, a former goods train station on the edge of today's HafenCity area, which was activated as a temporary "creative quarter" some years ago. Among other things, the site includes small workshops, a film studio, a music club, and the storage site of the Hanseatische Materialverwaltung (Hanseatic Material Administration), which loans out props for every sort of event. A further site for the symposium was a large hall on the third story of Kraftwerk Bille, a former power station in the heart of Hamburg's newly laid-out urban master plan (FHH 2015). Currently, it is used by self-organized cultural institutions and dynamic start-ups. Both of the above-mentioned spaces are located not only physically, but also discursively, in concrete processes of urban development. They evoke images of being creative and productive, while at the same time pointing towards an experimentally arranged open process.

The symposium shifted back and forth between these main sites, meaning that participants were often out and about, moving through urban space. On top of this, the majority of the guest participants of the conference were accommodated in a hotel in the heart of St. Pauli, an area marked not only by its role as the center for pleasure and entertainment, but also by quite well-known artistic interventions in urban planning (ParkFiction, PlanBude, etc). Finally, one more urban site was, to my mind, central to the staging of exchange in the symposium: a family-run Italian restaurant on a highway, not far from the Elbbrücken (Elbe Bridges), was chosen for the communal celebratory evening meal. A long table was set under a train bridge at the edge of a car park, facing onto a canal, surrounded by traces of urban infrastructure—a romantic scene, in what would otherwise be an inhospitable place. Everyone agreed that no urban planner could or would even want to plan such a space. Nonetheless (or perhaps precisely because of this?) experts from all participating disciplines were completely charmed by the site's view, the sun setting between concrete pillars, the barges on the canal, the oh-so-urban atmosphere. An unforgettable place, where ever-changing constellations of small and large groups of people chatted informally about the topic of city and how cities are produced.

Here, as at every other site of the symposium, exchange was staged, including the question of pleasure, of hospitality and friendliness, of good food and togetherness playing a central role. Accordingly, it was precisely this combination of sites on the supposed peripheries of the city that formed a central setting for discussion about the potential to traverse and transcend disciplinary boundaries.

Similar, the spatial settings intended for lectures, working groups, or discussion forums in any format also point towards the possibilities for staging spaces of exchange. For each and every phase of the symposium, walls were moved and units of space divided or reopened, table sizes varied, chairs placed, seating, viewing and speaking arrangements were shifted around to meet the required format for each working process. This constant reshuffling led to ever-new temporary constellations. In this process, the question of self-reflection—when and how to extract oneself from a group around a table—was ever-present, as was that of possible provocation—the refusal to sit in a circle of chairs, and instead (as one participant spontaneously did) to climb onto a table and address the others from above. By the spatial arrangements such situations were made possible, somtimes even forced into being.

As well as the furniture brought into each space, technological devices also play a role—one that often goes overlooked—in producing such settings. Though otherwise today scarcely seen, analog overhead projectors were omnipresent at this symposium, alongside the ubiquitous digital projector. The overhead projectors not only structured the event space with their cones of light, but also offered the possibility for spontaneous and immediately visible minute-taking. Further instruments for the staging of exchange included didactic methods and playful formats, reflecting how these elements are increasingly applied in participatory urban planning workshops. Accordingly, concepts and dreams were defined, and ideas compiled, with fat markers and butcher's paper, or with small Post-it notes.

The extent to which the content of the negotiated discursive positions was consistently worked through could be questioned. Certainly, in the moment of communication at a table, negotiation processes were constantly in motion: Who writes? Who translates what has just been said, into which central concepts? Who speaks, and how much time is there to continue discussing? Time, above all, is the crucial factor of the setting. How long is necessary for a particular question to be discussed? How long will a small group, thrown together for the occasion, be able to sustain the discussion? How long will they stick to the topic before they discover a

2.8.1

new one? The question of speed was highly important for every individual working phase, but also had great significance beyond this immediate framework. The entire three days were a state of exception for interdisciplinary exchange. How much time will be necessary in order to carry back these experiences into individual disciplines—to move from the edges, and to act again in the center?

A final and apparently inconspicuous instrument for the staging of exchange was the specific arrangement of participants who encountered one another, almost a casting of personalities. Even though the symposium was open to the public and around one-third of those present were interested listeners, the majority of participants were specifically invited and given a particular task. Invitations had been sent to members of the various networks of the event organizers. Many knew one another already from working situations; others met old friends after some years again. However, there were also new acquaintances and experts from the municipal administration, with artistic backgrounds or hailing from project-based architecture as well as people whose names were known to one another, and who would likely be seeing one another again at other up-coming interdisciplinary events. Each invited person had a task, or sometimes a couple of tasks to carry out during the course of the symposium: a presentation, a discussion input, or moderation at one of the working tables. This distribution of labor meant that not only were the majority of participants present for most of the symposium, but it also lent itself to a form of collective participation in the process. Each person was responsible for the unfolding of proceedings, as well as being a part of the discussion around the structure of experimental process, and the possibilities opened by a space that traverses—and allows exchange between—disciplines.

The Staging of Spaces of Exchange
After three days spent in a state of exception, it became apparent that the declared reasons for coming together—the definition of precise areas of work, areas of education, and even new professional labels such as "enabler"—did not quite succeed in creating a manifesto for an urban planning that would traverse or transcend disciplinary boundaries, let alone develop new utopians for the urban planning of the future. Such things are, of course, not so easily conjured up.

The days spent together did, however, demonstrate that staging spaces of exchange, and discussing disciplinary boundaries in the field of urban research, could destabilize one's own perspective. To leave the trusted comfort zone of the center, to open oneself to the edges of the disciplinary field, and to use this vantage point to cast a new gaze onto urban space, can trigger something and push it into motion. To begin with, only slight, still fragile vibrations might be sensed; further steps need time. Above all, these forms of exchange require an ease of movement, an ability to shuttle between spaces and places, and between thoughts and the physicality that space offers for opening new positions. Whether new professional communities for urban planning form out of this venture is yet to be seen.

For the question of the possibility to stage exchanges that might transcend disciplinary boundaries, this would mean that further moments of traversal or transcendence do not take place in a state of exception. Rather, staged and therefore focused encounters between disciplines are a prerequisite to finding new ways of understanding urban space. Such meetings, as constructive, *unlikely encounters,* should be taken seriously, and further expanded across the shared field for research and action: the city. This would mean also building various formats of spaces for such exchanges to take place in the praxis of urban planning.

There would be no need to discover new professions for conveying this task, but rather, the negotiation of various disciplinary perspectives should be accounted for and involved from the very beginning of each planning project. As an urban ethnographer, I continue to be fascinated by this movement between positions: of listening, observing, and participating at the edges of disciplines within the urban field.

2.8.1

References

FHH. Freie und Hansestadt Hamburg (2015). *Stromaufwärts an Elbe und Bille. Wohnen und urbane Produktion in Hamburg*. Hamburg.

Parkfiction. Accessed October 17, 2017. http://park-fiction.net.

Planbude. Accessed October 17, 2017. http://planbude.de.

Wildner, K. (2015). "Inventive Methods. Künstlerische Ansätze in der ethnographischen Stadtforschung." *Ethnoscripts* 17.1: pp. 168–185.

Urban Practices: Vocabularies for a Creative Science and a Reflective Design

Frank Eckardt

Knowledge in a knowledge society has become decentralized. In an unlimited net of information, combining thoughts, ideas, and concepts has become the norm for everybody researching the city. Decentralized knowledge not only incorporates but also exceeds existing forms of knowledge communication. As a result, the disciplined way of organizing progress in general knowledge is at stake. Despite unlimited horizons of exploration, the human conditions of knowledge creation are requiring a new organization of knowledge progress.

What the ongoing knowledge revolution means for science in general cannot yet be fully grasped; however, it can be observed that there are tendencies to repersonalize and relocalize knowledge. These tendencies, in turn, promote an understanding of the world that accepts a more local and personal range of exploration and explanation.

Researching cities in this way leads to a redefinition of scientific ethos that allows the inclusion or acceptance of parallel worlds of knowledge that might be not testable on a larger scale. This does not imply the refusal of argument and evidence nor does it deny the relevance of control and intersubjectivity. Rather, it opens the gate to fuzzy, confusing, unconventional, and local knowledge.

Urban knowledge is created in diverse settings of individual encounters and institutional frames. The generation of urban knowledge is based upon certain practices that are linked to processes of exchange. As long as they are narrated, they can be made accessible for research and design. Essentially, these practices are situation-based but as urban life is bound to the general logic of self-organization in society, they are not unlimited. It is rather the redefinition of global schemes of practices that makes up for the locale to progress to reach out to and have an impact on the urban conditions. In this sense, the urban has become the "global" or the "general" of the knowledge that is intended to be produced.

1.1.3 ◄

For the nonlocal, the entrance to urban knowledge depends on understanding the used vocabulary. Knowledge—in its modern and urban form—still depends on the narrative structure of organization. The recombination of knowledge under urban conditions follows the logic of fragmenting narratives. Authenticity is no longer produced by situating knowledge into a single narrative but by anchoring one's vocabularies in the diversity of urban perspectives.

2.8.2

Conclusion

Afterthoughts as Intentions and Hopes

AR: When we discuss the future of our professions, roles, responsibilities ... what must we change? How and what do we change?

YS: The professionalization of boundary-crossers, who move between various theoretical, practical, disciplinary, and thus methodological approaches, entails new ways to generate and impart knowledge.

YW: Despite, or perhaps due to, other kinds of institutionalization, variable networks, and a stronger self-conception, the question of financing remains. New regulations are needed for remuneration.

AR: But it also has to do with regard and appreciation. It is unacceptable for committed people who assume responsibility, shape their environment, and in the process create some of their own areas of responsibility to be so often pigeonholed with the indelible designation of "subculture." Here I mean appreciation in a double sense—also, and especially, monetary appreciation.

RT: I think that a very important aspect is that not just one of the three spheres of actors in urban development should bear the primary responsibility for designing cities, for instance, owing to their economic power. Especially when housing is again being more strongly promoted and constructed, the question of urbanity plays an important part. How can we develop our cities in the long term so that room for possibilities—not monostructures—continue to arise?

MK: This reality requires different, better training.

RT: Exactly. Training that broadens perspectives—and also broadens the generality of architects and planners into a multilayered, multiperspectival ability—to change one's standpoint and accept and take on the widest variety of viewpoints. And in this way, also to be able to shape processes actively—to be less a mere building block in the process.

MK: Again, we are not pleading for the abolition of the above-mentioned disciplines, but rather for openness in the direction of new fields of urban work. To this end, it will have to be possible to experiment at universities.

RT: Engaging in a new culture of interdisciplinary debate and work includes a new understanding of science and the kind of "science" to which architecture, urban design, and urban planning refer, could refer, and should refer.

YW: A discussion was launched in Germany postulating the term of a "transformative science," which could include the special methods; the arts, for instance, could offer to produce knowledge.

RT: But this ability also requires the ability to be critical. The participative "co-" can be all too quickly and too easily undermined, the common process turned into one dominated by individual interests. We must also train people to take a critical approach to fundamental social structures.

AR: What about no longer studying architecture, city planning, constructional engineering, or urban design in the future, but instead enrolling in a construction university and taking courses according to your own personal interests, which gradually form a very individual occupational profile, an individual profession? What if this could be supplemented by regularly held symposia, conferences, workshops, and parties that encourage sharing, promote communication between apparently solitary satellites flitting around, and stimulate the formation of a swarm?

MK: It's hard to introduce innovations at the same time that the restructuring of universities is seen by policymakers and ministerial bureaucracies as opportunities to try out new savings schemes. This inhibits curiosity and provokes the defense and justification of existing disciplinary structures. The new HafenCity University, founded as a thematically focused university for "Building Art and Metropolitan Development," is still suffering from this today and therefore remains beneath its possibilities.

AR: Yes, and considering that the regulation of courses of study is prevailing and intensifying ever since the Bologna process, the idea of this sort of free configuration of everyday academic life seems utopian. But does it have to remain utopian?

I champion the idea that it is primarily freedom that enables a passion for a profession to unfold and that it requires trust to be able to live this freedom. Trust in students, that they will find the right path, the right choice of courses for themselves. Trust in our cooperation partners, that they will "do a good job," and trust in collaboration.

To be continued:
by you and others!

Contributors

Authors

Markus Ambach is artist, curator, and author of several projects in public and urban spaces. His work focuses on building up a complex structure of urban practices, project rooms, and interventions in public spaces, that allow a controversial discussion of art within specific public contexts. He lives and works in Dusseldorf.
Aiming at the articulation of different urban relations, his strategies develop directly out of the significant qualities of the work's contexts resulting in projects like "B1A40 The beauty of the grand road," "The urban congress" or "From foreign countries in own towns." www.markusambachprojekte.de.

Renato Anelli is an architect and urban planner (PUC Campinas, 1982), and holds a master's in history (UNICAMP, 1990) and a PhD in architecture (FAU USP, 1995). He is a full professor of the history of architecture and urban design at the Institute of Architecture and Urban Planning of the University of São Paulo at São Carlos. He is also the former secretary of public works, transportation, and services in the São Carlos city government (2001–2004). As he is a full-time professor, he doesn't have a professional studio, but he is developing applied surveys and plans in his Arqbras research group, which includes undergraduate- and graduate-level researchers, at the University of São Paulo. He has been working on his research project, entitled "Urban Infrastructure as Urban Planning Strategy," since 2005.

Markus Bader studied architecture in Berlin and London. He graduated in 1996 from the Bartlett School of Architecture, London. Markus Bader's academic activities include guest professorships in Düsseldorf, Kassel, and Prague, complemented by many workshops and lectures held internationally. He has been professor at the Institute of Architecture and Urban Design at the UdK Berlin, Germany, since 2016.
raumlaborberlin was started in 1999 by Markus Bader, Andrea Hofmann, Jan Liesegang, and Christof Mayer as a commons of spatial practice. With Benjamin Foerster-Baldenius, Matthias Rick (†2012), Francecso Apuzzo, Axel Timm, Frauke Gerstenberg, and Florian Stirnemann, it has expanded to nine members currently. Through its practice raumlabor has developed and explored an extended concept of architecture and space beyond the built object. http://raumlabor.net/

Daniela Brahm is a visual artist based in Berlin, Germany. In 2004 together with artist Les Schliesser she initiated the project ExRotaprint in Berlin-Wedding; co-founded in 2007 the nonprofit ExRotaprint gGmbH; and has been a member of its planning team ever since. ExRotaprint is a model for an inclusive and nonprofit approach to urban development. She is a member of the initiative Stadt Neudenken and of the Round Table for Land and Real Estate Policy in Berlin. www.exrotaprint.de, www.danielabrahm.de

Frauke Burgdorff is an urban planner with expertise in alternative project development, neighborhood development, and process design. She has worked as an urban planner in Antwerp, a futurologist in Gelsenkirchen, and a member of the executive board of Montag Stiftung Urbane Räume; she founded her own agency for co-operative urban development, BURGDORFF STADT, in 2017.
BURGDORFF STADT designs integrated urban development processes and public participation processes. From the implementation of new housing areas in Berlin to the refurbishment of the Viktualienmarkt in Munich, from concepts for a new neighborhood-development strategy in Heidelberg to neighborhood-based programming of new infrastructure, BURGDORFF STADT always seeks inspiration in adjacent disciplines such as the arts, education, and organizational development.

ConstructLab is a collaborative construction practice, working on both ephemeral and permanent projects. It embraces the freedoms of a collaborative practice—the complexity of involvement and layers of reality, the shared hopes and worries occurring while experimenting with the unknown, and the collective intelligence that results from working together and confronting differences. To find out more about everything that happened and everybody who was involved in the Arch, visit the Arch blog: http://www.constructlab.net/category/the-arch/

Kirsten David holds a diploma in architecture and is a doctoral student at the HafenCity University of Hamburg (HCU). She researches and teaches at the chair of Construction Economics and focuses on building in existing buildings. In her research work, she analyzes the transdisciplinary framework conditions of the (energetic) modernization of rented housing stocks.

Christopher Dell is a composer, musician, and professor of urban forms of knowledge, organization theory, and relational forms of practice in the Urban Design research and teaching program at HCU as well as director of ifit, at the Institute for Improvisation Technology, Berlin. He has taught in London, Johannesburg, New York, and Arnheim and works in transdisciplinary constellations on conceptualizing relational forms of action with a view to render them fruitful for research and design.

Frank Eckardt is a political scientist and professor of urban sociology at the Bauhaus-Universität Weimar. https://www.uni-weimar.de/de/kontrast/architektur-und-urbanistik/professuren/stadtforschung

Liza Fior is a founding partner of muf architecture/art. She has lectured, published, and taught internationally, including at Central Saint Martins, Milan Politecnico, the AA, Yale University, and the RCA . She is a Mayors Design Advocate to Sadiq Khan, co-founder of We Are Here Venice, and mentor for arts-emergency.org.
muf is a London-based practice that works in the public realm (including museums). They take on "normal" briefs, but then bring unsolicited research. muf work mainly but not exclusively in east London, are the only UK winners of the European Prize for Public Space, and authored the British Pavilion at the Venice Biennale in 2010. http://www.muf.co.uk and http://www.morethanonefragile.co.uk

Saskia Hebert was trained as an architect, graduated from UdK Berlin in 1996 and co-founded subsolar* in 2001. In 2012 she received a doctorate and established the "lived/space/lab" at the UdK. Since 2015, she has been a professor ad interim teaching transformation design at HBK Braunschweig.
subsolar* In her office subsolar* architektur & stadtforschung, which she runs together with Matthias Lohmann, Saskia Hebert operates in the field of what she calls "urban transformation design." Here, she experiments with open, inclusive, interdisciplinary, and participatory formats in research and planning.

Melanie Giza studied design at TH Köln and urban design at HCU Hamburg. She works as a graphic designer and is currently registered in the Bauhaus-Universität Weimar's International Doctorate Program—European Urban Studies.

Hanna Katharina Goebel has a PhD in sociology and has also trained in cultural studies. She works as a post-doctorate lecturer in the fields of body and cultural sociology at Universität Hamburg. In urban studies her focus is on the relationship between architecture, urban spatialities, and the body/human movements. https://www.bw.uni-hamburg.de/personen/goebel-hanna-katharina.html

Monika Grubbauer is professor in history and theory of the city at HCU Hamburg and teaches across the three study programs—Urban Planning, Urban Design, and Metropolitan Culture. Her research focuses on the interdependencies between economic, social, and material processes of urban change. She has published widely on urban transformation and socioeconomic restructuring in different geographical contexts, with a particular focus on the role of architecture, planning, and construction. https://www.hcu-hamburg.de/master/stadtplanung/arbeitsgebiete-professuren/monika-grubbauer/

Camilla Guadalupi is a PhD fellow in urban and regional development at Politecnico di Torino, Italy. She has a background in urban planning and a strong interest in human geography. She is concerned with co-design, urban tactics, and activism, focusing the paradoxes of such experiences. http://www.dist.polito.it/personale/scheda/(nominativo)/camilla.guadalupi

Christoph Heinemann studied architecture at RWTH Aachen University of Technology and at the École d'Architecture de Paris la Villette from 1990 to 1997. He co-founded ifau with Susanne Heiss and Christoph Schmidt in 1998. He has been professor of architecture and the city at HCU Hamburg since 2017.
ifau (Institute for Applied Urbanism) is a Berlin-based working group of architects focusing on interrelated, interdisciplinary projects in the field of architecture and urban design. They are especially interested in process-oriented strategies and participative design methods. ifau realized numerous projects for arts institutions and recently the co-housing projects R50 and IBeB in Berlin. http://www.ifau.berlin.heimat.de

Dietrich Henckel held a full professorship of urban and regional economics at the Institute for Urban and Regional Planning at the TU Berlin until September 2017. His main topics of research are technological change and urban development, urban temporal structures, light pollution, and urban security and has numerous publications in these fields. He is a member of RSA, ARL, DASL, and DGfZP. http://www.econ-isr.tu-berlin.de/menue/ueber_uns/hochschullehrer/prof_dr_dietrich_henckel/

Jette Cathrin Hopp is a graduate architect and has been working with Snøhetta since 2005. She is part of the management group as project director and head of acquisitions and new projects. Jette has extensive experience in complex projects—both Norwegian and international—and has led major international project developments and competitions. She has lectured at several architectural symposia, sharing Snøhetta's philosophy and design ideas, and she is also used in jury work in several architecture competitions.

Snøhetta began as a collaborative architectural and landscape workshop, and has remained true to its transdisciplinary way of thinking since its inception. Today, Snøhetta has grown to become an internationally renowned practice of architecture, landscape architecture, interior architecture, and brand design. Comprised of two main studios in Oslo and New York City, the practice currently has more than 180 employees from thirty different nations. www.snohetta.com

Rainer Johann studied architecture and urbanism in Cologne and Delft and holds a PhD from HCU Hamburg. He worked at various architecture, urban design, and urban planning firms in Germany and the Netherlands. In 2007 Johann was named visiting professor at the Bauhaus-Universität Weimar and started his own practice as an urbanist in Berlin. He has been teaching and researching at the HCU Hamburg since 2008. He has also worked since 2017 for the Berlin Senate's department of housing and urban development. (Studio 3.111) www.rainerjohann.eu

Bernd Kniess is an architect, urban planner, and a professor of urban design at HCU Hamburg. His focus is on the negotiation and diagrammatic descriptions of the contemporary city. He directed the project University of the Neighbourhoods (UoN) from 2008 to 2014, and has been involved in Building A Proposition For Future Activities, a participatory process of planning and self-building a community building since 2015. He has been a member of the North-Rhine Westphalian Academy of the Arts and Sciences since 2009.

Michael Koch is an architect, urban planner, and professor of urban design and district planning at HCU Hamburg. After his studies in Hannover he was a co-founder of the architectural firm agsta and today is partner at yellow z (Zurich/Berlin, www.yellowz.net). Prior to his tenure at HCU he was professor of urban planning and urban design at Bergische Universität Wupptertal, visiting professor at various universities, and research fellow at ETH Zurich where he obtained his PhD. His projects, teaching, and research operate at the interface of architecture, urban design, and urban planning. He is a member of several advisory boards in Germany and Switzerland. (Studio 3.111)

Studio 3.111 Since its foundation, the Urban Design and District Planning Chair of Prof. Michael Koch, in the context of HCU Hamburg and recently known as Studio 3.111, has always stood for a multidisciplinary approach to town planning. The involvement of the Urban Design, Architecture and Metropolitan Culture perspectives— just to mention a few of them—assembled over the years professional collaborators with different theoretical and practical interests who enriched the chair's thinking, teaching, and research. The studio members often were involved in teaching and research on urbanistic problems and strategies of other chairs at HCU, but also national and international issues. In that sense this publication is based on these multiple urbanistic experiences and can be considered as both a reflection of building disciplinary bridges and an outlook to new urban professions.

Martin Kohler is a photographer and urbanist. He studied landscape architecture and environmental planning at the University of Hannover and at the Southern Australia University, Adelaide, travelled the world and has been working at the Creative Space for Technical Innovations since 2016. (Studio 3.111) www.mrtnklr.de

Jonas König is a research associate in urban economics at HCU Hamburg. His research focuses on online networks and the platform economy as well as on emigration and urban development. jonas.koenig@hcu-hamburg.de

Ana Paula Koury has been a professor at the graduate program in architecture and arbanism at the Universidade São Judas in São Paulo since 2008 and was a Fulbright Visiting Scholar in Global Cities CUNY in New York in the fall of 2016. She co-led the research project Planning and Participation: New Agenda for Urban and Environment Policies in Brazil from 2014 to 2016.
The Itaim Paulista Lab brings together professors and students of São Judas University and is supported by formal agreement with local government. The Lab is a pilot of co-operation to improve urban management skills in the metropolitan zone through collaboration between the university and the public authority. https://apkoury.wixsite.com/anapaulakoury

Andreas Krauth studied architecture at the TU München and the UdK Berlin. He has been a partner of Teleinternetcafe since 2011. Between 2008 and 2016 he worked as a project architect at raumlabor in Berlin. Parallel to his work with Teleinternetcafe he worked in 2013–14 as a research assistant at the Karlsruher Institut für Technologie and at the TU München. In 2016–17 he was guest lecturer at the UdK Berlin.
TELEINTERNETCAFE follows a multiperspectival approach and the principle of shared authorship both in practice and academia. The work operates at the interface of architecture and urban planning. It is characterized by process-oriented cooperative development strategies and an experimental approach to building and landscape typologies. An intensive engagement with the place and its situational qualities provides the starting point for the search for new and open forms of the city. teleinternetcafe.de

Jan Lange is a scientific assistant and doctoral candidate in European ethnology at the University of Tübingen. His currently ethnographic work is concerned with understanding how urban space is developed in informal projects through the collaboration of municipal authorities and urban communities. http://www.wiso.uni-tuebingen. de/faecher/empirische-kulturwissenschaft/personen/wiss-mitarbeiterinnen/jan-lange.html

Ton Matton studied urban planning in the Delft Technical University, graduating in 1991. Nowadays his work is situated somewhere between object-design, society-shaping, ecological urban planning, and artist-actionism. As a professor of space&designSTRATEGIES at the Kunstuniversität Linz he worked in 2015–16 with his team on the subjects "Cow," the social reanimation of a village and "NOT WELCOME!," an exhibition on refugee thematic.
Mattonoffice - semi-autarkic applied architectural thinking = trendy pragmatism In 2001 Ton Matton opened (together with partner Ellie Smolenaars) Werkstatt Wendorf in Mecklenburg Vorpommern, Germany. Working in various constellations he participated in a.o. Archilab (Orléans, France), Biennale Sao Paulo, Biennale Manifesta 2 (Ljubljana), Venice Biennale in Architecture, and Architecture Biennale Rotterdam. www.mattonoffice.org

Michael Obrist is an architect and partner of feld72 architekten zt gmbh. He has been a visiting professor of space and design strategies at the Kunstuniversität Linz since 2013. He has also taught at TU Vienna (housing and urbanism), TU Graz (urbanism), and was a professor at Summeracademy Salzburg and at the Architectural Association Visiting School Slovenia.
feld72 The work of feld72 pivots at the interface of architecture, applied urbanism, and art. The studio—with twenty-eight architects and urban planners—was founded in 2002 by Anne Catherine Fleith, Michael Obrist, Mario Paintner, Richard Scheich, and Peter Zoderer and is based in Vienna. Their work has been shown in the major exhibitions for architecture and urbanism worldwide. http://www.feld72.at/

Klaus Overmeyer trained as a gardener, is a landscape architect and pioneer in the field of user-driven spatial development. He founded the office Urban Catalyst. He has been a professor of landscape architecture at Bergische Universität Wuppertal since 2010.
Urban Catalyst was founded in 2004, originating from the EU-funded research project of the same name. Now the office is a collegially conducted business of nine associates, cooperatively designing and shaping spaces in transformation, at the interface of strategic planning, participation and communication, urban research, and policy advice. www.urbancatalyst.de

Timothy Pape is a practicing architect and urban design scholar with an MA in architecture and MSc in media and communication. He holds a PhD in cultural studies with a research interest in intercultural and interdisciplinary approaches towards aesthetic reflection of urban dynamic form. (Studio 3.111)

Dominique Peck joined the Urban Design research and teaching program at HCU in 2015 and works with architects, urban researchers, art-, music- and film-producers, graphic and web designers, and economists. He is concerned with shaping capacities and modes of realizing in the production of the urban, including the performance "Oktavistische Internationale" (Octavist International) and the project Building A Proposition For Future Activities.

Doina Petrescu is a professor of architecture and design activism at the University of Sheffield and co-founder of atelier d'architecture autogérée (aaa). Her main publications include *The Social (Re)Production of Architecture* (2017), *Learn to Act* (2017), *Altering Practices* (2007), and *Architecture and Participation* (2005). https://www.sheffield.ac.uk/architecture/people/academic/doina-petrescu
atelier d'architecture autogérée (aaa) is an activist platform that conducts practice-based research on participatory urban design, engaging with political ecology and civic resilience networks. aaa has received the Innovation in Politics Awards 2017, the Zumtobel Prize for Sustainability 2012, and the Curry Stone Design Prize 2011. www.urbantactics.org

PlanBude is a transdisciplinary team combining knowledge and practice from the fields of art, architecture, urban theory, cultural science, DJ-ing, activism, social work, community organizing, and planning. In a unique planning process, PlanBude opened its doors right at the construction site in the heart of St. Pauli, and offered innovative tools that allowed complex contributions by everybody. PlanBude is commissioned by the local administration, the district Hamburg-Mitte, but it is also a product of the right-to-the-city movements of Hamburg. PlanBude is now working on the realization of the "St. Pauli Code." www.planbude.de

Christine Preiser is a sociologist and has written her PhD about bouncers as guardians of urban nightlife. She is currently working on a research project about prostitution.

Carlo Ratti, an architect and engineer by training, is a professor at MIT where he directs the Senseable City Laboratory, and is a founding partner of the international design and innovation practice Carlo Ratti Associati. A leading voice in the debate on new technologies' impact on urban life, his work has been exhibited in several venues worldwide. **Carlo Ratti Associati (CRA)** is an international design and innovation practice based in Turin, Italy, with branches in New York and London. Drawing on Carlo Ratti's research at MIT, the practice is currently involved in many projects across the globe, embracing every scale of intervention, merging design with cutting-edge digital technologies. www.carloratti.com

Stefan Rettich is an architect and partner of KARO* architects. He has taught at the Bauhaus Kolleg in Dessau from 2007 to 2011 and since then has been professor of theory and design at the School of Architecture Bremen. In 2016 he was appointed professor of urban design at the University of Kassel. www.uni-kassel.de/go/staedtebau **KARO*** is a conceptual platform for communication, architecture, and spatial tactics based in Leipzig and Hamburg. The work of KARO* has been shown at various international exhibitions including the eleventh and twelfth Venice Biennales in Architecture, has been awarded the European Prize for Urban Public Space in 2010 and the Brit Insurance Design Award in 2011, and was shortlisted for the Mies van der Rohe Award in 2011. www.karo-architekten.de

Anna Richter has been a post-doctorate researcher in the Urban Design research and teaching program at HCU since 2013. She studied sociology and English literature in Bremen and New York and received a PhD from Leeds Metropolitan University. She is an editorial board member of *City* (Routledge) and currently concerned with researching methodology in urban design, trans- and interdisciplinary curriculum research, and the social turns in architecture and design debates.

Hannes Rockenbauch is an academic assistant at the department of city planning at the University of Stuttgart. As a political activist Rockenbauch was a member of the Faktencheck Stuttgart21 in 2010. Since 2004 Rockenbauch has been an elected member of the city council of Stuttgart for the group parteifreies Bündnis Stuttgart Ökologisch Sozial. http://soeslinkeplus.de/

Amelie Rost is an architect and co-owner of the architectural office Rost-Niderehe Architekten I Ingenieure. After a number of teaching assignments on urban design and interdisciplinary design projects, as well as contracts as a research assistant in the fields of urban design and architecture at HCU Hamburg, she is currently working on her doctoral thesis within the framework of the International Doctoral College Spatial Research Lab IDK III. (Studio 3.111) www.rost-niderehe.de

Jakob F. Schmid is an urban planner, initiator of the stadtnachacht network (www.stadtnachacht.de), author of the study stadtnachacht, and curator of the Nights conferences in Berlin. He has held several lectureships for urban planning and urban design at HCU Hamburg and HAWK. He currently works as an urban planner for the Free and Hanseatic City of Hamburg, urban design divison for the district of Eimsbüttel. Within his office Jakob Franz Schmid Stadtforschung & Entwicklung he worked several years as an urban planning consultant with a special focus on issues related with the evening and nighttime economy and spatial-temporal aspects. The office conducted the first nighttime economy study in Germany. (Studio 3.111) www.jakobfranzschmid.de

Tatjana Schneider is an educator and writer based in Sheffield, England. Her work explores notions of social (re)production and (re)appropriation as well as (spatial) agency. She was co-founder and director of the workers' cooperative Glasgow Letters on Architecture and Space, and the research and teaching collective Agency. She currently leads the research cluster Space, Culture, and Politics at the University of Sheffield. https://www.sheffield.ac.uk/ architecture/people/academic/tatjana-schneider

Yvonne Siegmund studied architecture in Munich and urban design in Hamburg. She worked on various construction projects before she changed her profession to the field of applied research. At the TUM she took part in developing strategies in a qualified densification study for the Munich region. Later she worked in teaching and research at the HCU Hamburg. Her PhD focuses on the effects of time aspects as driving forces in urban development. The time perspective is also key part in her photographs. (Studio 3.111) www.heyvisiona.com

Renée Tribble is an urban researcher and practitioner. She is also a shareholder and founding member of PlanBude. She studied architecture at Bauhaus-Universität Weimar and has worked as a freelance planner since. From 2008 to 2014 she taught at the HCU Hamburg. Currently she is completing her PhD about art and urban planning. (Studio 3.111)

umschichten is an artistic practice from Stuttgart using temporary architecture as an approach for immediate action. They create built interventions to display local needs, ideas, or passions. In the context of urban space umschichten visualizes theories, problems, or constellations of humans and materials. **Peter Weigand** and **Lukasz Lendzinski** are architects born in Stuttgart, Germany, and Zabrze, Poland. Formerly educated as carpenters they improved their professions by studying architecture and design at the Staatliche Akademie der Bildenden Künste Stuttgart. In 2007 they started working together as umschichten.

Urban Design Concerned with the urban as socially produced and historically developed, the research and teaching program Urban Design at HCU Hamburg engages with the contemporary-future urban society in the practice(d) forms of its co- and constant reproduction. Assembled as an interdisciplinary course and working with a wide range of methods and approaches, Urban Design aims to make visible and negotiable the knowledge of and about urban situations so as to unlock and demonstrate potentialities hidden therein. http://ud.hcu-hamburg.de/home

Viele Grüße von—Verein zur Förderung raumöffnender Kultur e.V., the Hamburg-based association, has existed since 2015 with the aim to explore the topic of opening up closed spaces for the public. The festival Hallo Festspiele—the association's first—is an artistic and experimental format of spatial development that led to a long-term use of the so-called Schaltzentrale—an experimental and artistic neighborhood bureau situated in the privately owned Kraftwerk Bille. www.vielegruessevon.org, www.hallo-festspiele.de

Dorothee Halbrock, cultural organizer and curator, initiated the collaborative development of Hallo Festspiele in Hamburg in 2014 and is working on the program and strategy of the association's projects. She was founding member and former curator of the MS Dockville Kunstcamp and Festival and will program the raumlabor project Floating University Berlin alongside Benjamin Foerster-Baldenius.

Julia Jost is a dramaturge and director. After studying philosophy and getting a degree in theatre directing in the class of Luk Perceval, she studied sculpture under Monica Bonvicini. In 2013 she began to work as a director's assistant at the Thalia Theatre in Hamburg. Since 2017 Julia Jost has worked at various theaters and off-spaces. For Viele Grüße von e.V. she develops different formats that combine discourse and performance.

Julia Lerch-Zajączkowska, an urban designer, is currently working within a research and exhibition project at Museum für Kunst und Gewerbe Hamburg. She was teaching in several formats at HafenCity University (Urban Design and Metropolitan Culture) and co-designed, curated, and programmed various projects. As a member of Hallo Festspiele and its partner project Schaltzentrale she focuses on collaboration and international exchange.

Tina Steiger received her degree in political science from the University of Florida and her master's in urban studies within the UNICA 4Cities Program. She has been an external lecturer at the University of Copenhagen and involved with the Hallo Festspiele in Hamburg since 2016. Currently based in Copenhagen, she works for Leadership Giving of the UN Refugee Agency.

Kai Vöckler is an urbanist and publicist in Offenbach, Germany. He is a founder member of Archis Interventions and program director South Eastern Europe (SEE) Network. He has worked on urban development projects in southeastern Europe and urban research projects in Europe and Asia. He is currently an endowed professor of Creativity in Urban Contexts at the Offenbach University of Art and Design, Germany. He is also spokesman for the LOEWE research cluster Infrastructure—Design—Society. www.kai.voeckler.de, www.seenetwork.org

Yvonne Werner is an urban planner and has worked at the HCU Hamburg at the department of urban development and district planning as a graduate assistant and taught in various projects. In her work she is concerned with practices of innovative planning offices in the context of their regulatory framework. (Studio 3.111)

Martin Wickel is professor of law and administration at the HCU Hamburg, where he has worked since the university's founding in 2006. He specializes in planning, building, and environmental law. https://www.hcu-hamburg.de/bachelor/stadtplanung/arbeitsgebiete-professuren/martin-wickel/

Kathrin Wildner is an urban anthropologist and did ethnographic fieldwork in New York City, Mexico City, Istanbul, Bogotá, and other urban agglomerations. As an urban researcher she teaches, publishes, and participates in transdisciplinary projects and international exhibitions. She is a founding member of metroZones (www.metrozones.info) and was visiting professor at the KHB Weißensee (2013–2015). Since 2012 she has been professor of cultural theory and practice at HCU Hamburg. www.kwildner.net

Filipa Matos Wunderlich holds a PhD in planning studies and is a lecturer in urban design and the director of the Master of Research in Interdisciplinary Urban Design at the Bartlett School, UCL. Filipa has an interdisciplinary background as an architect, urban designer, and musician. Before engaging with academia she worked as an architect and urban designer at KCAP in the Netherlands. Key research interests are temporality in urban places, urban rhythms and rhythmanalysis, sensory urbanism, and the design and use of alternative urban typologies.